BARUCH AND THE LETTER OF JEREMIAH

WISDOM COMMENTARY

Volume 31

Baruch and The Letter of Jeremiah

Marie-Theres Wacker

Carol J. Dempsey, OP
Volume Editor

Barbara E. Reid, OP
General Editor

A Michael Glazier Book

LITURGICAL PRESS
Collegeville, Minnesota

www.litpress.org

A Michael Glazier Book published by Liturgical Press

1   2   3   4   5   6   7   8   9

Library of Congress Cataloging-in-Publication Data

Wacker, Marie-Theres.
    Baruch and the Letter of Jeremiah / Marie-Theres Wacker ; Carol Dempsey, volume editor ; Barbara E. Reid, OP, general editor.
        pages   cm. — (Wisdom commentary ; Volume 31)
    "A Michael Glazier book."
    Includes bibliographical references.
    ISBN 978-0-8146-8155-8 — ISBN 978-0-8146-8180-0 (ebook)
    1. Bible. Baruch—Commentaries.   2. Epistle of Jeremiah—Commentaries.   I. Title.

BS1775.53.W33   2015
229'.5077—dc23   2015018746

Contents

Abbreviations

AB	Anchor Bible
ATD	Das Alte Testament Deutsch
BibInt	Biblical Interpretation Series
BZAW	Beihefte zur Zeitschrift für die Alttestamentliche Wissenschaft
CBET	Contributions to Biblical Exegesis and Theology
CBQ	*Catholic Biblical Quarterly*
DCLS	Deuterocanonical and Cognate Literature Studies
EBib	*Études bibliques*
EJL	Early Judaism and Its Literature
FRLANT	Forschungen zur Religion und Literatur des Alten und Neuen Testaments
HSM	Harvard Semitic Monograph
JBL	*Journal of Biblical Literature*
JSJ	*Journal for the Study of Judaism in the Persian, Hellenistic and Roman Periods*
JSOTSup	Journal for the Study of the Old Testament Supplement Series
LXX	Septuagint

MT   Masoretic Text

NAB   New American Bible

NEchtB   Neue Echter Bibel

NETS   A New English Translation of the Septuagint

NIB   New Interpreter's Bible

NJB   New Jerusalem Bible

OBO   Orbis Biblicus et Orientalis

OTE   *Old Testament Essays*

PAAJR   *Proceedings of the American Academy for Jewish Research*

SBL   Society of Biblical Literature

TH   Theodotion

WMANT   Wissenschaftliche Monographien zum Alten und Neuen Testament

WUNT   Wissenschaftliche Untersuchungen zum Neuen Testament

ZABR   *Zeitschrift für altorientalische und biblische Rechtgeschichte*

ZDMG   *Zeitschrift der deutschen morgenländischen Gesellschaft*

Contributors

Klaus Mertes, SJ, is a Jesuit priest and, since 2011, director of the Jesuit-run secondary school/Gymnasium Kolleg St. Blasien in St. Blasien, Southern Germany. Previously, he was director of another Gymnasium, Canisius-Kolleg, in Berlin. During that time, in 2010, he initiated the debate in Germany on sexual violence against boys by Catholic priests and became one of the spokespersons calling for a thorough investigation that would break the silence.

Prof. emerita Dr. Kyung-Sook Lee is a Methodist and an Old Testament scholar from Ewha University in Seoul, South Korea. Her doctorate in theology is from Goettingen, Germany. She served as dean of the Graduate School of Theology at Ewha and as vice president of Ewha Woman's University. She is an important voice for the development of Christian feminist biblical perspectives in her context.

Prof. Dr. Tal Ilan has held the position of professor of Jewish studies at Freie Universität Berlin, Germany, since 2003. Israeli-born, she grew up in a kibbutz in southern Israel and received her PhD at the Hebrew University in Jerusalem. She has written widely on women in the Second Temple period and is preparing a multivolume feminist commentary on the Talmud.

Dr. Antony John Baptist is a Catholic priest from Tamil Nadu, South India. He serves as secretary of the commission for Bible at Tamil Nadu

Bishops' Conference. In his research at the Asian Center for Cross-Cultural Studies in Madras, he reads the Bible from the context of Dalits and Dalit women.

Foreword

"Tell It on the Mountain"—or, "And You Shall Tell Your Daughter [as Well]"

Athalya Brenner-Idan
Universiteit van Amsterdam/Tel Aviv University

What can Wisdom Commentary do to help, and for whom? The commentary genre has always been privileged in biblical studies. Traditionally acclaimed commentary series, such as the International Critical Commentary, Old Testament and New Testament Library, Hermeneia, Anchor Bible, Eerdmans, and Word—to name but several—enjoy nearly automatic prestige; and the number of women authors who participate in those is relatively small by comparison to their growing number in the scholarly guild. There certainly are some volumes written by women in them, especially in recent decades. At this time, however, this does not reflect the situation on the ground. Further, size matters. In that sense, the sheer size of the Wisdom Commentary is essential. This also represents a considerable investment and the possibility of reaching a wider audience than those already "converted."

Expecting women scholars to deal especially or only with what is considered strictly "female" matters seems unwarranted. According to Audre Lorde, "The master's tools will never dismantle the master's house."[1] But this maxim is not relevant to our case. The point of this commentary is not to destroy but to attain greater participation in the interpretive dialogue about biblical texts. Women scholars may bring additional questions to the readerly agenda as well as fresh angles to existing issues. To assume that their questions are designed only to topple a certain male hegemony is not convincing.

At first I did ask myself: is this commentary series an addition to calm raw nerves, an embellishment to make upholding the old hierarchy palatable? Or is it indeed about becoming the Master? On second and third thoughts, however, I understood that becoming the Master is not what this is about. Knowledge is power. Since Foucault at the very least, this cannot be in dispute. Writing commentaries for biblical texts by women for women and for men, of confessional as well as non-confessional convictions, will sabotage (hopefully) the established hierarchy but will not topple it. This is about an attempt to integrate more fully, to introduce another viewpoint, to become. What excites me about the Wisdom Commentary is that it is not offered as just an alternative supplanting or substituting for the dominant discourse.

These commentaries on biblical books will retain nonauthoritative, pluralistic viewpoints. And yes, once again, the weight of a dedicated series, to distinguish from collections of standalone volumes, will prove weightier.

That such an approach is especially important in the case of the Hebrew Bible/Old Testament is beyond doubt. Women of Judaism, Christianity, and also Islam have struggled to make it their own for centuries, even more than they have fought for the New Testament and the Qur'an. Every Hebrew Bible/Old Testament volume in this project is evidence that the day has arrived: it is now possible to read *all* the Jewish canonical books as a collection, for a collection they are, with guidance conceived of with the needs of women readers (not only men) as an integral inspiration and part thereof.

In my Jewish tradition, the main motivation for reciting the Haggadah, the ritual text recited yearly on Passover, the festival of liberation from

1. Audre Lorde, "The Master's Tools Will Never Dismantle the Master's House," in *Sister Outsider: Essays and Speeches* (Berkeley, CA: Crossing Press, 1984, 2007), 110–14. First delivered in the Second Sex Conference in New York, 1979.

bondage, is given as "And you shall tell your son" (from Exod 13:8). The knowledge and experience of past generations is thus transferred to the next, for constructing the present and the future. The ancient maxim is, literally, limited to a male audience. This series remolds the maxim into a new inclusive shape, which is of the utmost consequence: "And you shall tell your son" is extended to "And you shall tell your daughter [as well as your son]." Or, if you want, "Tell it on the mountain," for all to hear.

This is what it's all about.

Editor's Introduction to Wisdom Commentary

"She Is a Breath of the Power of God" (Wis 7:25)

Barbara E. Reid, OP
General Editor

Wisdom Commentary is the first series to offer detailed feminist interpretation of every book of the Bible. The fruit of collaborative work by an ecumenical and interreligious team of scholars, the volumes provide serious, scholarly engagement with the whole biblical text, not only those texts that explicitly mention women. The series is intended for clergy, teachers, ministers, and all serious students of the Bible. Designed to be both accessible and informed by the various approaches of biblical scholarship, it pays particular attention to the world in front of the text, that is, how the text is heard and appropriated. At the same time, this series aims to be faithful to the ancient text and its earliest audiences; thus the volumes also explicate the worlds behind the text and within it. While issues of gender are primary in this project, the volumes also address the intersecting issues of power, authority, ethnicity, race, class, and religious belief and practice. The fifty-eight volumes include the books regarded as canonical by Jews (i.e., the Tanakh); Protestants (the "Hebrew Bible" and the New Testament); and Roman Catholic, Anglican, and Eastern Orthodox Communions (i.e., Tobit, Judith, 1 and 2 Maccabees, Wisdom of Solomon, Sirach/Ecclesiasticus, Baruch, including the Letter of Jeremiah, the additions to Esther, and Susanna and Bel and the Dragon in Daniel).

A Symphony of Diverse Voices

Included in the Wisdom Commentary series are voices from scholars of many different religious traditions, of diverse ages, differing sexual identities, and varying cultural, racial, ethnic, and social contexts. Some have been pioneers in feminist biblical interpretation; others are newer contributors from a younger generation. A further distinctive feature of this series is that each volume incorporates voices other than that of the lead author(s). These voices appear alongside the commentary of the lead author(s), in the grayscale inserts. At times, a contributor may offer an alternative interpretation or a critique of the position taken by the lead author(s). At other times, she or he may offer a complementary interpretation from a different cultural context or subject position. Occasionally, portions of previously published material bring in other views. The diverse voices are not intended to be contestants in a debate or a cacophony of discordant notes. The multiple voices reflect that there is no single definitive feminist interpretation of a text. In addition, they show the importance of subject position in the process of interpretation. In this regard, the Wisdom Commentary series takes inspiration from the Talmud and from *The Torah: A Women's Commentary* (ed. Tamara Cohn Eskenazi and Andrea L. Weiss; New York: Women of Reform Judaism, Federation of Temple Sisterhood, 2008), in which many voices, even conflicting ones, are included and not harmonized.

Contributors include biblical scholars, theologians, and readers of Scripture from outside the scholarly and religious guilds. At times, their comments pertain to a particular text. In some instances they address a theme or topic that arises from the text.

Another feature that highlights the collaborative nature of feminist biblical interpretation is that a number of the volumes have two lead authors who have worked in tandem from the inception of the project and whose voices interweave throughout the commentary.

Woman Wisdom

The title, Wisdom Commentary, reflects both the importance to feminists of the figure of Woman Wisdom in the Scriptures and the distinct wisdom that feminist women and men bring to the interpretive process. In the Scriptures, Woman Wisdom appears as "a breath of the power of God, and a pure emanation of the glory of the Almighty" (Wis 7:25), who was present and active in fashioning all that exists (Prov 8:22-31; Wis 8:6). She is a spirit who pervades and penetrates all things (Wis 7:22-23), and she provides guidance and nourishment at her all-inclusive table (Prov 9:1-5). In both postexilic biblical and nonbiblical Jewish sources, Woman Wisdom is often equated with Torah, e.g., Sir 24:23-34; Bar 3:9–4:4; 38:2; 46:4-5; 2 Bar 48:33, 36; 4 Ezra 5:9-10; 13:55; 14:40; 1 Enoch 42.

The New Testament frequently portrays Jesus as Wisdom incarnate. He invites his followers, "take my yoke upon you and learn from me" (Matt 11:29), just as Ben Sira advises, "put your neck under her [Wisdom's] yoke and let your souls receive instruction" (Sir 51:26). Just as Wisdom experiences rejection (Prov 1:23-25; Sir 15:7-8; Wis 10:3; Bar 3:12), so too does Jesus (Mark 8:31; John 1:10-11). Only some accept his invitation to his all-inclusive banquet (Matt 22:1-14; Luke 14:15-24; compare Prov 1:20-21; 9:3-5). Yet, "wisdom is vindicated by her deeds" (Matt 11:19, speaking of Jesus and John the Baptist; in the Lucan parallel at 7:35 they are called "wisdom's children"). There are numerous parallels between what is said of Wisdom and of the *Logos* in the Prologue of the Fourth Gospel (John 1:1-18). These are only a few of many examples. This female embodiment of divine presence and power is an apt image to guide the work of this series.

Feminism

There are many different understandings of the term "feminism." The various meanings, aims, and methods have developed exponentially in recent decades. Feminism is a perspective and a movement that springs from a recognition of inequities toward women, and it advocates for changes in whatever structures prevent full human flourishing. Three waves of feminism in the United States are commonly recognized. The first, arising in the mid-nineteenth century and lasting into the early twentieth, was sparked by women's efforts to be involved in the public sphere and to win the right to vote. In the 1960s and 1970s, the second wave focused on civil rights and equality for women. With the third wave, from the 1980s forward, came global feminism and the emphasis on the contextual nature of interpretation. Now a fourth wave may be emerging, with a stronger emphasis on the intersectionality of women's concerns with those of other marginalized groups and the increased use of the internet as a platform for discussion and activism.[1] As feminism has matured, it has recognized that inequities based on gender are interwoven with power imbalances based on race, class, ethnicity, religion, sexual identity, physical ability, and a host of other social markers.

Feminist Women and Men

Men who choose to identify with and partner with feminist women in the work of deconstructing systems of domination and building structures of equality are rightly regarded as feminists. Some men readily identify with experiences of women who are discriminated against on the basis of sex/gender, having themselves had comparable experiences; others who may not have faced direct discrimination or stereotyping recognize that inequity and problematic characterization still occur, and they seek correction. This series is pleased to include feminist men both as lead authors and as contributing voices.

Feminist Biblical Interpretation

Women interpreting the Bible from the lenses of their own experience is nothing new. Throughout the ages women have recounted the biblical stories, teaching them to their children and others, all the while interpreting them afresh for their time and circumstances.[2] Following is a very brief sketch of select foremothers who laid the groundwork for contemporary feminist biblical interpretation.

One of the earliest known Christian women who challenged patriarchal interpretations of Scripture was a consecrated virgin named Helie, who lived in the second century CE. When she refused to marry, her

---

1. See Martha Rampton, "Four Waves of Feminism" (October 25, 2015), at http://www.pacificu.edu/about-us/news-events/four-waves-feminism; and Ealasaid Munro, "Feminism: A Fourth Wave?," https://www.psa.ac.uk/insight-plus/feminism-fourth-wave.

2. For fuller treatments of this history, see chap. 7, "One Thousand Years of Feminist Bible Criticism," in Gerda Lerner, *Creation of Feminist Consciousness: From the Middle Ages to Eighteen-Seventy* (New York: Oxford University Press, 1993), 138–66; Susanne Scholz, "From the 'Woman's Bible' to the 'Women's Bible,' The History of Feminist Approaches to the Hebrew Bible," in *Introducing the Women's Hebrew Bible*, IFT 13 (New York: T & T Clark, 2007), 12–32; Marion Ann Taylor and Agnes Choi, eds., *Handbook of Women Biblical Interpreters: A Historical and Biographical Guide* (Grand Rapids, MI: Baker Academic, 2012).

parents brought her before a judge, who quoted to her Paul's admonition, "It is better to marry than to be aflame with passion" (1 Cor 7:9). In response, Helie first acknowledges that this is what Scripture says, but then she retorts, "but not for everyone, that is, not for holy virgins."[3] She is one of the first to question the notion that a text has one meaning that is applicable in all situations.

A Jewish woman who also lived in the second century CE, Beruriah, is said to have had "profound knowledge of biblical exegesis and outstanding intelligence."[4] One story preserved in the Talmud (b. Berakot 10a) tells of how she challenged her husband, Rabbi Meir, when he prayed for the destruction of a sinner. Proffering an alternate interpretation, she argued that Psalm 104:35 advocated praying for the destruction of sin, not the sinner.

In medieval times the first written commentaries on Scripture from a critical feminist point of view emerge. While others may have been produced and passed on orally, they are for the most part lost to us now. Among the earliest preserved feminist writings are those of Hildegard of Bingen (1098–1179), German writer, mystic, and abbess of a Benedictine monastery. She reinterpreted the Genesis narratives in a way that presented women and men as complementary and interdependent. She frequently wrote about feminine aspects of the Divine.[5] Along with other women mystics of the time, such as Julian of Norwich (1342–ca. 1416), she spoke authoritatively from her personal experiences of God's revelation in prayer.

In this era, women were also among the scribes who copied biblical manuscripts. Notable among them is Paula Dei Mansi of Verona, from a distinguished family of Jewish scribes. In 1288, she translated from Hebrew into Italian a collection of Bible commentaries written by her father and added her own explanations.[6]

Another pioneer, Christine de Pizan (1365–ca. 1430), was a French court writer and prolific poet. She used allegory and common sense to

---

3. Madrid, Escorial MS, a II 9, f. 90 v., as cited in Lerner, *Feminist Consciousness*, 140.

4. See Judith R. Baskin, "Women and Post-Biblical Commentary," in *The Torah: A Women's Commentary*, ed. Tamara Cohn Eskenazi and Andrea L. Weiss (New York: Women of Reform Judaism, Federation of Temple Sisterhood, 2008), xlix–lv, at lii.

5. Hildegard of Bingen, *De Operatione Dei*, 1.4.100; PL 197:885bc, as cited in Lerner, *Feminist Consciousness*, 142–43. See also Barbara Newman, *Sister of Wisdom: St. Hildegard's Theology of the Feminine* (Berkeley: University of California Press, 1987).

6. Emily Taitz, Sondra Henry, Cheryl Tallan, eds., *JPS Guide to Jewish Women 600 B.C.E.–1900 C.E.* (Philadelphia: JPS, 2003), 110–11.

subvert misogynist readings of Scripture and celebrated the accomplishments of female biblical figures to argue for women's active roles in building society.[7]

By the seventeenth century, there were women who asserted that the biblical text needs to be understood and interpreted in its historical context. For example, Rachel Speght (1597–ca. 1630), a Calvinist English poet, elaborates on the historical situation in first-century Corinth that prompted Paul to say, "It is well for a man not to touch a woman" (1 Cor 7:1). Her aim was to show that the biblical texts should not be applied in a literal fashion to all times and circumstances. Similarly, Margaret Fell (1614–1702), one of the founders of the Religious Society of Friends (Quakers) in Britain, addressed the Pauline prohibitions against women speaking in church by insisting that they do not have universal validity. Rather, they need to be understood in their historical context, as addressed to a local church in particular time-bound circumstances.[8]

Along with analyzing the historical context of the biblical writings, women in the eighteenth and nineteenth centuries began to attend to misogynistic interpretations based on faulty translations. One of the first to do so was British feminist Mary Astell (1666–1731).[9] In the United States, the Grimké sisters, Sarah (1792–1873) and Angelina (1805–1879), Quaker women from a slaveholding family in South Carolina, learned biblical Greek and Hebrew so that they could interpret the Bible for themselves. They were prompted to do so after men sought to silence them from speaking out against slavery and for women's rights by claiming that the Bible (e.g., 1 Cor 14:34) prevented women from speaking in public.[10] Another prominent abolitionist, Sojourner Truth (ca. 1797–1883), a former slave, quoted the Bible liberally in her speeches[11] and in so doing challenged cultural assumptions and biblical interpretations that undergird gender inequities.

---

7. See further Taylor and Choi, *Handbook of Women Biblical Interpreters*, 127–32.

8. Her major work, *Women's Speaking Justified, Proved and Allowed by the Scriptures*, published in London in 1667, gave a systematic feminist reading of all biblical texts pertaining to women.

9. Mary Astell, *Some Reflections upon Marriage* (New York: Source Book Press, 1970, reprint of the 1730 edition; earliest edition of this work is 1700), 103–4.

10. See further Sarah Grimké, *Letters on the Equality of the Sexes and the Condition of Woman* (Boston: Isaac Knapp, 1838).

11. See, for example, her most famous speech, "Ain't I a Woman?," delivered in 1851 at the Ohio Women's Rights Convention in Akron, OH; http://www.fordham.edu/halsall/mod/sojtruth-woman.asp.

Another monumental work that emerged in nineteenth-century England was that of Jewish theologian Grace Aguilar (1816–1847), *The Women of Israel*,[12] published in 1845. Aguilar's approach was to make connections between the biblical women and contemporary Jewish women's concerns. She aimed to counter the widespread notion that women were degraded in Jewish law and that only in Christianity were women's dignity and value upheld. Her intent was to help Jewish women find strength and encouragement by seeing the evidence of God's compassionate love in the history of every woman in the Bible. While not a full commentary on the Bible, Aguilar's work stands out for its comprehensive treatment of every female biblical character, including even the most obscure references.[13]

The first person to produce a full-blown feminist commentary on the Bible was Elizabeth Cady Stanton (1815–1902). A leading proponent in the United States for women's right to vote, she found that whenever women tried to make inroads into politics, education, or the work world, the Bible was quoted against them. Along with a team of like-minded women, she produced her own commentary on every text of the Bible that concerned women. Her pioneering two-volume project, *The Woman's Bible*, published in 1895 and 1898, urges women to recognize that texts that degrade women come from the men who wrote the texts, not from God, and to use their common sense to rethink what has been presented to them as sacred.

Nearly a century later, *The Women's Bible Commentary*, edited by Sharon Ringe and Carol Newsom (Westminster John Knox Press, 1992), appeared. This one-volume commentary features North American feminist scholarship on each book of the Protestant canon. Like Cady Stanton's commentary, it does not contain comments on every section of the biblical text but only on those passages deemed relevant to women. It was revised and expanded in 1998 to include the Apocrypha/Deuterocanonical books, and the contributors to this new volume reflect the global face of contemporary feminist scholarship. The revisions made in the third edition, which appeared in 2012, represent the profound advances in feminist biblical scholarship and include newer voices. In both the second and third editions, *The* has been dropped from the title.

---

12. The full title is *The Women of Israel or Characters and Sketches from the Holy Scriptures and Jewish History Illustrative of the Past History, Present Duty, and Future Destiny of the Hebrew Females, as Based on the Word of God.*

13. See further Eskenazi and Weiss, *The Torah: A Women's Commentary*, xxxviii; Taylor and Choi, *Handbook of Women Biblical Interpreters*, 31–37.

Also appearing at the centennial of Cady Stanton's *The Woman's Bible* were two volumes edited by Elisabeth Schüssler Fiorenza with the assistance of Shelly Matthews. The first, *Searching the Scriptures: A Feminist Introduction* (New York: Crossroad, 1993), charts a comprehensive approach to feminist interpretation from ecumenical, interreligious, and multicultural perspectives. The second volume, published in 1994, provides critical feminist commentary on each book of the New Testament as well as on three books of Jewish Pseudepigrapha and eleven other early Christian writings.

In Europe, similar endeavors have been undertaken, such as the one-volume *Kompendium Feministische Bibelauslegung*, edited by Luise Schottroff and Marie-Theres Wacker (Gütersloh, Gütersloher Verlagshaus, 1998; 3rd ed., 2007), featuring German feminist biblical interpretation of each book of the Bible, along with apocryphal books, and several extrabiblical writings. This work, now in its third edition, has recently been translated into English.[14] A multivolume project, *The Bible and Women: An Encylopaedia of Exegesis and Cultural History*, edited by Irmtraud Fischer, Adriana Valerio, Mercedes Navarro Puerto, and Christiana de Groot, is currently in production. This project presents a history of the reception of the Bible as embedded in Western cultural history and focuses particularly on gender-relevant biblical themes, biblical female characters, and women recipients of the Bible. The volumes are published in English, Spanish, Italian, and German.[15]

Another groundbreaking work is the collection The Feminist Companion to the Bible Series, edited by Athalya Brenner (Sheffield: Sheffield Academic Press, 1993–2015), which comprises twenty volumes of commentaries on the Old Testament. The parallel series, Feminist Companion

14. *Feminist Biblical Interpretation: A Compendium of Critical Commentary on the Books of the Bible and Related Literature*, trans. Lisa E. Dahill, Everett R. Kalin, Nancy Lukens, Linda M. Maloney, Barbara Rumscheidt, Martin Rumscheidt, and Tina Steiner (Grand Rapids, MI: Eerdmans, 2012). Another notable collection is the three volumes edited by Susanne Scholz, *Feminist Interpretation of the Hebrew Bible in Retrospect*, Recent Research in Biblical Studies 7, 8, 9 (Sheffield: Sheffield Phoenix Press, 2013, 2014, 2016).

15. The first volume, on the Torah, appeared in Spanish in 2009, in German and Italian in 2010, and in English in 2011 (Atlanta, GA: SBL). Four more volumes are now available: *Feminist Biblical Studies in the Twentieth Century*, ed. Elisabeth Schüssler Fiorenza (2014); *The Writings and Later Wisdom Books*, ed. Christl M. Maier and Nuria Calduch-Benages (2014); *Gospels: Narrative and History*, ed. Mercedes Navarro Puerto and Marinella Perroni (2015); and *The High Middle Ages*, ed. Kari Elisabeth Børresen and Adriana Valerio (2015). For further information, see http://www.bibleandwomen.org.

to the New Testament and Early Christian Writings, edited by Amy-Jill Levine with Marianne Blickenstaff and Maria Mayo Robbins (Sheffield: Sheffield Academic Press, 2001–2009), contains thirteen volumes with one more planned. These two series are not full commentaries on the biblical books but comprise collected essays on discrete biblical texts.

Works by individual feminist biblical scholars in all parts of the world abound, and they are now too numerous to list in this introduction. Feminist biblical interpretation has reached a level of maturity that now makes possible a commentary series on every book of the Bible. In recent decades, women have had greater access to formal theological education, have been able to learn critical analytical tools, have put their own interpretations into writing, and have developed new methods of biblical interpretation. Until recent decades the work of feminist biblical interpreters was largely unknown, both to other women and to their brothers in the synagogue, church, and academy. Feminists now have taken their place in the professional world of biblical scholars, where they build on the work of their foremothers and connect with one another across the globe in ways not previously possible. In a few short decades, feminist biblical criticism has become an integral part of the academy.

Methodologies

Feminist biblical scholars use a variety of methods and often employ a number of them together.[16] In the Wisdom Commentary series, the authors will explain their understanding of feminism and the feminist reading strategies used in their commentary. Each volume treats the biblical text in blocks of material, not an analysis verse by verse. The entire text is considered, not only those passages that feature female characters or that speak specifically about women. When women are not apparent in the narrative, feminist lenses are used to analyze the dynamics in the text between male characters, the models of power, binary ways of thinking, and dynamics of imperialism. Attention is given to how the whole text functions and how it was and is heard, both in its original context and today. Issues of particular concern to women—e.g., poverty, food, health, the environment, water—come to the fore.

---

16. See the seventeen essays in Caroline Vander Stichele and Todd Penner, eds., *Her Master's Tools? Feminist and Postcolonial Engagements of Historical-Critical Discourse* (Atlanta, GA: SBL, 2005), which show the complementarity of various approaches.

One of the approaches used by early feminists and still popular today is to lift up the overlooked and forgotten stories of women in the Bible. Studies of women in each of the Testaments have been done, and there are also studies on women in particular biblical books.[17] Feminists recognize that the examples of biblical characters can be both empowering and problematic. The point of the feminist enterprise is not to serve as an apologetic for women; it is rather, in part, to recover women's history and literary roles in all their complexity and to learn from that recovery.

Retrieving the submerged history of biblical women is a crucial step for constructing the story of the past so as to lead to liberative possibilities for the present and future. There are, however, some pitfalls to this approach. Sometimes depictions of biblical women have been naïve and romantic. Some commentators exalt the virtues of both biblical and contemporary women and paint women as superior to men. Such reverse discrimination inhibits movement toward equality for all. In addition, some feminists challenge the idea that one can "pluck positive images out of an admittedly androcentric text, separating literary characterizations from the androcentric interests they were created to serve."[18] Still other feminists find these images to have enormous value.

One other danger with seeking the submerged history of women is the tendency for Christian feminists to paint Jesus and even Paul as liberators of women in a way that demonizes Judaism.[19] Wisdom Commentary aims

17. See, e.g., Alice Bach, ed., *Women in the Hebrew Bible: A Reader* (New York: Routledge, 1998); Tikva Frymer-Kensky, *Reading the Women of the Bible* (New York: Schocken, 2002); Carol Meyers, Toni Craven, and Ross S. Kraemer, *Women in Scripture* (Grand Rapids, MI: Eerdmans, 2000); Irene Nowell, *Women in the Old Testament* (Collegeville, MN: Liturgical Press, 1997); Katharine Doob Sakenfeld, *Just Wives? Stories of Power and Survival in the Old Testament and Today* (Louisville, KY: Westminster John Knox, 2003); Mary Ann Getty-Sullivan, *Women in the New Testament* (Collegeville, MN: Liturgical Press, 2001); Bonnie Thurston, *Women in the New Testament* (New York: Crossroad, 1998).

18. Cheryl Exum, "Second Thoughts about Secondary Characters: Women in Exodus 1.8–2.10," in *A Feminist Companion to Exodus to Deuteronomy*, FCB 6 (Sheffield: Sheffield Academic Press, 1994), 75–97, at 76.

19. See Judith Plaskow, "Anti-Judaism in Feminist Christian Interpretation," in *Searching the Scriptures: A Feminist Introduction* (New York: Crossroad, 1993), 1:117–29; Amy-Jill Levine, "The New Testament and Anti-Judaism," in *The Misunderstood Jew: The Church and the Scandal of the Jewish Jesus* (San Francisco: HarperSanFrancisco, 2006), 87–117.

to enhance understanding of Jesus as well as Paul as Jews of their day and to forge solidarity among Jewish and Christian feminists.

Feminist scholars who use historical-critical methods analyze the world behind the text; they seek to understand the historical context from which the text emerged and the circumstances of the communities to whom it was addressed. In bringing feminist lenses to this approach, the aim is not to impose modern expectations on ancient cultures but to unmask the ways that ideologically problematic mind-sets that produced the ancient texts are still promulgated through the text. Feminist biblical scholars aim not only to deconstruct but also to reclaim and reconstruct biblical history as women's history, in which women were central and active agents in creating religious heritage.[20] A further step is to construct meaning for contemporary women and men in a liberative movement toward transformation of social, political, economic, and religious structures.[21] In recent years, some feminists have embraced new historicism, which accents the creative role of the interpreter in any construction of history and exposes the power struggles to which the text witnesses.[22]

Literary critics analyze the world of the text: its form, language patterns, and rhetorical function.[23] They do not attempt to separate layers of tradition and redaction but focus on the text holistically, as it is in its present

---

20. See, for example, Phyllis A. Bird, *Missing Persons and Mistaken Identities: Women and Gender in Ancient Israel* (Minneapolis: Fortress Press, 1997); Elisabeth Schüssler Fiorenza, *In Memory of Her: A Feminist Theological Reconstruction of Christian Origins* (New York: Crossroad, 1984); Ross Shepard Kraemer and Mary Rose D'Angelo, eds., *Women and Christian Origins* (New York: Oxford University Press, 1999).

21. See, e.g., Sandra M. Schneiders, *The Revelatory Text: Interpreting the New Testament as Sacred Scripture*, rev. ed. (Collegeville, MN: Liturgical Press, 1999), whose aim is to engage in biblical interpretation not only for intellectual enlightenment but, even more important, for personal and communal transformation. Elisabeth Schüssler Fiorenza (*Wisdom Ways: Introducing Feminist Biblical Interpretation* [Maryknoll, NY: Orbis Books, 2001]) envisions the work of feminist biblical interpretation as a dance of Wisdom that consists of seven steps that interweave in spiral movements toward liberation, the final one being transformative action for change.

22. See Gina Hens Piazza, *The New Historicism*, Guides to Biblical Scholarship, Old Testament Series (Minneapolis: Fortress Press, 2002).

23. Phyllis Trible was among the first to employ this method with texts from Genesis and Ruth in her groundbreaking book *God and the Rhetoric of Sexuality*, Overtures to Biblical Theology (Philadelphia: Fortress Press, 1978). Another pioneer in feminist literary criticism is Mieke Bal (*Lethal Love: Feminist Literary Readings of Biblical Love Stories* [Bloomington: Indiana University Press, 1987]). For surveys of recent developments in literary methods, see Terry Eagleton, *Literary Theory: An Introduction*, 3rd ed. (Minneapolis: University of Minnesota Press, 2008); Janice Capel Anderson and

form. They examine how meaning is created in the interaction between the text and its reader in multiple contexts. Within the arena of literary approaches are reader-oriented approaches, narrative, rhetorical, structuralist, post-structuralist, deconstructive, ideological, autobiographical, and performance criticism.[24] Narrative critics study the interrelation among author, text, and audience through investigation of settings, both spatial and temporal; characters; plot; and narrative techniques (e.g., irony, parody, intertextual allusions). Reader-response critics attend to the impact that the text has on the reader or hearer. They recognize that when a text is detrimental toward women there is the choice either to affirm the text or to read against the grain toward a liberative end. Rhetorical criticism analyzes the style of argumentation and attends to how the author is attempting to shape the thinking or actions of the hearer. Structuralist critics analyze the complex patterns of binary oppositions in the text to derive its meaning.[25] Post-structuralist approaches challenge the notion that there are fixed meanings to any biblical text or that there is one universal truth. They engage in close readings of the text and often engage in intertextual analysis.[26] Within this approach is deconstructionist criticism, which views the text as a site of conflict, with competing narratives. The interpreter aims to expose the fault lines and overturn and reconfigure binaries by elevating the underling of a pair and foregrounding it.[27] Feminists also use other postmodern approaches, such as ideological and autobiographical criticism. The former analyzes the system

---

Stephen D. Moore, eds., *Mark and Method: New Approaches in Biblical Studies*, 2nd ed. (Minneapolis: Fortress Press, 2008).

24. See, e.g., J. Cheryl Exum and David J. A. Clines, eds., *The New Literary Criticism and the Hebrew Bible* (Valley Forge, PA: Trinity Press International, 1993); Edgar V. McKnight and Elizabeth Struthers Malbon, eds., *The New Literary Criticism and the New Testament* (Valley Forge, PA: Trinity Press International, 1994).

25. See, e.g., David Jobling, *The Sense of Biblical Narrative: Three Structural Analyses in the Old Testament*, JSOTSup 7 (Sheffield: Sheffield University, 1978).

26. See, e.g., Stephen D. Moore, *Poststructuralism and the New Testament: Derrida and Foucault at the Foot of the Cross* (Minneapolis: Fortress Press, 1994); *The Bible in Theory: Critical and Postcritical Essays* (Atlanta, GA: SBL, 2010); Yvonne Sherwood, *A Biblical Text and Its Afterlives: The Survival of Jonah in Western Culture* (Cambridge: Cambridge University Press, 2000).

27. David Penchansky, "Deconstruction," in *The Oxford Encyclopedia of Biblical Interpretation*, ed. Steven McKenzie (New York: Oxford University Press, 2013), 196–205. See, for example, Danna Nolan Fewell and David M. Gunn, *Gender, Power, and Promise: The Subject of the Bible's First Story* (Nashville, TN: Abingdon, 1993); David Rutledge, *Reading Marginally: Feminism, Deconstruction and the Bible*, BibInt 21 (Leiden: Brill, 1996).

of ideas that underlies the power and values concealed in the text as well as that of the interpreter.[28] The latter involves deliberate self-disclosure while reading the text as a critical exegete.[29] Performance criticism attends to how the text was passed on orally, usually in communal settings, and to the verbal and nonverbal interactions between the performer and the audience.[30]

From the beginning, feminists have understood that interpreting the Bible is an act of power. In recent decades, feminist biblical scholars have developed hermeneutical theories of the ethics and politics of biblical interpretation to challenge the claims to value neutrality of most academic biblical scholarship. Feminist biblical scholars have also turned their attention to how some biblical writings were shaped by the power of empire and how this still shapes readers' self-understandings today. They have developed hermeneutical approaches that reveal, critique, and evaluate the interactions depicted in the text against the context of empire, and they consider implications for contemporary contexts.[31] Feminists also analyze the dynamics of colonization and the mentalities of colonized peoples in the exercise of biblical interpretation. As Kwok Pui-lan explains, "A postcolonial feminist interpretation of the Bible needs to investigate the deployment of gender in the narration of identity, the negotiation of power differentials between the colonizers and the colonized, and the reinforcement of patriarchal control over spheres where these elites could exercise control."[32] Methods and models from sociology and cultural anthropology

28. See Tina Pippin, ed., *Ideological Criticism of Biblical Texts: Semeia* 59 (1992); Terry Eagleton, *Ideology: An Introduction* (London: Verso, 2007).

29. See, e.g., Ingrid Rose Kitzberger, ed., *Autobiographical Biblical Interpretation: Between Text and Self* (Leiden: Deo, 2002); P. J. W. Schutte, "When *They, We,* and the Passive Become *I*—Introducing Autobiographical Biblical Criticism," *HTS Teologiese Studies / Theological Studies* 61 (2005): 401–16.

30. See, e.g., Holly Hearon and Philip Ruge-Jones, eds., *The Bible in Ancient and Modern Media: Story and Performance* (Eugene, OR: Cascade Books, 2009).

31. E.g., Gale Yee, ed., *Judges and Method: New Approaches in Biblical Studies* (Minneapolis: Fortress Press, 1995); Warren Carter, *The Gospel of Matthew in Its Roman Imperial Context* (London: T & T Clark, 2005); *The Roman Empire and the New Testament: An Essential Guide* (Nashville, TN: Abingdon, 2006); Elisabeth Schüssler Fiorenza, *The Power of the Word: Scripture and the Rhetoric of Empire* (Minneapolis: Fortress Press, 2007); Judith E. McKinlay, *Reframing Her: Biblical Women in Postcolonial Focus* (Sheffield: Sheffield Phoenix Press, 2004).

32. Kwok Pui-lan, *Postcolonial Imagination and Feminist Theology* (Louisville, KY: Westminster John Knox, 2005), 9. See also Musa W. Dube, ed., *Postcolonial Feminist Interpretation of the Bible* (St. Louis, MO: Chalice Press, 2000); Cristl M. Maier and

are used by feminists to investigate women's everyday lives, their experiences of marriage, childrearing, labor, money, illness, etc.[33]

As feminists have examined the construction of gender from varying cultural perspectives, they have become ever more cognizant that the way gender roles are defined within differing cultures varies radically. As Mary Ann Tolbert observes, "Attempts to isolate some universal role that cross-culturally defines 'woman' have run into contradictory evidence at every turn."[34] Some women have coined new terms to highlight the particularities of their socio-cultural context. Many African American feminists, for example, call themselves *womanists* to draw attention to the double oppression of racism and sexism they experience.[35] Similarly, many US Hispanic feminists speak of themselves as *mujeristas* (*mujer* is Spanish for "woman").[36] Others prefer to be called "Latina feminists."[37] Both groups emphasize that the context for their theologizing is *mestizaje* and *mulatez* (racial and cultural mixture), done *en conjunto* (in community), with *lo cotidiano* (everyday lived experience) of Hispanic women as starting points for theological reflection and the encounter with the divine. Intercultural analysis has become an indispensable tool for working toward justice for women at the global level.[38]

Carolyn J. Sharp, *Prophecy and Power: Jeremiah in Feminist and Postcolonial Perspective* (London: Bloomsbury, 2013).

33. See, for example, Carol Meyers, *Discovering Eve: Ancient Israelite Women in Context* (New York: Oxford University Press, 1991); Luise Schottroff, *Lydia's Impatient Sisters: A Feminist Social History of Early Christianity*, trans. Barbara and Martin Rumscheidt (Louisville, KY: Westminster John Knox, 1995); Susan Niditch, *"My Brother Esau Is a Hairy Man": Hair and Identity in Ancient Israel* (Oxford: Oxford University Press, 2008).

34. Mary Ann Tolbert, "Social, Sociological, and Anthropological Methods," in *Searching the Scriptures*, 1:255–71, at 265.

35. Alice Walker coined the term (*In Search of Our Mothers' Gardens: Womanist Prose* [New York: Harcourt Brace Jovanovich, 1967, 1983]). See also Katie G. Cannon, "The Emergence of Black Feminist Consciousness," in *Feminist Interpretation of the Bible*, ed. Letty M. Russell (Philadelphia: Westminster, 1985), 30–40; Renita Weems, *Just a Sister Away: A Womanist Vision of Women's Relationships in the Bible* (San Diego: Lura Media, 1988); Nyasha Junior, *An Introduction to Womanist Biblical Interpretation* (Louisville, KY: Westminster John Knox, 2015).

36. Ada María Isasi-Díaz (*Mujerista Theology: A Theology for the Twenty-first Century* [Maryknoll, NY: Orbis Books, 1996]) is credited with coining the term.

37. E.g., María Pilar Aquino, Daisy L. Machado, and Jeanette Rodríguez, eds., *A Reader in Latina Feminist Theology* (Austin: University of Texas Press, 2002).

38. See, e.g., María Pilar Aquino and María José Rosado-Nunes, eds., *Feminist Intercultural Theology: Latina Explorations for a Just World*, Studies in Latino/a Catholicism (Maryknoll, NY: Orbis Books, 2007).

Some feminists are among those who have developed lesbian, gay, bisexual, and transgender (LGBT) interpretation. This approach focuses on issues of sexual identity and uses various reading strategies. Some point out the ways in which categories that emerged in recent centuries are applied anachronistically to biblical texts to make modern-day judgments. Others show how the Bible is silent on contemporary issues about sexual identity. Still others examine same-sex relationships in the Bible by figures such as Ruth and Naomi or David and Jonathan. In recent years, queer theory has emerged; it emphasizes the blurriness of boundaries not just of sexual identity but also of gender roles. Queer critics often focus on texts in which figures transgress what is traditionally considered proper gender behavior.[39]

Feminists also recognize that the struggle for women's equality and dignity is intimately connected with the struggle for respect for Earth and for the whole of the cosmos. Ecofeminists interpret Scripture in ways that highlight the link between human domination of nature and male subjugation of women. They show how anthropocentric ways of interpreting the Bible have overlooked or dismissed Earth and Earth community. They invite readers to identify not only with human characters in the biblical narrative but also with other Earth creatures and domains of nature, especially those that are the object of injustice. Some use creative imagination to retrieve the interests of Earth implicit in the narrative and enable Earth to speak.[40]

Biblical Authority

By the late nineteenth century, some feminists, such as Elizabeth Cady Stanton, began to question openly whether the Bible could continue to be regarded as authoritative for women. They viewed the Bible itself as the source of women's oppression, and some rejected its sacred origin

---

39. See, e.g., Bernadette J. Brooten, *Love between Women: Early Christian Responses to Female Homoeroticism* (Chicago and London: University of Chicago Press, 1996); Mary Rose D'Angelo, "Women Partners in the New Testament," *JFSR* 6 (1990): 65–86; Deirdre J. Good, "Reading Strategies for Biblical Passages on Same-Sex Relations," *Theology and Sexuality* 7 (1997): 70–82; Deryn Guest, *When Deborah Met Jael: Lesbian Feminist Hermeneutics* (London: SCM Press, 2011); Teresa Hornsby and Ken Stone, eds., *Bible Trouble: Queer Readings at the Boundaries of Biblical Scholarship* (Atlanta, GA: SBL, 2011).

40. E.g., Norman C. Habel and Peter Trudinger, *Exploring Ecological Hermeneutics*, SBLSymS 46 (Atlanta, GA: SBL, 2008); Mary Judith Ress, *Ecofeminism in Latin America*, Women from the Margins (Maryknoll, NY: Orbis Books, 2006).

and saving claims. Some decided that the Bible and the religious traditions that enshrine it are too thoroughly saturated with androcentrism
and patriarchy to be redeemable.[41]

In the Wisdom Commentary series, questions such as these may be
raised, but the aim of this series is not to lead readers to reject the authority of the biblical text. Rather, the aim is to promote better understanding
of the contexts from which the text arose and of the rhetorical effects it
has on women and men in contemporary contexts. Such understanding
can lead to a deepening of faith, with the Bible serving as an aid to bring
flourishing of life.

Language for God

Because of the ways in which the term "God" has been used to symbol-
ize the divine in predominantly male, patriarchal, and monarchical
modes, feminists have designed new ways of speaking of the divine.
Some have called attention to the inadequacy of the term *God* by trying
to visually destabilize our ways of thinking and speaking of the divine.
Rosemary Radford Ruether proposed *God/ess*, as an unpronounceable
term pointing to the unnameable understanding of the divine that tran-
scends patriarchal limitations.[42] Some have followed traditional Jewish
practice, writing *G-d*. Elisabeth Schüssler Fiorenza has adopted *G*d*.[43]
Others draw on the biblical tradition to mine female and non-gender-
specific metaphors and symbols.[44] In Wisdom Commentary, there is not
one standard way of expressing the divine; each author will use her or
his preferred ways. The one exception is that when the tetragrammaton,
YHWH, the name revealed to Moses in Exodus 3:14, is used, it will be
without vowels, respecting the Jewish custom of avoiding pronouncing
the divine name out of reverence.

---

41. E.g., Mary Daly, *Beyond God the Father: A Philosophy of Women's Liberation* (Boston: Beacon, 1973).

42. Rosemary Radford Ruether, *Sexism and God-Talk: Toward a Feminist Theology*
(Boston: Beacon, 1983).

43. Elisabeth Schüssler Fiorenza, *Jesus: Miriam's Child, Sophia's Prophet; Critical Issues
in Feminist Christology* (New York: Continuum, 1994), 191 n. 3.

44. E.g., Sallie McFague, *Models of God: Theology for an Ecological, Nuclear Age* (Philadelphia: Fortress Press, 1987); Catherine LaCugna, *God for Us: The Trinity and Christian Life* (San Francisco: Harper Collins, 1991); Elizabeth A. Johnson, *She Who Is: The
Mystery of God in Feminist Theological Discourse* (New York: Crossroad, 1992). See
further Elizabeth A. Johnson, "God," in *Dictionary of Feminist Theologies*, 128–30.

Nomenclature for the Two Testaments

In recent decades, some biblical scholars have begun to call the two Testaments of the Bible by names other than the traditional nomenclature: Old and New Testament. Some regard "Old" as derogatory, implying that it is no longer relevant or that it has been superseded. Consequently, terms like Hebrew Bible, First Testament, and Jewish Scriptures and, correspondingly, Christian Scriptures or Second Testament have come into use. There are a number of difficulties with these designations. The term "Hebrew Bible" does not take into account that parts of the Old Testament are written not in Hebrew but in Aramaic.[45] Moreover, for Roman Catholics, Anglicans, and Eastern Orthodox believers, the Old Testament includes books written in Greek—the Deuterocanonical books, considered Apocrypha by Protestants. The term "Jewish Scriptures" is inadequate because these books are also sacred to Christians. Conversely, "Christian Scriptures" is not an accurate designation for the New Testament, since the Old Testament is also part of the Christian Scriptures. Using "First and Second Testament" also has difficulties, in that it can imply a hierarchy and a value judgment.[46] Jews generally use the term Tanakh, an acronym for Torah (Pentateuch), Nevi'im (Prophets), and Ketuvim (Writings).

In Wisdom Commentary, if authors choose to use a designation other than Tanakh, Old Testament, and New Testament, they will explain how they mean the term.

Translation

Modern feminist scholars recognize the complexities connected with biblical translation, as they have delved into questions about philosophy of language, how meanings are produced, and how they are culturally situated. Today it is evident that simply translating into gender-neutral formulations cannot address all the challenges presented by androcentric texts. Efforts at feminist translation must also deal with issues around authority and canonicity.[47]

---

45. Gen 31:47; Jer 10:11; Ezra 4:7–6:18; 7:12-26; Dan 2:4–7:28.
46. See Levine, *The Misunderstood Jew*, 193–99.
47. Elizabeth Castelli, "*Les Belles Infidèles*/Fidelity or Feminism? The Meanings of Feminist Biblical Translation," in *Searching the Scriptures*, 1:189–204, here 190.

Because of these complexities, the editors of Wisdom Commentary series have chosen to use an existing translation, the New Revised Standard Version (NRSV), which is provided for easy reference at the top of each page of commentary. The NRSV was produced by a team of ecumenical and interreligious scholars, is a fairly literal translation, and uses inclusive language for human beings. Brief discussions about problematic translations appear in the inserts labeled "Translation Matters." When more detailed discussions are available, these will be indicated in footnotes. In the commentary, wherever Hebrew or Greek words are used, English translation is provided. In cases where a wordplay is involved, transliteration is provided to enable understanding.

Art and Poetry

Artistic expression in poetry, music, sculpture, painting, and various other modes is very important to feminist interpretation. Where possible, art and poetry are included in the print volumes of the series. In a number of instances, these are original works created for this project. Regrettably, copyright and production costs prohibit the inclusion of color photographs and other artistic work. It is our hope that the web version will allow a greater collection of such resources.

Glossary

Because there are a number of excellent readily-available resources that provide definitions and concise explanations of terms used in feminist theological and biblical studies, this series will not include a glossary. We refer you to works such as *Dictionary of Feminist Theologies*, edited by Letty M. Russell with J. Shannon Clarkson (Louisville, KY: Westminster John Knox, 1996), and volume 1 of *Searching the Scriptures*, edited by Elisabeth Schüssler Fiorenza with the assistance of Shelly Matthews (New York: Crossroad, 1992). Individual authors in the Wisdom Commentary series will define the way they are using terms that may be unfamiliar.

Bibliography

Because bibliographies are quickly outdated and because the space is limited, only a list of Works Cited is included in the print volumes. A comprehensive bibliography for each volume is posted on a dedicated website and is updated regularly.

The link for this volume can be found at wisdomcommentary.org.

A Concluding Word

In just a few short decades, feminist biblical studies has grown exponentially, both in the methods that have been developed and in the number of scholars who have embraced it. We realize that this series is limited and will soon need to be revised and updated. It is our hope that Wisdom Commentary, by making the best of current feminist biblical scholarship available in an accessible format to ministers, preachers, teachers, scholars, and students, will aid all readers in their advancement toward God's vision of dignity, equality, and justice for all.

Acknowledgments

There are a great many people who have made this series possible: first, Peter Dwyer, director, and Hans Christoffersen, publisher of the academic market at Liturgical Press, who have believed in this project and have shepherded it since it was conceived in 2007. Editorial consultants Athalya Brenner-Idan and Elisabeth Schüssler Fiorenza have not only been an inspiration with their pioneering work but have encouraged us all along the way with their personal involvement. Volume editors Mary Ann Beavis, Carol J. Dempsey, Amy-Jill Levine, Linda M. Maloney, Ahida Pilarski, Sarah Tanzer, Lauress Wilkins Lawrence, and Seung Ai Yang have lent their extraordinary wisdom to the shaping of the series, have used their extensive networks of relationships to secure authors and contributors, and have worked tirelessly to guide their work to completion. Two others who contributed greatly to the shaping of the project at the outset were Linda M. Day and Mignon Jacobs, as well as Barbara E. Bowe of blessed memory (d. 2010). Editorial and research assistant Susan M. Hickman has provided invaluable support with administrative details and arrangements. I am grateful to Brian Eisenschenk and Christine Henderson who have assisted Susan Hickman with the Wiki. There are countless others at Liturgical Press whose daily work makes the production possible. I am especially thankful to Lauren L. Murphy, Andrea Humphrey, Lauress Wilkins Lawrence, and Justin Howell for their work in copyediting.

Author's Introduction

The book of Baruch (Bar) and the Epistle (or Letter) of Jeremiah (Ep Jer) are part of the larger corpus of Jewish Writings from the Second Temple period. Both transmitted in Greek, they do not belong to the Tanak but to the Septuagint tradition where they were regarded as two separate works. In the Latin tradition, the Epistle of Jeremiah was added to the book of Baruch as its sixth chapter. Catholic Bible editions like the New American Bible, the German *Einheitsübersetzung*, the French *Bible de Jérusalem*, the Italian *Bibbia CEI*, the Spanish *Biblia de la CEE*, but also the (Protestant) German revised *Luther–Bibel* or the Spanish Bible edition *Dios habla hoy* follow the Latin order, while ecumenical translations like the French *Traduction Oecuménique de la Bible* and the *Bible en français courant*, the German *Bibel in gerechter Sprache*, and the *Gute Nachricht–Bibel* (as well as its English counterpart, the *Good News Bible*) present the Letter of Jeremiah separate from the book of Baruch.

The Book of Baruch and the Epistle of Jeremiah as Part of a "Story" Told by the Septuagint

As the proper names indicate, the two booklets, Baruch and the Epistle of Jeremiah, connect with the biblical tradition through the prophet Jeremiah and his scribe and secretary Baruch. Both books introduce themselves as written texts, the one as "book" (Bar 1:1), the other as "epistle" (Ep Jer 1 = Bar 6:1). As such, they develop the motif of written messages or records already prominent in the book of Jeremiah: the prophet sent a letter to those who were about to be deported to Babylon (Jer 29 MT/36 LXX); Baruch was told to write down Jeremiah's words in a scroll (Jer 36 MT/43 LXX). The "Epistle" would then be another letter of Jeremiah, and Baruch would again write down words in a new situation.[1] In a historical-critical perspective, both writings are considered pseudepigraphs, using the names of Jeremiah and Baruch in and for times historically different from those of the prophet and his scribe but perceived (or constructed) as similar or comparable in terms of challenges and hopes.

A tentative first approach to the two writings—to be expanded by other readings—might explain them in their literary context, the books of the Corpus Ieremianum (Jeremiah, Lamentations, Baruch, and Epistle of Jeremiah) in the Septuagint. The relevant observation to start with concerns the different order of chapters in the Masoretic (MT) and the Greek (LXX) book of Jeremiah. In the Hebrew version, the "oracles against the nations" (Jer 46–52) conclude Jeremiah's message. The last of these oracles is against the Babylonian Empire, visualized as the country of the Chaldeans with its king but also as a woman figure representing the city of Babylon (Jer 50–51). The final chapter of the book (Jer 52) reports the conquest of Jerusalem by Babylonian troops. Hence, Jeremiah's message ends the way it began in chapter 1: his message is verified by the events he announced; he is a true prophet according to Deut 18:22. Therefore, in the logic of Deut 18, his last words concerning Babylon, foreshadowed in Jer 25, are credible and convey a message of hope: indeed, Jerusalem's destruction has to be told, but the empire that destroyed her does not escape its own destruction. The opposition or polarization between Jerusalem and Babylon appears to be a central message at the end of Jeremiah's book in its Hebrew shape.

In the Septuagint, the oracles against the nations are placed behind (more precisely: within) Jer 25, after Jeremiah's words against Judah and Jerusalem (2–24). The Greek book of Jeremiah closes, as does the Hebrew, with the account of Jerusalem's fall, but the preceding chapter tells about the spectacular revolt of the people in Egypt, led by women, against the prophet's call to abstain from the worship of the Queen of Heaven, a

---

1. For a broader discussion of the Jeremian "diaspora letters" as "epistolary communication," see Lutz Doering, "Jeremiah and the 'Diaspora Letters' in Ancient Judaism: Epistolary Communication with the Golah as Medium for Dealing with the Present," in *Reading the Present in the Qumran Library: The Perception of the Contemporary by Means of Scriptural Interpretation*, ed. Kristin De Troyer and Armin Lange (Atlanta, GA: SBL Press, 2005), 43–72.

goddess venerated since Judean times (Jer 44:1-30 MT/Jer 51:1-30 LXX).[2] The worship of the Queen of Heaven, thus, becomes the prototype of idolatry, Egypt the site of continuing apostasy, and women the spokespersons of revolt against the God of Israel. According to the narrative, Jerusalem's fall is interpreted as a consequence of Israel's blasphemy. Moreover, Jer 51 LXX has a final word addressed to Baruch, predicting that he would save just his life in these times of calamity (Jer 45 MT/51:31-35 LXX). Given the widely accepted hypothesis that most of the Septuagint originated in Hellenistic Alexandria, hence in Egypt, the composition of Jer LXX can be read as a critical voice against Jews in Alexandria who are fascinated by the goddess Isis, the Hellenistic "Great Goddess."[3]

This end of Jer LXX forms an apt platform for the book of Baruch with its opening scene in Babylonia and the message Baruch has to convey. At the river Sud, where the congregation listening to Baruch has gathered, there is no revolt but instead a mourning liturgy (Bar 1:5). The city is in ruins (Jer 52MT/LXX; Bar 1:2), and the joyful prophecy for Jerusalem (Bar 4:30–5:9) still concerns her future. The present is dominated by a prayer confessing transgression from God's commandments transmitted by Moses, and the only commandment spelled out is the one not to worship other gods (Bar 1:22).

According to the order in the two major Septuagint codices of Alexandrinus and Sinaiticus, the book of Lamentations follows Baruch and comes back to the present disaster. Lamentations is dominated by a female figure, the figure of Jerusalem and her moving laments, corresponding to the lament of mother Jerusalem in Bar 4:9-20. The last cry of the Jerusalemites is this: "Restore us to yourself, O YHWH, that we may be restored; renew our days as of old—unless you have utterly rejected us, and are angry with us beyond measure" (Lam 5:21-22).[4] The following text, Jeremiah's letter to those who will soon be deported from Jerusalem

2. The NRSV follows the MT unless otherwise noted. Note that the Greek text has βασίλισσα τοῦ οὐρανοῦ, "Queen of Heaven," clearly denoting a goddess, while the MT has מלכת השמים, vocalized as "work of heavens," an intentional distortion of the goddess.

3. A quite different voice is the Wisdom of Solomon, where the figure of wisdom beside God is central and seems to be shaped with a view toward the goddess Isis. See Silvia Schroer, "Wisdom: An Example of Jewish Intercultural Theology," in *Feminist Biblical Interpretation: A Compendium of Critical Commentary on the Books of the Bible and Related Literature*, ed. Luise Schottroff and Marie-Theres Wacker (Grand Rapids, MI: Eerdmans, 2012), 555–65.

4. The NRSV translates the divine name, YHWH, as "Lord." In quotations from the Hebrew Bible, I prefer to transliterate rather than translate that name. See also n. 13 on p. 23 below.

to Babylonia, reads like an explanation, a consolation, and an obligation: their exile is imperative, but limited, and in the meantime they have to resist the worship of the gods of Babylonia—or, with a slightly different emphasis, they must not repeat the revolt of those in Egypt who defended the worship of the goddess. Egypt and Babylonia melt into one site, the site of danger and failure but also of challenge.

In other Greek manuscripts as well as in the Syriac and in the Latin tradition, the Letter of Jeremiah follows the book of Baruch or is counted as the last chapter of that book. In this case, the Letter seems to be an answer to the exiles who sent Baruch's book to Jerusalem; it is a message coming from Jerusalem, the recognized center of Jewish identity—in ruins, as the book of Lamentations reflects, but with the altar still in function (Bar 1:10)—to those who will live in the diaspora and have to arrange their lives there for a long time.

The Septuagint translation and compilation of Early Jewish writings came into being before the invention of codices where each book has its fixed place between others. Considered as single scrolls, the sequence of the texts can easily be varied, with the book of Jeremiah as a kind of lead voice and Baruch, Lamentations, and the Epistle of Jeremiah as responding voices that would not only react to Jeremiah but might also be in dialogue with one another.[5] The central themes, however, are constant: Jerusalem and Babylon/Egypt; homeland and diaspora; God and other gods, with a certain emphasis on/against the worship of a/the goddess; acceptance of God's commandments or revolt/apostasy.

Textual Criticism and the Translational Character of the Texts

As there are, in both books, quite a number of difficulties or peculiarities in the Greek wording that can best be explained by assuming a Semitic *Vorlage*, it seems reasonable to admit a prior Hebrew (or Aramaic) edition of (at least parts of) the book of Baruch and of Jeremiah's letter. The NRSV translation at some points goes back to this hypothetical original in a

---

5. Only brief mention can be made of other voices inserting themselves into the tradition of Jeremiah and Baruch, including the (later) Syriac and Greek Apocalypses of Baruch or the *Paraleipomena Jeremiae* (also: 2, 3, 4 Bar), as well as 4QApocryphon Jeremiah. For more details, see Lutz Doering, "Jeremia in Babylonien und Ägypten: Mündliche und schriftliche Toraparänese für Exil und Diaspora nach 4QApocryphon of Jeremiah C," in *Frühjudentum und Neues Testament im Horizont Biblischer Theologie*, ed. Wolfgang Kraus and Karl-Wilhelm Niebuhr, WUNT 162 (Tübingen: Mohr Siebeck, 2003), 50–79, and relevant entries in John J. Collins and Daniel C. Harlow, eds., *The Eerdmans Dictionary of Early Judaism* (Grand Rapids, MI: Eerdmans, 2010).

Semitic language. Thus the NRSV does not consequently translate the Greek Septuagint text, but does use a Greek text with conjectures according to that hypothetical Semitic text. This is an accepted and well-founded text-critical procedure, but it is based heavily on the assumption that the translators into Greek had their linguistic limitations and sometimes missed the original meaning. An alternative approach would start from the assumption that the Greek translator(s) pondered over their *Vorlage* and in several instances decided against what was (seemingly) most evident in the original text. Instead, they probably chose the best reading according to their own logic. Therefore I will discuss the instances where NRSV decided against the Greek wording and show that there is meaning in the Greek text, not just mistake or corruption.

From the specifics of the textual tradition emerges another fundamental problem: as it is not possible to compare the Greek texts of Baruch and the Epistle of Jeremiah with their presumed *Vorlage*, it is difficult to know to what extent they were reworked. The translators might have rearranged their text and added or omitted phrases or paragraphs. They might rather have acted as editors. They might, as perhaps in the case of Jeremiah's letter, have created a new, smooth text, a translation oriented toward the target language, which means that a certain liberty to adapt meanings is *a priori* given. Therefore it remains extremely hypothetical to date translation or *Vorlage*, although neither could be dated to before the Hellenistic age. For the book of Baruch things are even more complex as it seems to be necessary to admit translation from a Semitic *Vorlage* as well as reference to the Septuagint of the book of Jeremiah.[6] What is evident is again the close connection seen or constructed between the writings of Jeremiah and his secretary.

Stages of Former Research

Scholarly research on Baruch and the Letter of Jeremiah is not abundant.[7] In the context of Protestant historical-critical interest in the Apocrypha and Pseudepigrapha through the nineteenth and beginning of the

6. See notes to Bar 1:9 and 2:25 below. To think of the same translator working on Jeremiah and Baruch appears too simple an explanation; Emanuel Tov, *The Septuagint Translation of Jeremiah and Baruch: A Discussion of an Early Revision of the LXX of Jeremiah 29–52 and Baruch 1:1–3:8*, HSM 8 (Missoula, MT: Scholars Press, 1976) convincingly combines translation and revision according to the Greek text of Jeremiah.

7. For a history of scholarly research on Baruch, see the extensive monograph by Rüdiger Feuerstein, *Das Buch Baruch. Studien zur Textgestalt und Auslegungsgeschichte*, Europäische Hochschul-Schriften XXIII/614 (Frankfurt: Peter Lang, 1997).

twentieth centuries, the two writings were treated in handbooks and collections[8] with a strong emphasis on original language, source criticism, and questions of date. On Baruch, two extensive commentaries along these lines—one by a Catholic, the other by a Protestant theologian—were published in nineteenth-century Germany;[9] on the Letter of Jeremiah, one monograph, the only one until now, appeared in 1913, interested mainly in knowledge of Babylonian culture expressed in the Letter.[10] Since the 1950s with the Catholic Magisterium's gradual opening to historical methods of exegesis, a number of commentaries and scholarly contributions on specific questions came from Catholics all over Western Europe.[11] Special mention has to be made of the project *L'univers de la Bible* with its Jewish-Christian-Muslim approach to the Bible, Baruch and the Letter of

---

8. The two major collections were provided by Emil Kautzsch (German) and Robert Charles (in English): Johann W. Rothstein, "Das Buch Baruch," 213–25, and Johann W. Rothstein, "Der Brief des Jeremia," 226–29, in *Die Apokryphen und Pseudepigraphen des Alten Testaments*, vol. 1, ed. Emil Kautzsch (Tübingen: Mohr, 1900 [repr. 1921]); Owen C. Whitehouse, "The Book of Baruch," 569–95, and C. J. Ball, "Epistle of Jeremy," 596–611, in *The Apocrypha and Pseudepigrapha of the Old Testament*, vol. 1, ed. Robert Charles (Oxford: Clarendon, 1913).

9. Heinrich Reusch (Cath.), *Erklärung des Buchs Baruch* (Freiburg i. Br.: Herder, 1853); Johann Jacob Kneucker (Prot.), *Das Buch Baruch. Geschichte und Kritik, Übersetzung und Erklärung auf Grund des wiederhergestellten hebräischen Urtextes* (Leipzig: Brockhaus, 1879), both with breathtaking linguistic competences. Another extensive commentary came from the Jesuit Joseph Knabenbauer, "Commentarius in Baruch," in *Commentarius in Danielem prophetam, Lamentationes et Baruch. Cursus Scripturae Sacrae* III/2 (Paris: Lethielleux, 1889), 433–520. He makes use already of publications about excavations in Mesopotamia.

10. Weigand Naumann, *Untersuchungen über den apokryphen Jeremiasbrief*, BZAW 25 (Gießen: Alfred Töpelmann, 1913). His aim is to show the knowledge of Babylonian cults, to plead for a Hebrew original, and to date Ep Jer in the period after Alexander the Great and his revitalization of Babylonian cults.

11. Mention can be made here only of some examples: Benjamin N. Wambacq, "Baruch," 365–84, and Benjamin N. Wambacq, "De Brief van Jeremias," 385–94, in *Jeremias – Klaagliederen – Baruch – Brief van Jeremias*, De Boeken van het Oude Testament (Roermond and Maaseik: J. J. Romen & Zonen, 1957); Luis Alonso Schökel, "Baruc," 123–65, and Luis Alonso Schökel, "Carta de Jeremias," 167–78, in *Daniel – Baruc – Carta de Jeremias – Lamentaciones*, Los Libros Sagrados 18 (Madrid: Ediciones Cristiandad 1976); Josef Schreiner, "Baruch," in *Klagelieder/Baruch*, NEchtB Altes Testament 14, ed. Josef G. Plöger and others (Würzburg: Echter, 1986), 43–84. Of particular interest is Heinrich Schneider, *Das Buch Daniel. Das Buch der Klagelieder. Das Buch Baruch. Die Hl. Schrift für das Leben erklärt*, Herders Bibelkommentar 9, vol. 2 (Freiburg: Herder, 1954), 131–62, who tries to explain Bar 1–6 for postwar German Catholicism.

Jeremiah included.[12] A turning point in the perception of Baruch is represented in the important study by the Swiss Protestant Old Testament scholar Odil Hannes Steck, who, in 1993, was the first to read this book as a carefully constructed unit and to rethink its logic built on a specific reception of the Tanak along the lines of a rereading of Jeremiah and Deuteronomy in its Deuteronomistic shape.[13] André Kabasele Mukenge, a Catholic Old Testament scholar from the Democratic Republic of Congo doing research in Belgium, pushed this approach further, combining it with fresh hypotheses on the redaction history of the book.[14] Today, Baruch and the Letter of Jeremiah are studied at the intersections of research fields on Second Temple Judaism, including new textual editions and translations,[15] in North America, Israel, and Western Europe and by scholars from different Christian and Jewish denominations. Unfortunately, the commentary by Sean Adams on Baruch and the Epistle of Jeremiah, based on the text of Codex Vaticanus,[16] could not be discussed

---

12. André Chouraqui, and others, "Lettre d'Irmeyahou/Lettre de Jérémie," in *L'univers de la Bible*, vol. 7 (Paris: Brepols, 1984), 453–64, richly illustrated and annotated from the perspective of the three monotheistic religions.

13. Odil Hannes Steck, *Das apokryphe Baruchbuch*, FRLANT 160 (Göttingen: Vandenhoeck & Ruprecht, 1993); Odil Hannes Steck, "Das Buch Baruch," in *ATD Apokryphen*, vol. 5, ed. Otto Kaiser and Lothar Perlitt (Göttingen: Vandenhoeck & Ruprecht, 1998), 9–68. Others before him tried to discover a certain unity—Schökel, *Baruc*, 126, e.g., saw already the conflux of four major literary traditions—but did not discover a similar coherent structure. Most commentators before Steck described the book of Baruch as a collection of pieces more or less well connected. A particular negative judgment comes from Carey A. Moore, "Epistle of Jeremiah," 317–32, and Carey A. Moore, "1 Baruch," 255–316, in *Daniel, Esther and Jeremiah: The Additions*, AB 44 (Garden City, New York: Doubleday, 1977), who sees in Baruch "no new or original religious idea" (259) and a thoroughgoing "theological and religious weakness" (261).

14. André Kabasele Mukenge, *L'unité littéraire du Livre de Baruch*, EBib, N.S. 38 (Louvain: Gabalda, 1998).

15. See in particular NETS (Tony S. L. Michael, "Barouch," and Benjamin G. Wright, "The Letter of Jeremiah," in *A New English Translation of the Septuagint*, ed. Albert Pietersma and Benjamin G. Wright, 2nd ed. [New York: Oxford University Press, 2009], 925–31 and 942–45); *Septuaginta deutsch* (Wolfgang Kraus and Georg Gäbel, "Baruch," and "Epistole Jeremiou," in *Septuaginta deutsch. Das griechische Alte Testament in deutscher Übersetzung*, ed. Wolfgang Kraus and Martin Karrer [Stuttgart: Deutsche Bibelgesellschaft, 2009], 1343–48 and 1358–61); Bible d'Alexandrie (Isabelle Assan-Dhôte and Jacqueline Moatti-Fine, "Baruch," in *Baruch, Lamentations, Lettre de Jérémie*, La Bible d'Alexandrie 25.2 [Paris: Cerf, 2005]).

16. See Sean Adams, *Baruch and the Epistle of Jeremiah: A Commentary Based on the Texts in Codex Vaticanus*, Septuagint Commentary Series (Leiden: Brill, 2014).

because it was published when my manuscript was already completed. Feminist or gender-sensitive studies on both books, though, are still rare[17] so that the reflections in this commentary will break new ground.

A New Hermeneutical Frame for Baruch and the Letter of Jeremiah: Feminism, Gender Sensitivity, and Empire or (Post)Colonial Criticism

From a closer look at women figures in biblical texts and reconstructions of women's daily life in biblical times, feminist biblical studies have moved to more complex perspectives and issues.[18] With the concept of gender, social constructions of women (and men) can be described and the problem of essentialism be raised. Feminist scholars are aware of their own contextual biases and limitations but also their privileges when reading biblical texts. Feminist scholars tend to reflect on their roles as readers who transmit specific meaning to a text and opt for new, decisively partial, and/or political readings. In particular, the notion of women (or men) is called into question in favor of a double differentiation relevant for literary and historical studies of biblical texts. The first considers social and economic structures in and behind the texts that bring some men closer to women in terms of human rights or social possibilities than to other men. Masculinity studies refer to this fact with the distinction between hegemonic masculinities and marginal or subordinate forms. The second differentiation concerns a critique of sex/gender analyses that stick to a naturally given system of two genders/sexes only and treat heterosexuality as socially normative. Queer studies can help to detect facts or structures in biblical texts going beyond that matrix. The designation "wo/men" might be a possible way to point to such more complex perspectives.

---

17. See Patricia K. Tull, "Baruch," 418–22, and Patricia K. Tull, "Letter of Jeremiah," 423–25, in *Women's Bible Commentary*, 3rd ed., ed. Carol A. Newsom, Sharon H. Ringe, and Jacqueline E. Lapsley (Louisville, KY: Westminster John Knox, 2012); Marie-Theres Wacker, "Baruch: Mail from Distant Shores," in Schottroff and Wacker, *Feminist Biblical Interpretation*, 431–38, who, independent from one another, developed the first feminist approaches to both writings. Other relevant studies concern specific topics only, like wisdom or Jerusalem as feminine figures.

18. For more details, see Barbara Reid's general introduction to this volume. In addition: Elisabeth Schüssler Fiorenza, *Wisdom Ways: Introducing Feminist Biblical Interpretation* (Maryknoll, NY: Orbis Books, 2001); Lisa Sowle Cahill, Diego Irarrázaval, and Elaine M. Wainwright, eds., *Concilium: Gender in Theology, Spirituality, and Practice* 48 (London: SCM Press, 2012).

Moreover, for writings from the Second Temple era, the perspectives of empire and/or (post)colonial criticism appear specifically relevant.[19] Historically, Jewish communities existed not only in Judaea but also in Egypt, Babylonia, and Western Asia, most of the time under the rule of large imperial powers (Ptolemies, Seleucids, Romans). Their arrangements with these political coordinates that shaped their daily life were manifold, including assimilation, submission, and resistance. The writings of that time reflect those struggles in the different ways they refer to tradition, the present, and their hopes but also in their styles of rhetoric between repetition of antagonistic structures and searching for new, often hybrid forms of thought and expression.

In a biblical commentary named Wisdom Commentary, the book of Baruch finds its due place not only as a biblical book for Christians from the Catholic or Orthodox traditions but also as a writing that has at its center a poem on wisdom (Bar 3:9–4:4). Baruch clearly relates intertextually to other biblical and early Jewish wisdom texts but hardly contributes to the feminine personification of wisdom so prominent in the books of Proverbs, Sirach, and Wisdom of Solomon. Instead, Baruch's strong feminine figure is Jerusalem, here again painted in well-known biblical— more precisely, prophetic—colors, but also with new traits (Bar 4:5–5:9). Baruch makes a discernible move from a community with all its enumerated male representatives, leaving women invisible or "included" in linguistic inferences (Bar 1–2), to a poem reflecting the hiddenness and accessibility of wisdom (Bar 3–4), and then finally to a view on the destiny of Jerusalem, the Woman-City (Bar 4–5). How, then, can this move be described?

The Letter of Jeremiah, on the contrary, has much to say about women. Interspersed with ironic mockeries of Babylonian idol worship, there are numerous side glances at women of different provenience and in diverse functions. The text is evidently rooted in the biblical traditions of idol mockery, but these do not include critical views on women. Therefore the Letter of Jeremiah's different interest may raise questions—and encourage the reader to examine the rhetoric and ideology of both writings. Both books feature fictitious locations: the Letter of Jeremiah in the

---

19. For a good introduction, see Musa W. Dube, *Postcolonial Feminist Interpretation of the Bible* (St. Louis, MO: Chalice, 2000); Hille Haker, Luiz Carlos Susin, and Éloi Messi Metogo, eds., *Concilium: Postcolonial Theology* 49 (London: SCM Press, 2013); Andreas Nehring, and Simon Tielesch, eds., *Postkoloniale Theologie: Bibelhermeneutische und kulturwissenschaftliche Beiträge* (Stuttgart: Kohlhammer, 2013).

conquered city of Jerusalem, where her inhabitants await deportation to Babylonia; and Baruch in Babylonia not long after Jerusalem's fall. Both books evoke a moment of extreme political and religious crisis. In both books, the two geographic antipodes are symbolic: for those who write Jeremiah's Letter, Jerusalem symbolizes the center of their identity overcome by a mighty empire;[20] for those who write the book of Baruch, the river Sud is a symbol of space within the vast Babylonian Empire where the deported live and orient their minds back to Jerusalem. Both writings, in their specific ways, struggle with the reality that part of the Jewish community lives outside Jerusalem and Judah and has to accommodate to this situation for a long time.

An appropriate approach to both books, then, is to use literary methods of analysis (structural, narrative, rhetorical, ideological) and try to combine feminist and gender-sensitive perspectives with attentiveness to "the colonial" on a multiplicity of levels: as a textual construction of the given situation as colonization, as a set of structures which influences the perspectives of those who are behind the text, as a problem of scholarly research on these books, and as a problem of present reception.

Voices

According to the concept of Wisdom Commentary, several voices besides that of the primary author are included. For each of the large parts in Bar 1–6 one other voice contributes three to five continuous passages. For Bar 1–2, known as the penitential prayer, Klaus Mertes, SJ, writes on the "guilt of fathers and rulers." He is the Jesuit priest who in 2010 initiated the debate in Germany on sexual violence against boys by Catholic priests and became one of the spokespeople who called for a thorough investigation that would break the silence.[21] In relation to Baruch's wisdom poem in Bar 3–4, Prof. Dr. Kyung-Sook Lee, a Methodist Old Testament feminist scholar from Ewha University in Seoul, South Korea, the largest women's university worldwide, contributes reflections on Christian and Buddhist/Confucian wisdom.[22] The speech by and to Jerusalem in Bar 4–5 is treated by Prof. Dr. Tal Ilan, an Israeli scholar

20. On the notion of "empire," see Elisabeth Schüssler Fiorenza, *The Power of the Word: Scripture and the Rhetoric of Empire* (Minneapolis: Fortress Press, 2007).

21. See Klaus Mertes, *Verlorenes Vertrauen. Katholisch sein in der Krise* (Freiburg: Herder, 2013).

22. See Kyung-Sook Lee, "1 & 2 Kings," in *Global Bible Commentary*, ed. Daniel Patte et al. (Nashville, TN: Abingdon, 2005), 105–18, and Kyung-Sook Lee, "Books of Kings:

teaching Jewish studies at Freie Universität Berlin, Germany. Prof. Ilan is well known for her efforts to integrate Jewish women into Second Temple and Rabbinic history[23] and for her project of a feminist commentary on the Talmud.[24] The idol mockery in the Letter of Jeremiah (Bar 6) is taken up by Dr. Antony John Baptist, a Catholic priest from Tamil Nadu, South India, who in his research at the Asian Center for Cross Cultural Studies in Madras reads the Bible from the context of Dalits and Dalit women. Dalit people belong to one of the lowest casts in India and sometimes are even considered "outcasts."[25] I am very grateful to P. Mertes, Dr. Lee, Dr. Ilan, and Dr. John Baptist for their willingness to be part of this enterprise!

Thanks

My involvement with Baruch and the Letter of Jeremiah dates back to the time I prepared the short commentary on both books for the one-volume feminist commentary *Kompendium feministische Bibelauslegung.*[26] The opportunity to translate Baruch and the Letter of Jeremiah for *Bibel in gerechter Sprache,*[27] an inclusive-language German translation of the Bible, and to revise these books for the official German Catholic *Einheitsübersetzung* helped to sharpen my sensibility for classical exegetical concerns related to these books as well as for gender-relevant questions. Thanks go to Sandra Schroer in Cologne, who helped to start the project with valuable bibliographical research, and to Dr. Johanna Erzberger and Leonie Leibold in Muenster, who provided countless books and articles and engaged in discussion with me on relevant topics. Verena Suchhart in Muenster provided competent assistance in formatting the

Images of Women without Women's Reality," in Schottroff and Wacker, *Feminist Biblical Interpretation*, 159–77.

23. See Tal Ilan, *Jewish Women in Greco-Roman Palestine: An Inquiry into Image and Status* (Tübingen: Mohr Siebeck, 1995); Tal Ilan, *Integrating Women into Second Temple History* (Tübingen: Mohr Siebeck, 1999).

24. Between the 2007 introductory volume—Tal Ilan et al., eds., *A Feminist Commentary on the Babylonian Talmud* (Tübingen: Mohr Siebeck, 2007)—and 2013, six volumes of the Feminist Commentary have appeared.

25. See Antony John Baptist, *Together as Sisters: Hagar and Dalit Women* (Delhi: ISPCK, 2012).

26. Wacker, "Baruch," 431–38.

27. Marie-Theres Wacker, "Das Buch Baruch," 1281–87; "Jeremiabrief," 1287–90, in *Bibel in gerechter Sprache. Taschenausgabe*, ed. Ulrike Bail, Frank Crüsemann, et al., 4th rev. ed. (Gütersloh: Gütersloher Verlagshaus, 2011).

footnotes and, together with Simone Bomholt, helped to compile the indexes. Martha M. Matesich kindly translated the contributions by Klaus Mertes. My thanks are, last but not least, to the general editor of Wisdom Commentary, Barbara E. Reid, OP, and to Carol J. Dempsey, OP, volume editor, for inviting me to contribute and for answering my innumerable questions.

Baruch

Introduction

The book of Baruch in its present form is a complex, multi-referential, hybrid composition, to reformulate Odil Hannes Steck's valuable insights in terms of literary-structural analysis.[1] It starts, after its heading, with a narrative: Baruch reads his book to the community of exiles gathered at the shores of a river in Babylonia (Bar 1:3-4). The reaction of the people is to have the book sent to the priests in the city of Jerusalem and to ask for a liturgy to be celebrated there (Bar 1:5-13). In terms of narrative space, the exiles build a communicative bridge between Babylonia and Jerusalem; they recognize Jerusalem as their religious center and point of orientation. As part of the liturgy, they want the book they send to be read out loud (1:14). What follows is a long penitential prayer (1:15–3:8), a poem searching for the traces of wisdom, framed by the exhortation to understand that Israel departed from the ways of wisdom but is able to return (3:9–4:4), and a speech addressed to the personified city of Jerusalem whose lament is cited, followed by a prophetic oracle of hope for her (4:5–5:9). These are common themes

---

1. See Odil Hannes Steck, *Das apokryphe Baruchbuch*, FRLANT 160 (Göttingen: Vandenhoeck & Ruprecht, 1993), and Odil Hannes Steck, "Das Buch Baruch," in *ATD Apokryphen*, vol. 5, ed. Otto Kaiser and Lothar Perlitt (Göttingen: Vandenhoeck & Ruprecht, 1998), 9–68.

in Second Temple Judaism and "have a protean quality that allows them to be applied to various situations."[2]

The book has no narrative conclusion, though, no mention that the message actually was sent out or arrived at its destiny. This brings us back to the overall structure: the very first two verses identify it as the book of Baruch, written shortly after the destruction of Jerusalem (Bar 1:1-2); the following verses (Bar 1:3-7) describe the exiles listening to Baruch and deciding to send the book to Jerusalem. In its present form, this description of the book being read out loud and the communication between Babylonia and Jerusalem being initiated by listening to it is part of the book of Baruch. Thus, the actual book of Baruch is a book about a book, its use in Babylon, and its intended transmission to Jerusalem.[3] This self-referential book evidently *was* transmitted, *was* read and listened to, and its open ending in Bar 5:9 might be understood as a hint to the auditors/readers to continue this transmission, to listen to it, to read it.[4]

There is, however, not only an open end but also an open beginning.[5] Most commentators think that the book which Baruch read out loud

---

2. Anthony J. Saldarini, "The Book of Baruch. Introduction, Commentary, and Reflections," in *Introduction to Prophetic Literature, the Book of Isaiah, the Book of Jeremiah, the Book of Baruch, the Letter of Jeremiah, the Book of Lamentations, the Book of Ezekiel*, ed. Leander E. Keck, NIB 6 (Nashville, TN: Abingdon Press, 2001), 929–82, at 933, gives this as a reason why the book's dating remains open (between pre-Hasmonaean times until after 70 CE). Already Luis Alonso Schökel, "Baruc," in *Daniel – Baruc – Carta de Jeremias – Lamentaciones*, Los Libros Sagrados 18 (Madrid: Ediciones Cristiandad 1976), 126, saw the presupposed situation as general and repeatable.

3. In commentaries preceding Steck, like Schökel, "Baruc," 128, or Benjamin N. Wambacq, "Baruch," in *Jeremias – Klaagliederen – Baruch – Brief van Jeremias*, De Boeken van het Oude Testament (Roermond and Maaseik: J. J. Romen & Zonen, 1957), 368, this complexity was reason to consider Bar 1:2-14 or Bar 1:3-14 a secondary addition. André Kabasele Mukenge, *L'unité littéraire du Livre de Baruch*, EBib, N.S. 38 (Louvain: Gabalda, 1998), 413–15, uses a narratological approach when describing Bar 1:3-4 as "mise en abîme" (mirror text).

4. See Rüdiger Feuerstein, *Das Buch Baruch. Studien zur Textgestalt und Auslegungsgeschichte*, Europäische Hochschul-Schriften XXIII 614 (Frankfurt: Peter Lang, 1997), 404.

5. In my short commentary on Baruch (Marie-Theres Wacker, "Baruch: Mail from Distant Shores," in *Feminist Biblical Interpretation: A Compendium of Critical Commentary on the Books of the Bible and Related Literature*, ed. Luise Schottroff and Marie-Theres Wacker [Grand Rapids, MI: Eerdmans, 2012], 431–38) I saw the necessity to decide on a clear beginning; now I agree with Egbert Ballhorn, "Baruch—pseudepigraphe Kommunikation," in *Gesellschaft und Religion in der spätbiblischen und deuterokanonischen Literatur*, ed. Renate Egger-Wenzel, Thomas Elßner, and Vincent Reiterer, DCLS 20 (Berlin and Boston: De Gruyter, 2014), 229–52, who argues that the open beginning corresponds to the open ending.

according to Bar 1:3 is identical to the three parts that follow the narrative introduction: the prayer, the wisdom poem, and the speech on Jerusalem's past and future. As indeed there is no further metanarrative hint within the book, this is one possible option. Alternatively, the prayer recited in the "we form" could be seen as a separate message sent along with the book, which would then mean that "the book" comprises only the sapiential poem (3:9–4:4) and the Jerusalem part (4:5–5:9), both coming from the voice of an individual. In that case, the exiled community would ask the Jerusalemites to pray for them (1:13), suggesting the words of that prayer (1:15b–3:8), and, after having recited the prayer (1:14), to listen to the book (3:9–5:9).[6]

Consequently, what is meant to be "the book" has a multiplicity of referents in Bar 1–5. It might refer, on a first level, to the voice admonishing Israel to follow the paths of wisdom, as this is the precondition to put an end to Jerusalem's sorrow and to let her see the return of her children (3:9–5:9). Or "the book of Baruch" might refer to the three parts—the prayer, the sapiential admonition, and the Jerusalem part—as the presumed book Baruch read out (1:15–5:9). On a second level, it might refer to the book as it stands, including the narrative introduction.

There is a further level, a level zero: the wisdom poem ends up with a reference to the "book of the law" as wisdom given to Israel (4:1-4). Embedded in Baruch's book comprising the story of the transmission of that book, the wording of the book transmitted includes the mention of another book: the Torah of Moses. In addition to that, a closer look into the parts of the actual book of Baruch reveal all of them in rich intertextuality with the Torah in a twofold sense: more specifically as the *Chumash*/Pentateuch, and in a broader sense as referring to the three parts of the Jewish Scriptures, the Tanakh, consisting of the five Books of Moses (Torah); the Prophetical Books (Nevi'im); and the Writings (Ketuvim).

Although the structure of the whole book seems to follow a logic nourished by a rereading of Jeremiah,[7] the penitential prayer is closest

6. Some older commentaries, reconstructing the textual growth of the book by using stylistic arguments, suggest that the original book of Baruch must be found in the prayer 1:15b–3:8 only.

7. "In Bar haben Einleitung, Bußgebet, Mahnrede, auch Bar *4f in Jer 36 eine Grundlage, alle vier Teile von Bar in Jer 29 und das Buch Baruchs mit seinen drei Teilen in Jer 32! Sie bilden die Leittexte aus Jer, an denen sich die Bar-Formulierung grundlegend orientiert" (Steck, *Das apokryphe Baruchbuch*, 88). English: The introduction, penitential prayer, admonition, also Bar *4 [an earlier version of Bar 4] in Bar have a basis in Jer 36; all four parts of Bar have a basis in Jer 29; and the book of Baruch with its three parts has a basis in Jer 32! They form the key texts of Jer to which Baruch's formulation is basically oriented."

to the Mosaic Torah, the wisdom poem closest to (wisdom) writings, and the Jerusalem part is imbued with allusions to prophetical books. This might point to different original sources for each part of the book.[8] With its actual compositional form, the book of Baruch is—or claims to be—a Tanakh in its own right, and if the inversed sequence of the parts is taken into account, a *Takhan*. With a different vocalization, this term is equivalent to *Tikkun* (= mending; healing), a notion of some importance in the much later kabbalah and there related to the whole creation.

It therefore makes sense to read the claim of Baruch's book as offering a guide to "mend" or to "heal" a distorted community. A feminist and gender-sensitive reading of Baruch's book might start from this claim and take it seriously. Is this book a guide inclusive enough to heal the whole community? Whose healing is considered? Who is excluded? What are the "remedies"? And who is offered as the "healer"?

8. The older commentaries focus on the reconstruction of such sources. The actual book of Baruch is nevertheless a hybrid compositional unity as Steck (*Das apokryphe* and *Baruch*) and Mukenge (*L'unité littéraire*) have convincingly shown.

Baruch 1:1-15a

Connecting Babylon and Jerusalem

The Book's Heading and Introduction (1:1-2)

A "written document" (βιβλίον) and its "wording" (λόγοι) is at the center of Bar 1:1-2, in relation to two significant places: written in Babylon, with a view to Jerusalem, the conquered and destroyed city. Implicitly, one gets the notion that Babylon is a place of exile, with, for readers having in mind the book of Jeremiah, at least the two dimensions of a space of forced deportation but also of escape. The one who wrote down the words is named and identified by his genealogy but is grammatically subordinated. By contrast, particular attention is given to the date: a specific day connected to Jerusalem's capture and burning, so that one might think of a commemoration day[1]—which is not restricted to the destruction of the temple but devoted to the city as a whole. From the outset, time and space of Baruch's writing are indissolubly tied to time and space of this key event.

According to the Greek book of Jeremiah, Baruch, the secretary-scribe of the prophet, receives the very last oracle of God that Jeremiah has to

---

1. See remark above concerning the text of 1:2.

Bar 1:1-2

[1]These are the words of the book that Baruch son of Neriah son of Mahseiah son of Zedekiah son of Hasadiah son of Hilkiah wrote in Babylon, [2]in the fifth year, on the seventh day of the month,[2] at the time when the Chaldeans took Jerusalem and burned it with fire.

transmit before the fall of Jerusalem is told. It is an oracle of doom as it has to repeat the message of Jerusalem's end, but at the same time, for Baruch, it means survival "every place to which you may go" (Jer 45:5 MT/51:35 LXX). Baruch 1:1 develops this motif and finds Baruch in Babylonia, probably imagining that after he had been forced to go, together with Jeremiah, to Egypt (Jer 43:5-7 MT/50:5-7 LXX), he found his way to the Babylonian Golah. His genealogy verifies that he is Jeremiah's secretary, the son of Neriah. According to a vivid description in Jer 36 MT (43 LXX), Jeremiah used Baruch to write down his words and to read them out before a huge assembly in Jerusalem, thus trying to give more emphasis to his message.

Baruch appears as a "second-order prophet" who did not himself receive the word of God but is necessary for its transmission, and who uses a new medium, not immediate oral announcement, but oral delivery of a written message. The book of Baruch, in turn, makes use of this concept. Baruch's words neither have divine origin nor did he receive them prophetically. But from the very beginning, the first line being in close parallel to the beginning of Jeremiah's letter (Jer 29:1 MT/36:1 LXX), these words "walk" in the footsteps of Jeremiah. Readers familiar with Jeremiah's book could listen to Baruch or read his book as a prolongation of Jeremiah's prophecies, especially as the book of Jeremiah provides a telling story: when King Jehoiakim had burnt the scroll Baruch read out, the scribe rewrote the whole scroll at the prophet's dictation, so that none of Jeremiah's former words could be forgotten—"and many similar words were added to them" (Jer 36:32 MT/43:32 LXX). In Jeremiah's time, his scroll was updated, and, similarly, Baruch's writing could have been seen as another updating, its authority as derived from Jeremiah, God's prophet. On the other hand, the ability to write seems to add to someone's authority. In the book of

2. The month is not specified. Many commentators discuss text-critical issues here. Odil Hannes Steck, *Das apokryphe Baruchbuch*, FRLANT 160 (Göttingen: Vandenhoeck & Ruprecht, 1993), 17–19, tries to keep the text as it stands and relates the month to the "time when the Chaldeans took Jerusalem" (see 2 Kgs 25:8).

TRANSLATION MATTERS

1:1 *These are the words of the book*: The Greek text starts with καί, "and," connecting Baruch's writing to the preceding book of Jeremiah.

Baruch, the scribes are self-confident—able to write, learned in authoritative books—as they take up, rework, and actualize Jeremiah's prophetical words. They imagine themselves in the context of Jerusalem in ruins, hence in a situation where new structures have to emerge, where traditions are threatened with loss if they are not written down and updated.

Baruch's genealogy, indicated in Bar 1:1, does not limit itself to his father, as is the case in the book of Jeremiah, but is unusually long. Hellenistic-Jewish texts tend to have such complex genealogies[3] so that Baruch's genealogy becomes one of many other indications that his book was composed in Hellenistic times. From a gendered perspective, the genealogy's androcentrism has to be pointed out, a mirror of a society where the rights of fathers and sons are superior to those of women and daughters. Much research on gender in the society of ancient Israel has been done, revealing that a simple notion of "patriarchy" runs short of more complex structures of female agency.[4] Nevertheless, in law and public representation, women were seen and kept as inferior or dependent, and they did not have official access to the type of education necessary to become scribes.[5] This is not unique to ancient Israel and can be explained historically. The problem is rather the seemingly "natural" givenness or even divine revelation of such constructions of asymmetry in a text that became normative for two religions, Judaism and Christianity. Christianity in particular has contributed to stabilizing laws and customs that subordinate women (and children) under the authority of men. Therefore women's movements have had to go back over and over again to the Bible and read it on their own. It is interesting to see that, today, Muslim women start to reread their Holy Scripture in order to free it from interpretations discriminatory for women, and in some Western contexts questions are raised even concerning the Qur'an's alleged homophobia.

---

3. See Mordechai in Esth 2:5 MT/LXX; Add Esth A, 1 or Judith in Jdt 9:1.

4. Carol L. Meyers, "Was Ancient Israel a Patriarchal Society?," *JBL* 133 (2014): 8–27.

5. See especially Tal Ilan's research for Hasmonaean to mishnaic periods: *Jewish Women in Greco-Roman Palestine: An Inquiry into Image and Status* (Tübingen: Mohr Siebeck, 1995), 190–204.

Liturgies in Exile and in Jerusalem (1:3-15a)

Baruch 1:1-2 can be understood as a superscription opening a book. Its closest parallel, Jer 29:1 MT/36:1 LXX, opens a letter Jeremiah sends from Jerusalem to those in Babylonia. What follows in Jeremiah is the wording of the Letter, while what follows in Bar 1:3-7 presupposes the superscription as part of the narrative. The book of Baruch starts with a report of its own reading. Right at the book's beginning the crucial importance of written (and oral) communication and tradition becomes already evident.

According to the narrative, starting with 1:3, Baruch reads out his book, and the community reacts with rites that could be understood as mourning rites or penitential rites (1:5). The people collect money and send it to Jerusalem (1:6-7). Before specifying its purpose, the information is given by means of a parenthesis (1:8-9) that the precious vessels of the temple taken by the Babylonians[6] are brought back to their land of origin. Such restoration of temple property was probably considered a necessary precondition to the exiles asking the priests in Jerusalem along with the people there to prepare offerings (1:10).[7] Again these rites seem to have a double meaning: the offerings accompany the prayers for the foreign rulers (1:11-12) and also the intercessory prayers for those who confess to have sinned (1:13-14). As a last element in this proposed liturgy comes the reading of the book the exiles are going to send to Jerusalem along with the money. They ask for a repeated reading at specific memorial or feast days; they want to give permanent dignity and authority to the book they themselves have listened to.

Baruch, who had written down (Bar 1:1-2) and is now reading out his text (1:3), performs two modes of communication that are both essential for the spirit of this biblical book: what is written down has to be made heard, and what has been heard can be transmitted to other audiences when written down. How Baruch himself received what he communicates is not explicitly revealed; in particular, the designation "prophet" is not used for him. The fact, however, that his book was transmitted as part of the Jeremian corpus and opens with the conjunction "and" allows for the implication that it was considered as drawing on Jeremiah's prophecy written down by Baruch his secretary (Jer 36:32 MT/43:32 LXX). And vice

---

6. See 2 Kgs 25:13-15/Jer 52:17-19.

7. See Anthony J. Saldarini, "The Book of Baruch: Introduction, Commentary, and Reflections," in *Introduction to Prophetic Literature, Isaiah, Jeremiah, Baruch, Letter of Jeremiah, Lamentations, Ezekiel*, ed. Leander E. Keck, NIB 6 (Nashville, TN: Abingdon Press, 2001), 929–82, at 944.

Bar 1:3-15a

[3]Baruch read the words of this book to Jeconiah son of Jehoiakim, king of Judah, and to all the people who came to hear the book, [4]and to the nobles and the princes, and to the elders, and to all the people, small and great, all who lived in Babylon by the river Sud.

[5]Then they wept, and fasted, and prayed before the Lord; [6]they collected as much money as each could give, [7]and sent it to Jerusalem to the high priest Jehoiakim son of Hilkiah son of Shallum, and to the priests, and to all the people who were present with him in Jerusalem. [8]At the same time, on the tenth day of Sivan, Baruch took the vessels of the house of the Lord, which had been carried away from the temple, to return them to the land of Judah—the silver vessels that Zedekiah son of Josiah, king of Judah, had made, [9]after King Nebuchadnezzar of Babylon had carried away from Jerusalem Jeconiah and the princes and the prisoners[8] and the nobles and the people of the land, and brought them to Babylon.

[10]They said: Here we send you money; so buy with the money burnt offerings and sin offerings and incense, and prepare a grain offering, and offer them on the altar of the Lord our God; [11]and pray for the life of King Nebuchadnezzar of Babylon, and for the life of his son Belshazzar, so that their days on earth may be like the days of heaven. [12]The Lord will give us strength, and light to our eyes; we shall live under the protection of King Nebuchadnezzar of Babylon, and under the protection of his son Belshazzar, and we shall serve them many days and find favor in their sight. [13]Pray also for us to the Lord our God, for we have sinned against the Lord our God, and to this day the anger of the Lord and his wrath have not turned away from us. [14]And you shall read aloud this scroll that we are sending you, to make your confession in the house of the Lord on the days of the festivals and at appointed seasons.

[15a]And you shall say:

versa: the secretary-scribe and his reading are part of a public ceremony that brings together those "who came to the book" as Bar 1:3 could more literally be rendered. "This book" (1:3; βίβλος) does not appear to refer to Baruch's writing (1:1; βιβλίον) but rather refers to a text already authoritative for the community assembled, so that Baruch's reading meets an audience gathered for a liturgy or catechesis or both—at least that might have been the idea of the Greek translator. In a supposed Hebrew original, however, the situation could have been more mundane, a simple public gathering to listen to a message received like Jeremiah's letter sent from Jerusalem (Jer 29 MT/36 LXX).

8. Text-critical matter: The Greek word δεσμώτης, "prisoners," is also found in Jer 24:1 MT=LXX and Jer 36:2 LXX/29:2 MT in a very similar list of deported persons

TRANSLATION MATTERS

1:3 *who came to hear the book*: τῶν ἐρχομένων πρὸς τὴν βίβλον, literally: "who came to the book/writing."

1:3-4 *read . . . to*: ἀνέγνω . . . ἐν ὡσὶ, literally: "read into the ears of."

1:7 *the high priest Jehoiakim*: Ἰωακεὶμ . . . τὸν ἱερέα, literally: "the priest Jehoiakim."

1:8 *Baruch took the vessels*: The Greek text leaves open who transfers the vessels to Jerusalem. Syntactically the priest Jehoiakim mentioned in v. 7 is the best candidate.

1:14 *scroll*: The same Greek word, βιβλίον, is used here and in vv. 1, 2 (where NRSV translates "book"); the "book" was probably in the form of a "scroll."

1:14 *to make your confession*: alternatively the Greek infinitive ἐξαγορεῦσαι could refer to the book: "to make it known"; "to read it out."

The community of exiles comes into view twice: first, the people as a whole headed by its king who is called by his name to give honor to him[9] but also to refer, within the narrative, to the situation indicated in the book's superscription (Bar 1:3); then, the people classified by age (or wealth), preceded by a hierarchy of nobles, close to the royal court, and authorities related to the ordinary people (1:4), hence a more differentiated social structure. All of them are involved in a similar way, by their ears, as the reading is in Greek literally "into the ears" of them (repeated five times in 1:3-4), appealing to their physical and mental attention, as Baruch already did when Jeremiah had told him to write down and then read out "into the ears" of everybody all the words of his prophecy (Jer 36 MT/43 LXX). All of them share a common living area in Babylonia connected to a river named Sud whose geography is unknown and whose name might serve a typological function indicating a place of assembly or council meeting (סוד, [*sud* or *sod*] = "assembly" or "council"?).[10]

---

and might have found its way from there into the book of Baruch. In Jeremiah, the Hebrew text reads מסגר, "blacksmith," an important group of professionals the Babylonians would have had reason to deport. The book of Baruch refers to the Greek, not the Hebrew, text of Jeremiah here.

9. On the concept of honor and shame in the book of Baruch, see below (on Bar 1:15b–2:10).

10. Some commentators, like Ivo Meyer, "Das Buch Baruch und der Brief des Jeremia," in *Einleitung in das Alte Testament*, ed. Erich Zenger and Christian Frevel,

In contrast to the rather complex picture of the social stratification, there is no gender differentiation, neither among those from the royal court, nor among the people. This is even more remarkable as the book of Jeremiah knows about the mother of the king who together with Jeconiah was deported to Babylonia (Jer 29:2 MT). The Greek translation (Jer 36:2 LXX) includes eunuchs along with other officials, the Second Book of Kings adds Jeconiah's wives (2 Kgs 24:15), and the first song of Lamentations mourns that "young women and young men have gone into captivity" (Lam 1:18). Baruch 1:3-4 has its focus on only the male members of the community. Indeed, among "all the people, small and great" (1:4) women and girls as well as persons who are seen as non-male may be included, but the text does not grant them visibility. The implicit authors of Baruch's book do not have a recognizable interest in non-male recipients of their message. Therefore, Bar 1:3-4 is open to an inclusive reading along the lines of Deut 31:12 or Josh 8:35, where a public reading of the Torah reaches men and women, little children and old people, and even the foreigners within Israel, but it is also open to tendencies of exclusion or hierarchization, as in Jer 29:1-32, where Jeremiah's letter goes to the (male) authorities who then have to ensure what has been suggested.

The community's reaction, after having listened to the reading, is twofold, one addressed to God, the other to Jerusalem. Before God, referred to as κύριος, "Lord,"[11] a frequent rendering of the divine name YHWH in the Septuagint, there is weeping, fasting, and praying, a ritual reaction in case of distress. If this reaction is seen in simple chronological sequence to the reading, it becomes part of the ceremony or liturgy the community is performing—at the commemoration day of the city's destruction (Bar 1:2). If the reaction is seen as caused by what the community heard, then the content of Baruch's book must have provoked it. Maybe both perspectives do not rule out each other: what follows explains the people's reaction and seems to be a writing appropriate for such a memorial day, be it the wisdom speech and the Jerusalem oracle only (3:9–5:9) or be it this part preceded by the prayer (1:15b–3:8 and 3:9–5:9). Read against the background of Jer 36 MT/43 LXX, Baruch's words now finally find the reaction Jeremiah's words read out by his scribe in Jerusalem did not find.

8th ed. (Stuttgart: Kohlhammer, 2012), 585–91, at 587, with reference to Jer 52:11 MT, suggest an emendation to Hebrew: סור ("departure").

11. κύριος is used in Bar 1:5–3:8 only. See comment in part 5.

For Jerusalem, there is a collection of silver money whose recipients are listed (Bar 1:7), thus characterizing the community of Jerusalem as an organization with a single priest as head (identified by name and genealogy but without the title "high priest") and a body of priests differentiated from the rest of the people, hence a hierocratic structure. By way of keyword association with "silver," a parenthetical note (1:8-9) recalls the silver vessels of the temple that had been brought back from Babylon to Jerusalem, and introduces an important detail: the Judeans in Babylon[12] were by force "carried away from their home" in Jerusalem. The Greek verb used here (ἀποικίζω; Bar 1:9; see also 2:14) may allude, for a Greek-speaking audience, to "living in a colony," hence a foundation to expand into new soils, mostly with trading interests.[13] The context in Bar 1, however, brings into the foreground the meaning of the underlying Hebrew verb גלה (here in its Hif'il form), which carries a strong connotation of violence, including rape of women. The community in Babylonia sees itself not as colonizers with ties to the metropolis but as deported people oriented toward their mother city.[14]

This community formulates a message to be sent to Jerusalem, quoted in direct speech (Bar 1:10-14).[15] They explain the intended use of the money: to purchase material for appropriate sacrificial animals, grain, and incense offerings. They specify the type of offerings and combine it with their specific purpose: that related prayers be performed. After the dramatic remembrance of Jerusalem's destruction, the first request of prayer comes as a surprise, as it entrusts the ruler of Babylon and his son, their lives, and the stability of their kingdom, to the protection of Israel's God. The exiled community seems to resign itself to its fate; the people accept Jeremiah's letter (Jer 29:4-7 MT/36:4-7 LXX) advising them to make the best of their situation, which is expected to last for a long

---

12. See text-critical matters related to Bar 1:9. See also Jer 29:2 MT/36:2 LXX.

13. For more information on colonization in antiquity, including Greek and Hellenistic colonies, see Walter Eder et al., "Colonization," *Brill's New Pauly*, ed. Hubert Cancik and Helmuth Schneider (Brill Online, 2006), http://referenceworks.brillonline .com/entries/brill-s-new-pauly/colonization-e618410; for a more classical work, see Alexander John Graham, *Colony and Mother City in Ancient Greece*, 2nd ed. (Chicago: Ares Publishers, 1983).

14. See also the comments on Bar 2:30, 32 (ἀποικισμός); 3:7-8 (ἀποικία) below.

15. By translating 1:10 "La carta decía así" ("The letter said the following"), Alonso Schökel underlines the written communication; the biblical text itself, however, does not specify this. Luis Alonso Schökel, "Baruc," in *Daniel—Baruc—Carta de Jeremias—Lamentaciones*, Los Libros Sagrados 18 (Madrid: Ediciones Cristiandad 1976), 133.

period of time. Jeremiah 29:10 MT predicts seventy years. In contrast, however, to Jeremiah's letter asking the people to pray for the peace of "the city" (Jer 29:7 MT) or "the land" (Jer 36:7 LXX), Bar 1:11 focuses on the king and his son, the same king who "carried away all of them" (1:9), and 1:12 underlines the will to be obedient slaves in the service of the court. The community's wish to pray for the oppressor[16] might be an inevitable *captatio benevolentiae*[17] but sounds like a second submission after the first, the forced one; it sounds like colonized language.[18] A slight tone of resistance might be heard when the community asks God to give them "strength and light to our eyes" (1:12) to survive their exile.

The second request for prayer addressed to the Jerusalemites turns to the community of exiles itself. They need offerings and prayers because they recognize their situation as a consequence of their guilt. The enduring wrath of God reflects the enormous dimensions of the sins committed. Jerusalem's destruction and the deportation of her inhabitants is interpreted here in line with deuteronomistic theology—also attested by the book of Jeremiah—as a consequence of Israel's revolt against her God, a concept shaping the book of Baruch as a whole. The confession of sins turns the ceremony at the river Sud into a penitential liturgy, with weeping and fasting (Bar 1:5) as related elements. Likewise, what ought to be done in Jerusalem gets the shape of such a liturgy (1:14)[19] in which reading Baruch's scroll aloud must take a central place. The altar of the temple as a site of God's former presence is still thought to be an appropriate site for sin offerings that are trying at least to mitigate God's wrath, as well as for prayers of supplication and for the public reading of a writing that

16. It is true that, according to Bar 1:2, the Chaldeans, not the Babylonians, burned the city of Jerusalem, and if Bar 1:8-9 is taken to be a secondary addition, as some commentators suggest, one could avoid such a reading. The text as it stands, though, reveals a perspective of colonized people adapting to the oppressor.

17. Steck, *Das apokryphe Baruchbuch*, 46, refers to Ezra 6:10 and 7:23 for the order of the Persian King Darius to pray for the king. Alonso Schökel, *Baruc*, 135, sees in the prayer an act of political prudence and at the same time a religious act, as the exiles accept the foreign ruler as their punishment and hope that the oppressor turns into a protector when the sinners had been forgiven. Schökel tries to reconstruct the logic of the text; at any rate, there is no political rebellion but submission to the actual fate.

18. Josef Schreiner, "Baruch," in *Klagelieder/Baruch*, NEchtB Altes Testament 14, ed. Josef G. Plöger and others (Würzburg: Echter, 1986), might have felt this problem when he refers to "the prayer for the oppressor" (56) and considers Bar 1:11-12 as a later addition.

19. See Translation Matters of 1:14 for a different explanation.

is meant to provoke similar reactions in Jerusalem as it did in Babylon. This again is a confirmation that Baruch's writing must be related to this concern of sin, wrath, resignation, suffering, and maybe hope.

If the last part of the community's exhortation to the Jerusalemites can be understood as part of a hendiadys "read aloud" (1:14) and "say" (1:15a), the following prayer may well be considered as the beginning of Baruch's words read aloud.[20] Another possibility is to see the prayer as part of the general message sent to Jerusalem, created by those at the river Sud as their reaction to the book and as their suggested introduction before the Jerusalemites listen to the book starting with 3:9. In Babylonia, then, the prayer would have followed the book consisting of Bar 3:9–5:9 as an apt reaction to it; in Jerusalem, this prayer would become the first "text" of what is now the book of Baruch.[21] In Jerusalem, the sequence of penitential prayer, exhortation and consolation/good news would correspond to a liturgical order to be repeated.

20. The verb ἐξαγορεύω in v. 14, meaning "to act out" and in the LXX sometimes "to confess," would underline this interpretation.

21. There is textual evidence that already in late antiquity/the Early Middle Ages the sequence of Bar 1:1-4 + 3:9–5:9 + 1:5–3:8 (hence the prayer including the decision to send the book to Jerusalem at the end of the present book of Baruch) was considered an apt one: three Latin codices from tenth-century Spain have this textual sequence (see Rüdiger Feuerstein, *Das Buch Baruch. Studien zur Textgestalt und Auslegungsgeschichte*, Europäische Hochschul-Schriften XXIII/614 [Frankfurt: Peter Lang, 1997], 51–55). According to Feuerstein they are of no further textual-critical relevance, while Mukenge (André Kabasele Mukenge, *L'unité littéraire du Livre de Baruch*, EBib, N.S. 38 [Louvain: Gabalda, 1998], 398), without knowing Feuerstein's critical assessment, uses one of them, Codex Legionensis, to argue for a literary development of the book of Baruch with a first stage comprising 1:1-3 + 3:9–5:9 only, and for the insertion of 1:15b–3:8 and the narrative part 1:4-15a. Such a redactional critical hypothesis was already developed in the nineteenth-century by critics like Johann Jacob Kneucker (*Das Buch Baruch*, Geschichte und Kritik, Übersetzung und Erklärung auf Grund des wiederhergestellten hebräischen Urtextes [Leipzig: Brockhaus, 1879], 16–20) and followed, for example, by Owen C. Whitehouse ("The Book of Baruch," in *The Apocrypha and Pseudepigrapha of the Old Testament*, vol. 1, ed. Robert Charles [Oxford: Clarendon, 1913], 571) without using textual criticism. It is interesting to see that from different methodological points of view a narrative sequence as suggested here was able to gain plausibility.

Baruch 1:15b–3:8

The Exiles' Prayer

The prayer as a whole, perceived as a unified composition, has two clearly discernible parts. Baruch 1:15b–2:10 refers to God in a narrative mode; 2:11-35 and 3:1-8 address God in direct speech. Both parts are spoken by the community, with 3:1-8 being begun by an individual voice. Again, these formal differences might point back to different sources, but in its present composition this prayer has a well-built dynamic and a distinctive "narrative." It starts with gathering the community before God, while direct communication with God comes in a second step. This gradual movement corresponds well to what is expressed in the prayer: in the presence of God, the first expression by the people has to be self-accusation combined with acknowledgment of God's justification or a theodicy. Only then can God be addressed directly with a cry for help, a recognition of the guilt of former generations, a remembrance of God's words of promise and hope to the people, and a final declaration of being prepared for a different attitude. The exiles' prayer in Bar 1:15b–3:8 builds on biblical models, with common form- or genre-specific features, especially the penitential prayers in Neh 9 and Dan 9; it combines them with Jer 32:16-44 MT (39:16-44 LXX)[1] but has its own structure and profile.[2]

---

1. For a detailed discussion, see Odil Hannes Steck, *Das apokryphe Baruchbuch*, FRLANT 160 (Göttingen: Vandenhoeck & Ruprecht, 1993), 81–115.

2. For the complex recent methodological discussion on the origin, development, and impact of penitential prayers in postexilic Israel, see Mark Boda, Daniel K. Falk, and Rodney A. Werline, eds., *Seeking the Favor of God*, 3 vols., EJL 21–23 (Atlanta, GA:

Confession of Guilt and Theodicy (1:15b–2:10)

Right from the outset, the prayer intones its main motif expressed in two opposite concepts: justice on the side of God; shame with those who have gathered. Shame seems to be visible on their faces; or shame prevents them from lifting their faces. The repetition in Bar 2:6 reads like a refrain and divides the first part of the prayer into two stanzas, the former unfolding the community's self-accusation, the second a short review affirming what has been said and insisting on God's justification.[3]

Those who represent the community are made visible or expose themselves in their geographically and socially determined groups (Bar 1:15b–16). The summary mention of the "people of Judah and inhabitants of Jerusalem" (1:15b), a Jeremian formula adapted in Daniel's prayer (Dan 9:7),[4] refers back as well to those exiled as to those in Jerusalem who will receive the book and pray this prayer (again). Shame, thus, is not only on the side of the exiles but also on those who are still in Jerusalem: the people, although actually torn apart, form a unity. As a first step, there is confession of guilt including "the people," hence everybody. In a second step, however, "kings, rulers, priests, prophets, fathers" are enumerated, the political, cultic-religious, and familial authorities (1:16). The series of plurals seems to include not only the living generations but former generations too. The formula recalls Nehemiah's prayer accusing "our kings, our officials, our priests, and our ancestors" for not having kept the commandments of God (Neh 9:34).[5] Both prayers underline a

---

SBL, 2006, 2007, 2008). For discussion of the penitential prayer in Bar 1–3, see Michael Floyd, "Penitential Prayer in the Second Temple Period from the Perspective of Baruch," in *Seeking the Favor of God*, vol. 2: *The Development of Penitential Prayer in Second Temple Judaism*, EJL 22 (Atlanta, GA: SBL, 2007), 51–81, and Pieter M. Venter, "Penitential Prayers in the Books of Baruch and Daniel," *OTE* 18 (2005): 406–25.

3. With Steck, *Das apokryphe Baruchbuch*, 76.

4. The formula "people of Judah and inhabitants of Jerusalem" clearly goes back to the Hebrew איש יהודה וישבי ירושלים, which is found only in 2 Kgs 23:2 // 2 Chr 34:30; Dan 9:7; and in Jer 4:4; 11:2; 18:11; 17:25; 35:13. See also, with reversed sequence, Jer 36:31 MT/43:31 LXX; and is translated mostly by ἄνδρες Ἰούδα καὶ κατοικοῦντες Ἰερουσαλὴμ (Jer 4:4; 11:2; 18:11; 17:25; Jer 43:31 γῆ=land) or even by ἀνήρ Ἰούδα . . . (4 Kgdms 23:2; 2 Chr 34:30 has Ἰούδα only). But cf. Dan 9:7 LXX and Jer 35:13 MT/42:13 LXX where ἄνθρωπος is used instead of ἀνήρ and takes on the sense of איש = everybody (see also Bar 6:15), while the other instances quoted understand איש as "man/male." The Greek ἄνθρωπος, in turn, can designate a male; see, e.g., 1 Sam 1:1.

5. While Nehemiah mentions "our prophets" as part of the community in misery (Neh 9:32), Bar 1:16 includes them among those who are shamed. Maybe "Baruch"

[15b]The Lord our God is in the right, but there is open shame on us today, on the people of Judah, on the inhabitants of Jerusalem, [16]and on our kings, our rulers, our priests, our prophets, and our ancestors, [17]because we have sinned before the Lord. [18]We have disobeyed him, and have not heeded the voice of the Lord our God, to walk in the statutes of the Lord that he set before us.

[19]From the time when the Lord brought our ancestors out of the land of Egypt until today, we have been disobedient to the Lord our God, and we have been negligent, in not heeding his voice. [20]So to this day there have clung to us the calamities and the curse that the Lord declared through his servant Moses at the time when he brought our ancestors out of the land of Egypt to give to us a land flowing with milk and honey. [21]We did not listen to the voice of the Lord our God in all the words of the prophets whom he sent to us, [22]but all of us followed the intent of our own wicked hearts by serving other gods and doing what is evil in the sight of the Lord our God.

[2:1]So the Lord carried out the threat he spoke against us: against our judges who ruled Israel, and against

specific responsibility of those having authoritative roles. Therefore the Greek πατέρες in Bar 1:16 should be taken literally and be translated as "fathers."[6] At the foreground here is not the inclusive perspective of former generations as a whole ("ancestors," as the NRSV puts it) but a precise designation of those in power.

What follows is a self-accusation structured by the opening as well as concluding confession "we have sinned" (Bar 1:17; 2:5),[7] the twofold explanation "we . . . have not heeded the voice of the Lord our God" (1:18, 21), and its repetition "in not heeding his voice" (1:19b; 2:5b). Thus, the subject of disobedience and its consequences is developed twice, telling Israel's distorted story with its God from its very beginnings according to the deuteronomistic frame.

Baruch 1:18-20 as a first approach goes back to Israel's exodus from Egypt. The exodus is linked to the Promised Land, remembering, on the one hand, these foundational givens provided by God and, on the other

---

would count himself among these prophets.

6. Carey A. Moore, "1 Baruch," in *Daniel, Esther, and Jeremiah: The Additions*, AB 44 (Garden City, NY: Doubleday, 1977), 278, discusses a translation of "ancestors" as including all generations, but the authoritative aspect seems stronger for him, hence a translation as "fathers" would be more apt.

7. See Deut 1:41; Jer 8:14; 16:10; 1 Sam 7:6.

Bar 1:15b–2:10 (cont.)

our kings and our rulers and the people of Israel and Judah. ²Under the whole heaven there has not been done the like of what he has done in Jerusalem, in accordance with the threats that were written in the law of Moses. ³Some of us ate the flesh of their sons and others the flesh of their daughters. ⁴He made them subject to all the kingdoms around us, to be an object of scorn and a desolation among all the surrounding peoples, where the Lord has scattered them. ⁵They were brought down and not raised up, because our nation sinned against the Lord our God, in not heeding his voice.

⁶The Lord our God is in the right, but there is open shame on us and our ancestors this very day. ⁷All those calamities with which the Lord threatened us have come upon us. ⁸Yet we have not entreated the favor of the Lord by turning away, each of us, from the thoughts of our wicked hearts. ⁹And the Lord has kept the calamities ready, and the Lord has brought them upon us, for the Lord is just in all the works that he has commanded us to do. ¹⁰Yet we have not obeyed his voice, to walk in the statutes of the Lord that he set before us.

hand, the treaty[8] that God concluded with Israel and the curses bound to that treaty in case it is not observed.[9] This concept resembling ancient Western Asian vassal treaties portrays God as a sovereign declaring his will to a people under his control and relies on curses as a specific form of powerful speech; deviation from the prescriptions of the treaty will almost automatically trigger negative consequences as uttered in the curse. God does not have to punish the people directly since their deeds cause events that can be regarded as punishments. Moses is seen in Bar 1:20 as mediator of the divine curse embedded in the treaty, probably indicating his role as mediator of the whole treaty ceremony with its commandments, its blessings, and its curses; moreover, he appears as an obedient servant (παῖς) of his God.

The second approach (Bar 1:21–2:5b) considers Israel's further history. After the death of Moses, Israel had her prophets as mediators of God's will (1:21), according to Deut 18:18 and its promise of a prophetic succession in the footsteps of Moses. Again, there is a confession of guilt, this time substantiated by the problem of cultic polytheism, a central concern of deuteronomistic theology as detectable in the book of Jeremiah

8. I try to avoid the term "covenant" in favor of "treaty" to underline the concept of obedience and blessings/curses.

9. See in particular Deut 28–29.

TRANSLATION MATTERS

1:15 *Open shame on us*: ἡμῖν δὲ αἰσχύνη τῶν προσώπων is rendered more literally: "shame with regard to the face," "we blush with shame," or "we cannot show our faces because of shame," or, as in NJB: "we have only the look of shame we bear."

1:15 *people of Judah*: literally: a person (ἄνθρωπος) in Judah.

1:16, 19, 20; 2:6 *ancestors*: τοῖς πατράσιν, literally: "fathers."

1:21 *We did not listen to the voice of the Lord our God*: καὶ οὐκ ἠκούσαμεν τῆς φωνῆς κυρίου τοῦ θεοῦ ἡμῶν is the same Greek formula as in 1:18; hence, better: "we have not heeded the voice of the Lord our God."

2:1 *carried out the threat*: ἔστησεν . . . τὸν λόγον, literally: "put into force the word" (see also 2:24).

2:2 *threats*: not in the Greek text.

2:5 *our nation*: ἡμάρτομεν . . . ἡμῶν, literally: "we sinned."

2:7 *with which the Lord threatened us*: ἃ ἐλάλησε κύριος ἐφ᾽ ἡμᾶς, literally: "which the Lord pronounced over us."

---

too, so that Jeremiah, in turn, becomes one of the prophets Bar 1:21 has in mind. For Israel's history after Moses, God's "threat he spoke against us" (2:1), which was the curse linked to "what is written in the law of Moses" (2:2), concerns the people as a whole, but again, in a specific way, its rulers (2:1). The recourse to the time of the judges (2:1) underlines the "wicked hearts" of Israel's people, since all this time other prophets succeeded Moses, from Deborah (Judg 4–5) to Huldah (2 Kgs 22).[10] Political subjugation and humiliation appear, on the one hand, as a self-produced consequence, as the result of permanent revolution against the treaty concluded between God and Israel. On the other hand, while in Bar 1:20-22 an automatic progression from curse, to refusal of obedience, and finally to misery was apparent, now it is God who "puts into force" his word (ἔστησεν, 2:1). It is God who delivers the people to their enemies (2:4); it is God who implemented the series of curses in Deut 28, probably remembered as one of the most terrible experiences of extreme famine in the besieged city (2:3): children were the first victims as parents decided to slaughter them for their own survival (Deut 28:52-57).

---

10. On Deborah and Huldah as prophets like Moses, see Irmtraud Fischer, *Gotteskünderinnen. Zu einer geschlechterfairen Deutung des Phänomens der Prophetie und der Prophetinnen in der Hebräischen Bibel* (Stuttgart: Kohlhammer, 2002), 109–30, 158–88; Klara Butting, *Prophetinnen gefragt. Die Bedeutung der Prophetinnen im Kanon aus Tora und Prophetie*, Biblisch-feministische Texte, no. 3 (Wittingen: Erev-Rav-Hefte, 2001), 99–189.

On the Guilt of Fathers and Rulers, Part 1

The prayer of Baruch mentions the guilt or "iniquity of the fathers and the rulers" with unequivocal clarity. A subject is thus addressed which has acquired a highly explosive nature in the Catholic Church in recent years.

Survivors of sexual abuse by Catholic priests report that the abuse has two aspects for them: the act of violence in the narrow sense of the word, and the failure of those in authority (those responsible for personnel, bishops) who choose to listen with half an ear, cease to listen at all, become annoyed, keep quiet about everything, cover things up, put pressure on the victims, relocate the perpetrators, protect the offenders instead of the victims, prolong the proceedings, protect the institution, and so on. The second aspect of the abuse is just as painful for the survivors as the first. It is connected to the experience of total defenselessness and the defeat of justice in the church. The basic trust in the Catholic system from which the survivors come is shaken; the church-related talk about God is contaminated since it (potentially or actually) arouses the experiences of violence over and over again; the struggle against the senses of shame and guilt exhausts the victims and wears them out. There is loss of home and exclusion.

When, at some time or other, the "iniquity of the rulers and fathers" does begin to be revealed before a wider public, this certainly does not yet mean that the guilt is also acknowledged. Not to admit one's own guilt, however, is not a "guiltless" omission; instead, it has problematic social consequences: scapegoats have to be found —the victims, the press, those fouling the nest. This leads to new violence within the church, the community, and the family. A fight about the interpretation of history ensues. The refusal by the "rulers and fathers" to acknowledge their guilt divides the church from top to bottom— between the allegedly loyal and allegedly disloyal, between friends and enemies. That is precisely what is so distinct about the guilt of those who occupy positions of power: their deeds and omissions affect the entirety of the church in an especially intense way.

The meaning of power and institution consists in the protection against violence. Power is misused when it is exercised to worm one's way into the confidence of one's charges in order to then take advantage of this confidence for one's own narcissistic interests. Power is also misused when it is exercised to protect oneself from the people whom one should actually be protecting and who are starting to fight the abuse of power. Finally, power is also misused when it is exercised to keep up an outward appearance which does not correspond to the inner reality. The powerful like having homage paid to them. Yet, the more ostentatious the homage of the masses, the

more likely it is that the inner reality is marked by abuse of power. This also holds true for many a liturgical staging in the Catholic Church.

Klaus Mertes

The sensitively gendered perception of the weakest among the people, the sons and daughters, stands in contrast to the anonymity of those who committed this horrible deed. At the same time, the common "we" marks this past as the memory of all those who are now performing the prayer; the (fictitious) situation five years after the destruction of Jeru-salem does not rule out the possibility that such parents—fathers and also mothers according to the underlying reference Deut 28:52-57—are among the exiles at the river Sud. They know and confess that such distortion of elementary family solidarity ultimately falls back on them as their own fault—and they repeat what will be the central affirmation in the second stanza of the prayer's first part (2:6-10): on God's side is justice and the right to set orders; God is justified, there is no doubt.

The logic of opposition between shame and righteousness structuring Bar 1:15b–2:10 is not evident for contemporary Western thought.[11] Clearly, the situation of the Jews in the Babylonian community is one of calamity, of misery. This misery is seen as a result of God's justice and a consequence of transgressions committed. To connect it with shame adds the aspect of humiliation, of the loss of a former status of respect. The society of ancient Israel was, according to the Hebrew Bible, largely an honor-shame society, and that seems even truer for Hellenistic times. The honor-shame system focuses on the spaces/places of individuals in a society. High ranks correspond to receiving much honor and to the right and the power to reclaim honor. People in high ranks receive respect and signs of esteem in the public, but also in the private, sphere. Masters have the right to beat their servants and slaves, but not vice versa. In

11. A very concise introduction to honor-shame theories and their critical evaluation for biblical studies, in particular prophetical books, is provided by Johanna Stiebert, *The Construction of Shame in the Hebrew Bible: The Prophetic Contribution*, JSOTSup 346 (Sheffield: Sheffield Academic Press, 2002). Her insistence that God's "function in the honor/shame dynamic" has to be included (p. 96) is particularly valuable for the analysis of a text like Baruch's penitential prayer.

traditional societies with patriarchal structures, women have their own honor but are also markers of honor of their fathers, brothers, or husbands. Women's behavior has to correspond to what is considered appropriate, often termed as modesty or decency.

In a system of honor and shame, human transgressions of God's orders disrespect God's honor. It is likely that in early Judaism veneration of other gods besides the one God could be considered a particularly onerous form of disrespect. Those who did so would deserve shame and would find themselves ashamed and humiliated as an expression of God's justice. Because they dared attack God's superior status, they would be made to "lose face," which brings the visual aspect to the foreground. Others look down on those who are humiliated; looking at someone with scorn and derision is part of shaming that person. The Jewish community in Babylonia felt surrounded by other people who might look at their humiliation and disdain them (2:4). The verbal self-exposition of those praying corresponds to what is expressed by "shame."

In all three monotheistic religions, the system of honor and shame has played a key role in the relationships among the community, the individual, and God but also in familial and public relations. The honor-shame system might help to protect traditional values, but it runs contrary to the idea of equality among humans and of freedom of reasonable choices for individual life. Usually girls and women suffer most in this system. As a structure to model a faithful relation to God, the honor-shame system is in conflict with individual development of a mature conscience and self-responsibility. On the other hand, Bar 1:15b–2:10 reveals, at least on a textual level, a remarkable implication within this system of honor and shame. The prayer's beginning assembles a community structured hierarchically, a society supposed to function according to the rules of honor and shame. Before God, however, all are equal in their sins, all blush with shame, all recognize God's honor and attest to God's justice. Nobody tries to shirk responsibility; all admit to being guilty. Until this day, in public confessions of guilt pronounced by secular or religious institutions, such an admission of common and all-embracing guilt, including not only individual members but equally the institutional structures and their leaders, is not the norm.[12]

---

12. Heinrich Schneider, *Das Buch Daniel. Das Buch der Klagelieder. Das Buch Baruch*, Die Hl. Schrift für das Leben erklärt, Herders Bibelkommentar 9/2 (Freiburg: Herder, 1954), 149, is an example of distinguishing between "all" who have to confess their guilt and "the church," like mother Jerusalem carrying the "robe of righteousness

Remembering/Re-Membering God's Mercy (2:11–3:8)

After this theodicy the prayer changes to direct speech, combined with a syntactical signal indicating a new turn in the development of thought. Four parts may be distinguished: a threefold cry for help (2:11-18), a repeated self-accusation (2:19-26), a reminder of words of hope (2:27-35), and a final cry for mercy (3:1-8).

Cry for Help (2:11-18)

"And now" is a marker that introduces a shift of perspective or argument. Now the community addresses God directly by using two epithets: "Lord" (κύριος) and "God of Israel" (ὁ Θεὸς Ἰσραὴλ). "Lord" underlines God's dominance and power and is, for Greek-speaking Jewish readers or listeners, also reminiscent of the divine name YHWH.[13] "God of Israel" points to the relationship between God and his people. As a foundational experience of such divine power acting in and for Israel, the exodus is remembered in a language combining formulae from Daniel's prayer (Dan 9:15) and Jeremiah's invocation (Jer 32:21 MT; 39:21 LXX). All prayers interpret Israel's exodus from Egypt as God's action for his people but above all as a spectacular theophany with Israel's God becoming well-known and respectable—in Israel, among other nations, and probably also in the cosmic realm. It is in recognizing this that the community once again confesses its transgressions, accumulating three verbs: ἡμάρτομεν, "we have sinned"; ἠσεβήσαμεν, "been ungodly"; and ἠδικήσαμεν, "done wrong" (2:12). These verbs emphasize the gravity of the people's guilt, and they serve to rhetorically humiliate those who speak before the face of their divine benefactor. The community again admits God's justice (1:15b; 2:6) when it now recognizes its actions, saying, "we have committed injustice" (ἠδικήσαμεν, 2:12; better than "done wrong" against God's "righteous ordinances," δικαιώματα, 2:12); they are now ready to accept God's will as expression of justice and righteousness.

What follows is a series of four imperatives pleading with God for help in a situation described by decimation, dispersion, and dependence

---

and the diadem of God's glory" (Bar 5:2) without reflecting on the church as institution and the problem of "structural sins."

13. This is why gender-sensitive translators would hesitate to render κύριος as "Lord." The German *Bibel in gerechter Sprache* has developed an elaborate system of circumscriptions for κύριος and for YHWH. In contrast to Dan 9:15 and its analogous shift, however, Bar 2:11 does not add the epithet δεσπότης, "master."

Bar 2:11-18

[11]And now, O Lord God of Israel, who brought your people out of the land of Egypt with a mighty hand and with signs and wonders and with great power and outstretched arm, and made yourself a name that continues to this day, [12]we have sinned, we have been ungodly, we have done wrong, O Lord our God, against all your ordinances. [13]Let your anger turn away from us, for we are left, few in number, among the nations where you have scattered us. [14]Hear, O Lord, our prayer and our supplication, and for your own sake deliver us, and grant us favor in the sight of those who have carried us into exile; [15]so that all the earth may know that you are the Lord our God, for Israel and his descendants are called by your name.

[16]O Lord, look down from your holy dwelling, and consider us. Incline your ear, O Lord, and hear; [17]open your eyes, O Lord, and see, for the dead who are in Hades, whose spirit has been taken from their bodies, will not ascribe glory or justice to the Lord; [18]but the person who is deeply grieved, who walks bowed and feeble, with failing eyes and famished soul, will declare your glory and righteousness, O Lord.

from foreign powers: "let your anger turn away from us," "hear our prayer," "deliver us," "grant us favor" (2:13-14). This situation is traced back to God's anger or wrath poured out on Israel, a concept of deuteronomistic historiography again linked to God's (violated) honor. While in the preceding passage the curse embedded in the words of God's Torah was in the foreground, now God as *auctor*, or more precisely a power within God as *auctor*, comes into view. Consequently, it is only God who can change the given situation. The community appeals to God's "own sake": it cannot be in God's interest to see his people humiliated, as this could fall back to himself as a question of his limited power to care for those upon whom God's name is called (2:15), hence what is his property.[14] God's divinity is at stake—divinity defined as powerful theophany.

With Bar 2:16-18 comes a new sequence of imperatives—"look down," "consider us," "incline your ear," "hear," "open your eyes," and "see"—preceded by an invocation. These verses continue the anthropomorphic way of imagining God's body[15] as was already the case in 2:11. In the past,

14. Steck, *Das apokryphe Baruchbuch*, 103–4.

15. On God's body, see Gerlinde Baumann, "Das göttliche Geschlecht. JHWHs Körper und die Genderfrage," in *Körperkonzepte im Ersten Testament. Aspekte einer Feministischen Anthropologie*, ed. Hedwig-Jahnow-Forschungsprojekt (Stuttgart: Kohlhammer, 2003), 220–49; Gerlinde Baumann, "Die 'Männlichkeit' JHWHs: Ein

TRANSLATION MATTERS

2:12 *we have done wrong*: ἠδικήσαμεν, literally: "we have committed injustice."

2:12 *against all your ordinances*: ἐπὶ πᾶσι τοῖς δικαιώμασι σου, literally: "against all your righteous ordinances."

2:15 *for Israel and his descendants are called by your name*: ὅτι τὸ ὄνομά σου ἐπεκλήθη ἐπὶ Ἰσραὴλ, καὶ ἐπὶ τὸ γένος αὐτοῦ, literally: "for your name is called upon Israel and his descendants."

2:17 *ascribe glory*: δώσουσι δόξαν, alternatively: "give honor."

2:18 *declare your glory*: δώσουσί σοι δόξαν, alternatively: "give honor to you."

God's fighting for Israel has been done by "arm" and "hand"; in the present, God's "eyes" and "ears" make him a deity "facing" those who cry to her. Apparently, God's hoped-for attention has to be re-membered! God's "holy dwelling" (οἶκος = "house"; 2:16) cannot be the temple in Jerusalem; the idea seems to be that God has a house in the heavens from where God can see the people in Jerusalem and Babylonia alike and where prayers reach the deity. Although Jerusalem with its altar remains the place for offerings (1:10), hence a privileged space of communication between Israel and her God, the book of Baruch, building on figures like Daniel, opens up a possibility to communicate with God wherever somebody wants to do so. From this perspective, the community gathered at the river Sud looks like an early form of "synagogue."

God is asked to "face" those supplicating as they are the only ones left who are able to give honor to God by ascribing glory and justice to God (Bar 2:18-19). Those who are dead belong to a realm far from God; the book of Baruch does not see the world of the dead as permeable to the world of God, in contrast to Dan 12:1-3 or 2 Macc 7 or, differently, Wis 3:1-4, although Baruch uses a terminology that reveals the attempt to transfer Jewish-Hebrew anthropology into Jewish-Greek thinking. According to Bar 2:17, the dead are considered to be "in Hades," in the

---

Neuansatz im Deutungsrahmen altorientalischer Gottesvorstellungen," in *Dem Tod nicht glauben. Sozialgeschichte der Bibel: Festschrift für Luise Schottroff zum 70. Geburtstag*, ed. Frank Crüsemann, Marlene Crüsemann, and Claudia Janssen (Gütersloh: Gütersloher Verlagshaus, 2004), 197–213; Silvia Schroer and Thomas Staubli, "Der göttliche Körper in der Miniaturkunst der südlichen Levante. Einblick in theologisch vernachlässigte Daten," in *"Gott bin ich, kein Mann". Beiträge zur Hermeneutik der biblischen Gottesrede*, ed. Ilona Riedel-Spangenberger and Erich Zenger (Paderborn: Schöningh, 2006), 124–55; Andreas Wagner, *Gottes Körper. Zur alttestamentlichen Vorstellung der Menschengestaltigkeit Gottes* (Gütersloh: Gütersloher Verlagshaus, 2010).

netherworld, their "spirit" (πνεῦμα) separated from their "entrails" (σπλάγχνα); hence their "breath of life" (Hebrew: רוח) vanished from the interior of the human body (Hebrew: מֵעִים) and lost forever. Therefore only those still among the living, those who are praying, are capable of honoring God, of recognizing God's justice and righteousness. But even their life is in danger. In Bar 2:18, they characterize themselves in correspondence to their misery, using formulae and images from Deut 28:65 in combination with Jer 38:12, 25 LXX. They refer to themselves by the term ψῦχή, which definitively has to be rendered as "person" (Hebrew: נפש) and which does not (yet) have the platonic connotation of immortal soul against mortal body. On the contrary, one could say ψῦχή describes the person as weak, as fainting away like a shadow, as close to the netherworld.

The logic of thought, then, seems to be the following: it cannot be in God's interest to lose the people of Israel completely, as there would not be anybody left to give honor to the deity. God is dependent on Israel.[16] Because Israel is not a strong community but rather humiliated, they ask to be "seen" and "considered" by God. But there is more: the person "who walks bowed and feeble" (Bar 2:18) has confessed her guilt and bows by free choice, demonstrating that she is ready to admit God's righteousness and God's righteous commandments. Hence, she is a person different from the earlier generations with their "wicked hearts" (1:22; 2:8). It is perhaps not a pure coincidence that the speech switches from the collective "we" to a form of talking about an individual, making visible every single member of the assembly. This person, these persons, do what deuteronomistic historiography interprets as actions that provide the people with a new chance and a new hope in response to the exile experience: they are ready to give heed to God's voice, to remember their prophets remembering the words of God's Torah.

Guilt of the Fathers and Rulers (2:19-26)

Again the prayer falls back on Israel's history. The focus, now, is not on confession of sins, although there is self-accusation, but on admission of guilt and therefore total dependence on God's mercy, because justice is what happened with Jerusalem's fall, in perfect concordance to what was to be expected.

---

16. For a similar logic, see the prayer of Esther, Esth C, 19–22 LXX.

[19]For it is not because of any righteous deeds of our ancestors or our kings that we bring before you our prayer for mercy, O Lord our God. [20]For you have sent your anger and your wrath upon us, as you declared by your servants the prophets, saying: [21]Thus says the Lord: Bend your shoulders and serve the king of Babylon, and you will remain in the land that I gave to your ancestors. [22]But if you will not obey the voice of the Lord and will not serve the king of Babylon, [23]I will make to cease from the towns of Judah and from the region around Jerusalem the voice of mirth and the voice of gladness, the voice of the bridegroom and the voice of the bride, and the whole land will be a desolation without inhabitants.

[24]But we did not obey your voice, to serve the king of Babylon; and you have carried out your threats, which you spoke by your servants the prophets, that the bones of our kings and the bones of our ancestors would be brought out of their resting place; [25]and indeed they have been thrown out to the heat of day and the frost of night. They perished in great misery, by famine and sword and pestilence.[17] [26]And the house that is called by your name you have made as it is today, because of the wickedness of the house of Israel and the house of Judah.

The prayer notes that it was God who moved death-bringing forces, indicated by the double expression "anger and wrath" (Bar 2:20), against Israel, just as it was God who was behind the words of those prophets preaching submission to Babylon in order to avoid deportation and the devastation of the land. Again, the "ancestors" (literally "fathers") along with the "kings" (Bar 2:19; see also 1:16) are mentioned as the authorities with their specific guilt. By quoting the prophecy of Jeremiah, his very emotional description of the end of any joy (Jer 7:34; 16:9; 25:10), and his announcement of desolation[18] as the word of God, the prayer recognizes Jeremiah as a true prophet in the footsteps of Moses (Deut 18:21-22). Disregard of the prophetical-divine order entails what Jeremiah prophetically announced as God's negative reaction. The curse declared through

17. Text-critical matter: "pestilence" translates a conjectured Hebrew *Vorlage* and not the Greek text as it stands. The Greek text has "through famine and through sword [ῥομφαία] and through sending off [ἀποστολῇ]." If one takes "sending off" in the sense of "dispersion," the expression makes sense. A similar formula with famine, μαχαίρα instead of ῥομφαία (both Greek nouns meaning "sword") and ἀποστολή is found in Jer 39:36 LXX, which renders Jer 32:36 MT ("sword, hunger, pestilence"). Baruch 2:25 seems to allude again to Jeremiah's prayer in Jer 32 MT/39 LXX but then follows Jer 39:36 LXX instead of the Hebrew. The case is similar to 1:9; see the comment there.

18. The formula εἰς ἄβατον, "into desolation" is found only in Jeremiah and Baruch.

TRANSLATION MATTERS

2:19, 21, 24 *ancestors*: πατέρες, literally: "fathers."

2:24 *carried out your threats*: ἔστησας τοὺς λόγους σου, literally: "put into force your words" (see also 2:1).

2:26 *the house that is called by your name*: τὸν οἶκον, οὗ ἐπεκλήθη τὸ ὄνομά σου ἐπ᾽αὐτῷ, literally: "the house upon which is called your name."

Moses (Bar 1:20) and the words spoken by the prophets after Moses (2:24) function in the same way; they come into force under determined conditions, and they are experienced as the expression of God's anger. As proof of this connection, the prayer mentions desecration of graves, a fate Jeremiah announced to all inhabitants of Jerusalem and Judah (Jer 8:1) and in particular to King Jehoiakim, who cut into pieces and burned the scroll on which Baruch had written Jeremiah's words concerning Jerusalem (Jer 36:30 MT; 43:30 LXX). In the context of the whole prayer this motif might be seen in correspondence to the horrible famine during the siege of Jerusalem when parents slaughtered and ate their own children (Bar 2:3). In remembering the end and beginning of life, a shameful treatment of the dead, and a horrible and no less shameful treatment of children, the horrors of the city's fall are evoked. The picture is completed by a general formula embracing all who died at that time[19] and by a brief glance at the temple imagined in ruins. The prayer brings into view the "house" of God in Jerusalem only after the affirmation that there is another "house" from where God's "eyes" and "ears" can perceive those who are praying. So there is hope for God's mercy.

In Bar 2:19-26, the prayer is in line with Jeremiah's preaching of nonresistance against Babylon, in contrast to his prophetical opponents who supported the anti-Babylonian party (see esp. Jer 28). For Jeremiah, remaining in the land was the value to defend in a situation of hopeless military inferiority, requiring surrender and submission to Babylonian forces. His opponents, on the other hand, cherished the hope that continued resistance would bring about a liberating blow or possibly a (relative) political autonomy. The prayer of the exiles admits that Jeremiah's prophecy was right: they are ready not only to avoid resistance or revolution but actively to recommend the foreign rulers to God (Bar 1:11-12); they not only confess as wrong their rebellion against the true prophet but also express their lasting relation to Jerusalem and the

---

19. See text-critical remark on Bar 2:25.

On the Guilt of Fathers and Rulers, Part 2

Sexualized violence in the church takes place in the context of a moral set of rules and church structures. The moral doctrine of the church, of course, condemns sexualized violence. But is this remark sufficient for comprehending the inscrutable contradiction between the stringency of the doctrine and the monstrous breach of the rules by some of its teachers, including the deafness of those in authority to whom the assaults have been reported as well as the halfhearted pursuit of a criminal prosecution or the failure to carry one out at all?

Sexuality is especially susceptible to abuse of power because, in an intimate encounter, people are particularly vulnerable and in need of protection. Sexualized violence against one's charges makes it clear that an intimate encounter is only ethically correct when there is no imbalance of power between the lovers. Perpetrators often claim that the victims had "consented" or had "wanted it." But what do "consent" and "wanting" mean in a relationship of dependency in which there is a person in power and a person under his charge?

This imbalance of power is expressed in sexualized violence, not only in the church, but also in society: more than 95 percent of sexual abusers are men; the majority of the victims of sexual abuse are women and girls; the majority of sexual abusers are heterosexuals; in the case of priests who are perpetrators, the largest group of victims is the group of post-pubescent boys.

The "rulers and fathers" in the church tend not to call the structural, systemic contexts into question when seeking a deeper understanding of sexualized violence in the church. In the end, this happens at the expense of the clarification and prevention of sexualized violence. The refusal to permit the questioning of the system corresponds objectively to the power interests of the "rulers and fathers," even if they subjectively think they are defending a holy order. Precisely this, however, is also part of the iniquity of "the rulers and fathers." One can denounce these inquiries on their part by alleging that sexual abuse is being exploited for purposes of internal church politics. But in the end that too is nothing other than a further trick to evade the pressing questions.

Klaus Mertes

land surrounding it. In that they refer to Jeremiah's prayer after his purchase of a piece of land—with Baruch as witness (Jer 32 MT/39 LXX)[20]—they underline their hope to return to the place of their origin.

---

20. See, e.g., Bar 2:11 and Jer 39:21 LXX; Bar 2:25 and Jer 39:36 LXX.

The exiles' description of Jerusalem in ruins corresponds well to what the recipients of their message in Jerusalem experienced. It even seems that this part of the prayer reflects better the Jerusalemite perspective than a Babylonian one, perhaps providing evidence of the prayer's origin in Jerusalem. The Jerusalemites alike, according to the (fictitious) date, have to endure foreign dominion; they cannot cast it off because it is part of the curse clinging to them. Thus, the prayer presumes the same political options open to both the exiles and to those who still live in the city and its surroundings. Jeremiah's action is a sign of hope for the Jerusalemites too. The book of Baruch considers this movement of thought relevant to its own time in the Hellenistic age. It suggests that the Hellenistic Empire is also the effect of an enduring divine curse, but there is hope for its end.

Remembering God's Promises (2:27-35)

With Bar 2:27 the prayer takes a decisively positive turn, pointing to God's "equity" (ἐπιείκεια) and "compassion" (οἰκτιρμός) already perceptible in the assembly. Again, this turn is shown to occur according to what was announced by Moses, hence with reference to the Torah, and again in a wording that combines motifs of the Pentateuch and allusions to Jeremiah.

The actual situation is dispersion and decimation (2:29) because of having been a "stiff-necked people" (2:30). This is a characteristic attributed to Israel in the Pentateuch when the people erected and venerated the golden calf,[21] the first act of idolatry, in immediate proximity to the declaration of the Ten Commandments with the prohibition of images and other gods. The penitential prayer, however, is an expression of a changed attitude that has grown out of the experiences of exile, a turn back to their hearts (2:30) that Moses had considered possible in his speeches to the people on the shores of the Jordan River (Deut 4:29-30; 30:1-2). Now the people are willing and able to recognize "the Lord their God" (2:31). This expression does not point to a monotheistic denial of other gods but is a profession within Israel of their God only, of their one and only God. As such, the formula resembles more the Priestly-Levitical declarations than the Isaianic formulae.[22] In Jer 24:5-7, "the Lord

---

21. See Exod 33:3, 5; 34:9; Deut 9:6, 13.

22. See part 5 below and as general background Marie-Theres Wacker, *Von Göttinnen, Göttern und dem einzigen Gott: Studien zum biblischen Monotheismus aus feministisch-theologischer Sicht*, Theologische Frauenforschung in Europa 14 (Münster: Lit, 2004).

²⁷Yet you have dealt with us, O Lord our God, in all your kindness and in all your great compassion, ²⁸as you spoke by your servant Moses on the day when you commanded him to write your law in the presence of the people of Israel, saying, ²⁹"If you will not obey my voice, this very great multitude will surely turn into a small number among the nations, where I will scatter them. ³⁰For I know that they will not obey me, for they are a stiff-necked people. But in the land of their exile they will come to themselves ³¹and know that I am the Lord their God. I will give them a heart that obeys and ears that hear; ³²they will praise me in the land of their exile, and will remember my name ³³and turn from their stubbornness and their wicked deeds; for they will remember the ways of their ancestors, who sinned before the Lord. ³⁴I will bring them again into the land that I swore to give to their ancestors, to Abraham, Isaac, and Jacob, and they will rule over it; and I will increase them, and they will not be diminished. ³⁵I will make an everlasting covenant with them to be their God and they shall be my people; and I will never again remove my people Israel from the land that I have given them."

their God" is found in a context similar to the one developed in Bar 2:30b-31 and indeed underlines the new mutual relation between Israel and its God. Again, corporeal images seem to be indispensable: the heart, center of volition and planning; and the ears, the organ to listen with and to prepare for comprehension. Both have to undergo a transformation pursued by God (2:31). Both organs will be listening,[23] and the first effect is praising, done by the lips, and remembering "by heart" the only appropriate way of praising, which is pronouncing God's name from the heart. As a corresponding measure there is another remembering: the transgression of the ancestors, with the metaphor of "the ways" (2:33), hence done with heart and feet, a memory to put at a distance.

With Abraham, Isaac, and Jacob, a different set of ancestors comes into view in Bar 2:34. These fathers—their families included—are remembered as part of Israel's story not yet damaged by disobedience to God's commandments. They received the promise of the land by a divine oath, a concept particularly frequent in the book of Deuteronomy but also seen in Jer 32:22 MT (39:22 LXX). This promise quoted as a divine word pronounced through Moses can now be activated and related to those who

---

23. The verb, according to the Greek text as it stands, refers to both organs. See 2:31 in Translation Matters. A "listening heart" is an allusion to Solomon who asked God for a "listening heart" at the beginning of his rule (1 Kgs 3:9) and got a "wise and discerning" heart (1 Kgs 3:12).

TRANSLATION MATTERS

2:27 *kindness*: ἐπιείκεια, better: "equity."

2:30 *they will come to themselves*: ἐπιστρέψουσιν ἐπὶ καρδίαν αὐτῶν, more literally: "they will turn back to their hearts/minds."

2:31 *a heart that obeys*: "that obeys" is conjectured; καρδία, literally: "a heart."

2:34 *I will bring them again*: ἀποστρέψω αὐτοὺς, literally: "I will turn them back again."

2:34 *ancestors*: πατέρες, literally: "fathers."

2:35 *I will make . . . with them*: στήσω αὐτοῖς, more literally: "I will put into force . . . for them" (see also 2:1; 2:24).

---

are praying with "listening hearts" (1 Kgs 3:9). This is what those exiled in Babylon hope for: to return to the land of promise and to rule over it (2:34). The Greek text employing the verb κυριεύω ("to rule") connects that hope even to the divine epithet κύριος ("ruler"). And there is another intensification: they hope for an "everlasting covenant" combining their indissoluble relation to God and to the land. The fact that only here in the book of Baruch the term "covenant" (διαθήκη) is used gives additional weight to this statement (2:35).[24]

The "land" (γῆ) promised or given to Israel by God is the counter-space to the "land of their exile" or displacement (ἀποικισμός, 2:30, 32). In the book of Jeremiah, this term refers to other nations only in announcing to them their exile.[25] On the one hand, the community praying in the book of Baruch compares itself humbly to these foreign nations. On the other hand, it becomes clear that a nation living on its own soil is a common concept in antiquity. The term ἀποικισμός—in classical Greek one of the terms designating settlements of a colony, hence revealing the perspective of colonizers—is used in Baruch and Jeremiah from the perspective of colonized people deported to serve the colonizers or to prevent revolutions against the colonial authority in the occupied regions (see Jer 41 MT/48 LXX). The hope of return to the country promised to

---

24. Franz Heinrich Reusch, *Erklärung des Buchs Baruch* (Freiburg: Herder, 1853), 158–62, uses the mention of a covenant to expand on Israel as the first people of the covenant replaced by the church, hence for the classical Christian theology of supersession.

25. See Jer 46:19; 48:11; 43:11 (26:19; 31:11; 50:11 [2] LXX). The Septuagint has, together with Bar 2:30, 32, only these six instances for ἀποικισμός.

the "fathers" is then the hope for an end of living under occupation. It seems that this passage of the prayer puts into the foreground the perspective of the exiles. But the political implications for those in Jerusalem are evident: they would be among those who rule over the land and will never again be removed from it. If there is actual exploitation of the land by foreign rulers, as Nehemiah's prayer assumes (Neh 9:36-37), then the Jews remaining in Jerusalem can hope for an end of that. Moreover, the prayer considers the people of Israel to be united without rivalries between those who return and those who remained.

In a sense, this prayer is fueled by and stimulates the hope for an independent state of the Jewish people in the country around Jerusalem. In contrast especially to the books of the Maccabees, the prayer does not call for resistance or an armed fight but rather leaves the realization of this hope to God's intervention. Because the prayer does not reflect on inhabitants of that state other than those belonging to Israel, it leaves room for divergent political-religious concepts of coexistence.

Cry for Mercy (3:1-8)

After the remembered vision of a happy future, the last part of the prayer turns back to the situation at hand. By an identically worded invocation of God (3:1, 4) the text is divided into two units: 3:1-3, 4-8. This invocation combines "God of Israel" with two epithets emphasizing God's dominion and infinite power.

The first unit of this section of the prayer (Bar 3:1-3) is an invocation that serves to emphasize the immense difference between God and those who pray and characterize themselves as troubled and needy. Again, the supplicants use the individualizing terms "soul" and "spirit" to point to their individual selves as weak and fainting away. Again, every single member of the assembly, "the soul . . . the wearied spirit" (3:1), tends to become visible in his or her misery. A repeated confession of sin is associated with a cry for mercy, and the contrast between God's dominion and the continued downfall of the people (3:3) can be seen once more as many individual acts of self-humiliation and of giving honor to God.

But then, in Bar 3:4, the prayer moves on to a new argument, introducing a distinction between the "sinners," characterized again as those who "did not heed the voice" of God (1:18-19; 2:5), and their descendants, their "children" to whom the calamities provoked by the deeds of the ancestors "have clung" (3:4; see also 1:20) and who feel already dead

Bar 3:1-8

³:¹O Lord Almighty, God of Israel, the soul in anguish and the wearied spirit cry out to you. ²Hear, O Lord, and have mercy, for we have sinned before you. ³For you are enthroned forever, and we are perishing forever. ⁴O Lord Almighty, God of Israel, hear now the prayer of the people of Israel, the children of those who sinned before you, who did not heed the voice of the Lord their God, so that calamities have clung to us. ⁵Do not remember the iniquities of our ancestors, but in this crisis remember your power and your name. ⁶For you are the Lord our God, and it is you, O Lord, whom we will praise. ⁷For you have put the fear of you in our hearts so that we would call upon your name; and we will praise you in our exile, for we have put away from our hearts all the iniquity of our ancestors who sinned against you. ⁸See, we are today in our exile where you have scattered us, to be reproached and cursed and punished for all the iniquities of our ancestors, who forsook the Lord our God.

when they speak of themselves as "the deceased of Israel," the literal translation of τῶν τεθνηκότων Ἰσραὴλ (3:4). And it is precisely that difference they ask God to respect, referring to God's "hand" (NRSV: "power") and "name" (3:5), to God's mighty deeds for Israel, and to the people ready to praise God's name (3:6-7). They add a decisive perspective: they do not deny their own guilt included in the foregoing confessions[26] but insist that, as opposed to their ancestors, they are willing to turn away from "all the iniquities of our ancestors" (3:7). Again, the literal rendering of πατέρες would be "fathers," but here the focus is on predecessors, not on male authoritative figures. Mothers might have joined in these iniquities—and mothers along with the fathers are willing to turn away from what they did wrong.

26. The relative clause in 3:4, "who did not heed the voice," seems to refer to "the sinners," hence the ancestors of those who pray, but it is possible to refer the phrase to those praying too. Nevertheless, 3:4 seems to underline the difference between the ancestors = sinners and their children who are prepared to "heed." Jonathan A. Goldstein ("The Apocryphal Book of I Baruch," *PAAJR* 46–47 [1928–29/1979–1980], 179–99) sees a sharp distinction made between the ancestors = rebels and "us (repentant Israel)" and concludes: "as a typical sectarian Jew, then, the author of Baruch viewed himself and his group as the 'true Israel'" (199). Over against the more "inclusive" perspectives other interpreters find in the book of Baruch, Goldstein underlines the "exclusivity" of the message: repentance, Torah, and promise of land go together for Baruch's "true Israel."

TRANSLATION MATTERS

3:1 *the soul . . . the spirit*: ψυχή . . . πνεῦμα, literally: "a soul . . . a spirit."

3:4 *the people of Israel*: τῶν τεθνηκότων Ἰσραὴλ, literally: "the deceased of Israel."

3:5 *your power*: χειρός σου, literally: "your hand."

3:7 *ancestors*: πατέρες, literally: "fathers."

On the Guilt of the Fathers and Rulers, Part 3

The term "fathers" includes the aspect of being "forefathers." The consequences of the iniquity of the forefathers pass over to subsequent generations. God does show mercy by inflicting punishment for the iniquity of the forefathers only "to the third and the fourth generation," not for all eternity. Nevertheless, the consequences of the iniquity of forefathers cannot be confined to their generation.

How does this punishment for the iniquity of the forefathers to the third and the fourth generation present itself in concrete terms? The survivors of sexual abuse often begin to speak only decades later when, in their struggle to survive, they have reached dry land or at least see the saving shore ahead of them. By then the perpetrators are frequently already dead, have disappeared, or have dodged the issue—and those who were in authority at the time are no longer in office. Hence the survivors usually encounter not the forefathers but the ruling sons. These sons are tempted to indicate to the survivors that they have nothing to do with the sins of the forefathers. The victims thus find no one to talk to who assumes responsibility and indicates to them that they have come to the right person with their grievance, their accusation, and their demands.

The responsibility that the ruling sons assume for the acts and omissions of their once ruling forefathers does not have to be limitless. Talk about the "third and fourth generation" is an expression of this fact. But the limit to responsibility can be found only in a process in which, first of all, responsibility is assumed—through clarification, acknowledgment of the inflicted pain, help, and prevention.

The church as the people of God is guided in particular by the demand for solidarity among the generations, also with regard to the dark sides of its own history. It sees itself as a "communion of saints," a communion of the living and the dead. Consequently, with the death of the forefathers, the church cannot set a limit beyond which it assumes no responsibility for the dead "saints" who have sinned

> (which, by the way, makes it clear that "holiness" arises from the sanctification of the sinners by God and not as a result of their own moral achievement). In this respect, the "we" of the whole church in the confession of sins is correct—it is a "we" that does not dissociate itself from the iniquity and guilt of the "rulers and fathers."
>
> *Klaus Mertes*

Therefore, the community's present situation, described as being far from their homes (ἀποικία), again using a Greek term in the sense of its underlying Hebrew connotations,[27] no longer corresponds to their actions. There is a discrepancy between God's promises and the actual situation; therefore God has to intervene! Instead of the prayer ending with "a response and closure,"[28] it ends with this implicit perspective of hope.

It is interesting to see how the question of guilt and its consequences is dealt with here (Bar 3:1-8). The experience of a collective disaster can be accepted as an expression of God's wrath, although the mention of the children slaughtered for their parents might already demand a critical distance to this concept. The prayer's oscillation between collective and individual voices paints a community with every single member made visible, showing the readiness of every individual to turn back from the "sins of the fathers" and at the same time questioning the ongoing misery. The prayer thus develops critical reflections on the "guilt of the fathers" and its impact on the next generation, reflections like those in the background of Jer 31:29-30 (38:29-30 LXX), or, similarly, in Ezek 18:2. Both prophets ask if it is acceptable when "the parents have eaten sour grapes, and the children's teeth are set on edge." Both have a divine oracle quote this proverb to declare it ineffective: a new generation willing to break with the iniquities of former generations shall have the chance of a new beginning. As modern readers look back on a century of horrible wars, this divine promise is an invitation to face our past in order to under-

---

27. In classical Greek, ἀποικία signifies "colony" (Bar 2:30, 32; ἀποικισμός). This Greek term usually translates the Hebrew גולה—"deportation" or exile. Heard with this background the desire to "be home" is nothing less than a call for human dignity.

28. Anthony J. Saldarini, "The Book of Baruch. Introduction, Commentary, and Reflections," in *Introduction to Prophetic Literature, the Book of Isaiah, the Book of Jeremiah, the Book of Baruch, the Letter of Jeremiah, the Book of Lamentations, the Book of Ezekiel*, ed. Leander E. Keck, NIB 6 (Nashville, TN: Abingdon Press, 2001), 929–82, at 957.

stand the structures behind the developments that led there. It is an invitation to distance ourselves from any rhetorical attempt to involve God on the sides of warring parties. This prayer is an invitation not to lose courage when realizing that the shadows of the past are still bearing down on us and cannot easily be overcome.

Baruch 3:9–4:4

Where Wisdom Is to Be Found

A new and different voice enters the stage after the narrator reporting about the Babylonian community gathered at the river Sud (Bar 1:2-9), formulating a message (1:10-14), and suggesting a long prayer of penitence, supplication, and hope to be recited in Jerusalem (1:15–3:8). Baruch 3:9 marks a switch in the direction of speech; an imperative introduces a new extensive passage with a clear subject of its own and a distinctive conclusion (4:2-4). Within the context of the book, Bar 3:9–4:4 can be heard and interpreted in different ways: as a unit in itself; as an answer to the preceding prayer; as admonition speech to prepare the prophetical voice for Jerusalem; and as part of the book as it exists now, the book for Babylon and Jerusalem, for two communities separated geographically but united ideologically. All of these readings reveal specific dimensions of the text and do not exclude one another.

Baruch 3:9–4:4 is marked by its poetical rhythm; nearly in its entirety, it consists of pairs of parallel lines (bicola). Its subject is wisdom, her place, her accessibility; many of the literary traditions it draws on are rooted in biblical Wisdom literature. Following thematic and formal indications,[1] a threefold structure can be noticed. The first section, 3:9-14,

---

1. Odil Hannes Steck, *Das apokryphe Baruchbuch*, FRLANT 160 (Göttingen: Vandenhoeck & Ruprecht, 1993), 123–26, relying on genre considerations, sees a somewhat different structure; for him, the three addresses to Israel are the most relevant signals.

is marked by imperatives inviting Israel to listen and to learn. A second, longer passage comprises verses 15-31. The questions in 3:15 correspond to those in 3:29-30 and find a negative answer in 3:31. The third passage, 3:32–4:4, has the positive answer and takes up again the imperative mode of the beginning. Thus, the poetical speech addressed to Israel develops in a complex way one fundamental idea: wisdom can be found nowhere among humans, only with God. Different terms are used to describe, to circumscribe, to explore the meaning of "wisdom": besides σοφία, a common translation of the Hebrew חכמה for wisdom, there is "prudence" (φρόνησις), "understanding" (σύνεσις), and "knowledge" (ἐπιστήμη). These terms can be interpreted as mutually complementary as all are connected to the wisdom metaphor of finding her "way" or "paths."

The poem is in dense intertextual relation to other Wisdom writings. The most striking feature of Bar 3:9–4:4, from a feminist perspective, though, is the intertextual preference given to the Wisdom poem of Job 28 with its concept of wisdom hidden and imperceptible[2] over against the traditions of personified wisdom in the book of Proverbs, Ben Sira, and the book of Wisdom.[3] The reasons and effects of such preference have to be considered.

Learning Wisdom (3:9-14)

The opening imperative "Hear, . . . O Israel" recalls spontaneously, for an audience or for readers living with the Torah, the analogous formula used in Moses' last speech and only there in the entire Hebrew Bible (Deut 5:1; 6:4; 9:1; 20:3; 27:9). Those who confessed to have transgressed the commandments of God are now invited to listen to these ordinances immediately connected to "life" and, in the parallel, synonymous line, to "prudence" (φρόνεσις), one aspect of the larger field of "wisdom." In one single verse, Torah from Sinai (in its deuteronomic shape) and wisdom are merged, and the twofold imperative merges obedience to the Torah with learning as a "disciple" of wisdom: Moses

2. For an extensive comparison between Job 28 and Bar 3:9–4:4, see Odil Hannes Steck, "Israels Gott statt anderer Götter—Israels Gesetz statt fremder Weisheit. Beobachtungen zur Rezeption von Hi 28 in Bar 3, 9–4,4," in *„Wer ist wie du, Herr, unter den Göttern?" Studien zur Theologie und Religionsgeschichte Israels*, ed. Ingo Kottsieper (Göttingen: Vandenhoeck & Ruprecht, 1994), 457–71.

3. Abundant feminist research has been done on personified wisdom. A concise introduction is provided in Gerlinde Baumann, "Personified Wisdom. Contexts, Meanings, Theology," in *The Writings and Later Wisdom Books*, ed. Christl Maier and Nuria Calduch Benages, The Bible and Women 1.3 (Atlanta, GA: SBL, 2014), 57–75.

Bar 3:9-14

⁹Hear the commandments of life,
O Israel;
give ear, and learn wisdom!
¹⁰Why is it, O Israel, why is it that
you are in the land of your
enemies,
that you are growing old in a
foreign country,
that you are defiled with the dead,
¹¹that you are counted among
those in Hades?
¹²You have forsaken the fountain
of wisdom.

¹³If you had walked in the way of
God,
you would be living in peace
forever.
¹⁴Learn where there is wisdom,
where there is strength,
where there is understanding,
so that you may at the same time
discern
where there is length of days,
and life,
where there is light for the
eyes, and peace.

TRANSLATION MATTERS

3:9 *hear the commandments of life, O Israel*: the Greek word order corresponds to "Hear, O Israel, the commandments of life," recalling Deut 6:4.

3:9 *learn wisdom*: γνῶναι φρόνησιν, better: "understand wisdom," to catch the same Greek word γνῶναι, "understand/ing," in 3:9 and 3:14.

3:9, 14 *wisdom*: the Greek φρόνεσις as distinct from σοφία = "wisdom," hence better: "prudence" (NAB) or "insight" (NETS).

turns into a wisdom teacher; the voice using deuteronomic and sapiential forms, styles, and motifs of speech brings together the authority of both traditions. This double introductory line comprises, in a nutshell, the theo-logic of the whole speech: wisdom and God's commandments are one.

With the name of "Israel" and the plural verb (literally) to "give heed" (ἐνωτίσασθε, 3:9), a collective people is addressed, and by the singular forms of all other verbs in the passage, every single member of the community is addressed, as often happens in the book of Deuteronomy. The wisdom teacher of Bar 3:9-37 might also have had in mind Prov 4:1 LXX where a voice admonishes "children" (παῖδες) to listen to the "learning" or, literally, "pedagogics" (παιδεία) of their father. It is clear, then, that in Bar 3:9 a male voice is speaking. The audience is not specified and might, as in the prayer, be imagined in an inclusive way ("children") or restricted to the "sons" distancing themselves from their "fathers" (Bar 3:4-8).

Which Wisdom?
Whose Wisdom? Part 1

The backdrop to this text was the situation in which the Israelites were living in the land of their historical enemy. As a Korean woman living in a country whose history includes a thirty-six-year-long (1910–1945) colonization by Japan, for which we are yet to receive a proper apology for its inhumane violent occupation, the outcry from Israel has a familiar ring. Even today, issues such as the "comfort women" (Jung-Sin-Dae) who were taken in sexual slavery for the Japanese army during the Second World War, and the contention of dominium over Dok-Do (Dakeshima), have escalated the political and emotional conflict and tension between Korea and Japan. In this context, it could be argued that the song concerning wisdom in Baruch is ours indeed.

This poem explains that the difficulties and problems of the Israelites are caused by themselves forsaking the fountain of wisdom, the way of God. One of the most accessible and easily available means for an oppressed people to seek help, when they are under the rule of another nation, is to pray to God on whom they have always relied. Before requesting deliverance from the other nation, however, reflection and repentance is necessary. This is because they believe their penitence is required for God to hear and forgive them. At a difficult time, Israel affirmed the power of their omnipotent God, by confessing their guilt. In other words, at the catastrophic time of having "shared the defilement of the dead and been numbered with those that lie in the grave" (3:10-11), they confess their guilt to God and profess their absolute dependence on him, by praising him as their only god. It is a similar political situation to what was experienced by Koreans at the end of the Chosun Dynasty, when the powerful surrounding nations like Russia, China, and Japan invaded, making the land their battle ground. At that time, the Dong-Hak movement arose from the traditional Korean national religion, and the Maitreya faith emerged from Korean Buddhism.

To understand the wisdom poem in Baruch, it is essential to comprehend such historical backgrounds. To ignore and generalize the faith-based, historical, confessional nature of this text as a simple statement would be imprudent. Each people has its own religious faith to facilitate unity and purity, but when other people are forced to adopt it, there may be a war between nations or religions.

Kyung-Sook Lee

The overall structure of the passage is concentric.[4] Baruch 3:9 and 3:14 frame the passage: imperatives open both verses: 3:9 ("hear") and 3:14 ("learn" or literally "give ear"); both verses name "prudence" (φρόνεσις) as the curriculum to be learned; both verses insist that "understanding" prudence is important (the infinitive γνῶναι, "understand/ing," appears in both verses); and both verses suggest that "life" is a fruit of learning. The central verse (3:12) has a different poetical form, not a bicolon, but one single line, and it is the only verse in the introductory passage that uses the noun σοφία for wisdom. This verse, an accusation by way of a statement, points to a fundamental problem that has to be dealt with: "You have forsaken the fountain of wisdom." The preceding verses, 3:10-11, raise rhetorical questions concerning those addressed and reveal the actual situation as miserable; the following verse, 3:13, describes the opportunity missed when wisdom was not strived for. "Living in peace" as status not achieved stands in contrast to living in the foreign country of the enemies (3:10), and walking in the way of God seems to be the contrary of being "counted among those in Hades" (3:11), making the spaces directed by God and the space of death antipodes.

The metaphor of a "fountain [or source] of wisdom" (3:12) with its associations of living, thirst-quenching water is frequent in Wisdom literature and often connected to life.[5] The composite expression "source of wisdom" refers either to wisdom as source or to wisdom flowing from a source different from her. Thus the reproach of 3:12 might aim at Israel leaving behind wisdom as her source of life or her (divine) source out of which wisdom flows. The difference is in the perception of the figure of wisdom and the degree of allowing her her own specific contours in relation to God. In both cases, wisdom and God are related—a subject the speech or poem will develop further.

Israel's situation as presumed by the voice speaking is shaped by enmity, foreignness, death, and defilement (Bar 3:10-11). Living in Babylonia means to live in a hostile country, to remember every day the humiliation of being defeated and deported. It means, for too long a time already, to live in a foreign country opposed to the country where one was rooted and where the ancestors are buried, to live a no-life at the borders of death.

---

4. This is a decisive argument for me to see 3:9-14 as a first unit and not to follow Steck, *Das apokryphe Baruchbuch*, 123–28, who links 3:14 with 3:15.

5. For example, see "source of life" in Prov 10:11; 13:14; 14:27; 16:22; Sir 21:13; the "source of wisdom" in Prov 18:4 MT becomes a "source of life" in Prov 18:4 LXX.

The opposition of death and life is a characteristic of Wisdom literature. In wisdom logic, as is well-documented in the book of Proverbs, for example, the terms of death and life sum up the alternative of a wisdom-oriented life or a life refusing wisdom. In this context, to be wise means life, while acting the fool prepares for death. Baruch 3:10-11 together with its counterpart in 3:13 goes beyond this wisdom logic and enlarges it by combining it with the logic of defilement and purity (a concern relevant also for the Epistle of Jeremiah): living in a foreign country is as defiling—in the sense of not being able to approach the sphere of the divine—as touching corpses. Death is not a realm of the God of Israel, and the God of Israel has no relation to countries of other people.[6] To put it differently, Israel's actual situation is portrayed as a space outside the blessings or protection of God, mingling metaphorical and real spaces ("ways"; 3:13), making Babylonia an impossible space to live in, implying that a worthwhile life is possible only in the land of origin. These gloomy perspectives urge the audience to long for a better future. The framing imperatives (3:9, 14) show them a way out.

Similarities are apparent between the community's prayer in Bar 1:15–3:8 and the Wisdom song in Bar 3:9-14. Both texts merge collective and individual perspectives, and both address the whole community and every single member of "Israel." The prayer characterized the community's situation as wasting away at the borders of Hades (2:17) and being in "exile"—torn away "from home" (ἀποικίζω, 2:14; ἀποικισμός, 2:30, 32; ἀποικία, 3:7-8). Those who pray know that if their ancestors had walked in the ways of God's commandments their situation would be different, and they are ready to listen to the "commandments of life," having confessed their guilt. The voice rising up in 3:9 refers to the community's exile in a foreign context for a long time and turns it into a problematic situation (3:10-11), thus kindling the hope for an end of this desperate condition. They hoped for "light to our eyes" (1:12) and are offered such "light" now (3:14).[7] On the other hand, this voice is differ-

---

6. Again, like in the prayer (Bar 2:17), the Greek translators use the term *Hades* corresponding to the Hebrew *Sheol* as designation for the realm of the dead, and again, there is no hint of a belief that God's power extends beyond the limits of death.

7. Looking forward to the end of the poem with its identification of wisdom and the book of God's commandments, "light for the eyes" gains another very pragmatic dimension: those who want to study the book need light to read! In premodern cultures where sources of light were limited to sunlight, moonlight, and oil lamps, "light" has quite a different quality, and splendid light can easily become a metaphor (or reality!) related to God.

ent, speaking in poetical rhythms, insisting on rhetorical oppositions, and moving on to the new subject area of knowing/insight/wisdom. The community of prayer turns into a community of disciples.

Read from the presupposition that Bar 3:9-14 forms part of Baruch's book read out at river Sud, the speaker would be Baruch, Jeremiah's scribe, reminding the exiles of their fate as uprooted people. Ultimately, then, his voice reveals not so much the perspective of the exiled community as the perspective of a Jerusalemite. At any rate, the following speech leaves the perspective of exile behind; its audience is "Israel" wherever they might be.

Wisdom Hidden (3:15-31)

The audience being in an attentive mood, the speaker's voice continues with another set of questions. They introduce a new line of thought, the subject of learning wisdom, put in the sapiential metaphor of "finding her place" (Bar 3:15) or "her paths/way" (3:20-21, 23, 27, 31), showing how difficult, even impossible, this turns out to be. The eyes of the speaker seem to inspect huge periods and spaces, each time with a negative result. Three such steps or stages can be distinguished (3:16-21, 22-23, 24-28), before the initial questions are taken up to resume the investigation (3:29-31).

Opening Questions (3:15)

These questions belong to the style of rhetoric engaging the audience directly. As such they are not specific to sapiential discourse but part of it. The two parallel questions in Bar 3:15 do not mention the object of inquiry but only allude to it by a feminine pronoun. Hearers or readers are referred back to the beginning of the speech talking about prudence and wisdom. At the same time, those readers might connect the first question with Job 28:12, asking where wisdom is to be found, and they might connect the second one about the "storehouses" (θησαυροί) of wisdom with the book of Proverbs (2:4; 3:14; 8:21 LXX) or Sir 1:25, reflecting on the "treasuries [θησαυροί] of wisdom." The questions personify wisdom; they give her a space where she stores her wealth. This corresponds to the image of Wisdom in the book of Proverbs, where she is presented as a wealthy and eloquent person, an attractive female, a counsellor of kings, and even at the side of God the creator (Prov 8:22-31). While in the book of Proverbs she is present, she makes a public

Bar 3:15

¹⁵Who has found her place?
And who has entered her
storehouses?

appearance, she offers herself, according to Bar 3:15 it seems to be more difficult to have access to her.

Powerful Rulers—Without Wisdom (3:16-21)

The series of questions continues to introduce a first group of persons who are possible candidates to find or possess wisdom: powerful rulers. In the Hebrew Bible, King Solomon is considered to be a wise ruler, as is his neighbor Hiram of Tyre (1 Kgs 5) and, of course, the Queen of Sheba (1 Kgs 10). One characteristic of the rulers focused on in Bar 3:16-17 is their control of human beings, but with even more emphasis on their dominion in the realm of animals, including the whole space between earth and heaven. One explanation might be a reference to Job 28:21. If Job's wisdom poem states that wisdom was hidden before every living being and before the birds of heaven, Bar 3:16-17 focuses on humans dominating every living being between heaven and earth, insinuating that such rulers have a chance to access wisdom.

Dominion in the realm of animals is a prerogative of monarchs, demonstrated especially when they go hunting.[8] The motif of a "master (or mistress) of animals" is frequent on seals and other objects from Egypt, the Levant, and Mesopotamia, ranging from the second and far into the first millennium BCE.[9] Often they represent a god or a goddess. Dominion over animals seems to be an expression of a god-like aura of a ruler, underlining their power. The way Bar 3:17a formulates it, however, might contain a criticism of those who "made sport of the birds of the air." If this were the case the text would comprise a second level of argumentation, bringing in suspicion with regard to such power games.

8. Already Joseph Knabenbauer, "Commentarius in Baruch," in *Commentarius in Danielem prophetam, Lamentationes et Baruch*, Cursus Scripturae Sacrae III/2 (Paris: Lethielleux, 1889), 481, refers to Assyrian monuments showing kings as hunters.

9. See Christoph Uehlinger, "'Powerful Persianisms' in Glyptic Iconography of Persian Period Palestine," in *The Crisis of Israelite Religion: Transformation of Religious Tradition in Exilic and Post-Exilic Times*, ed. Bob Becking and Marjo Korpel (Leiden: Brill, 1999) 134–82.

Bar 3:16-21

¹⁶Where are the rulers of the nations,
and those who lorded it over
the animals on earth;
¹⁷those who made sport of the
birds of the air,
and who hoarded up silver and
gold
in which people trust,
and there is no end to their
getting;
¹⁸those who schemed to get silver,
and were anxious,
but there is no trace of

their works?
¹⁹They have vanished and gone
down to Hades,
and others have arisen in their
place.
²⁰Later generations have seen the
light of day,
and have lived upon the earth;
but they have not learned the way
to knowledge,
nor understood her paths,
nor laid hold of her.
²¹Their descendants have strayed
far from her way.

TRANSLATION MATTERS

The meaning of Bar 3:16-18 can be determined in more than one way. The NRSV translation makes the "rulers of the nations" immoderate and greedy with no ifs, ands, or buts, so that it becomes obvious that no wisdom can be ascribed to them. I would rather insist on the ambivalence of the wording and translate more openly:

- 3:16 Where now are the rulers of the nations and those who were masters of the beasts of earth,
- 3:17 those who sported with the birds of heaven, those who stored up silver and gold on which people rely, and there is no end of their possessions,
- 3:18 those who worked so carefully in silver, and there is no fathoming out of their works?

Another characteristic of the rulers focused on in Bar 3:16-17 is wealth, visible in treasures of precious metals. Wealth in the biblical world is legitimate, even necessary, for a ruler: the story about the Queen of Sheba meeting King Solomon is full of admiration for her riches but underlines even more her admiration of Solomon's immeasurable wealth (1 Kgs 10). Wealth as an expression of power is part of the ancient world's culture, although excess would be regarded critically.[10] Baruch 3:17b underlines the rulers' power materialized in their enormous cache of

10. See the "law of the king," Deut 17:17.

valued possessions. The motif of "storing up" could have been attracted by the mention of wisdom's "storehouses" (3:15). Again, there might be a critical undertone, indicating at the outset that those who accumulate precious metals do not understand that wisdom cannot be exchanged for gold or jewels (see Job 28:15-19) and that the only real precious treasure is indeed wisdom. Readers familiar with philosophical terminology could even hear more: there is no "end [τέλος] to their getting," i.e., no final good in the possessions they store (Bar 3:17b).

The motif of wealth might, for its part, have inspired the next mention of those who occupy themselves with silver (3:18: silversmiths?) and produce works of art too wonderful and mysterious to be fathomed. The Bible speaks of craftsmen like Bezalel (Exod 31) who are invested with a divine spirit of wisdom (σοφία; Bar 3:12, 23), understanding (σύνεσις; Bar 3:14, 23), and knowledge (ἐπιστήμη; Bar 3:20) to work with silver and gold and other kinds of craft (Exod 31:2-5 LXX). Suspicious readers would ask themselves whether all those wonderful works are not in vain as "there is no trace of their works" to be found (Bar 3:18b).

Which Wisdom? Whose Wisdom? Part 2

The poem of wisdom in the passage states: if Israel seeks the wisdom given to them by God and walks within the way of wisdom, they will walk in light and glory. This statement is a significant theological proposition. In times of suffering, it is natural and intrinsic for an individual, or a group, or a people to seek the wisdom to overcome adversity through self-examination. When Koreans lost their sovereignty, their religious leaders—whether from a newly established religion, such as Dong-Hak or Chun-Do-Gyo, or traditional religions, such as Buddhism, Confucianism, or even Shamanism—claimed that Koreans must walk in "the way of God," "the way of Universe," in order to be liberated from Japan's occupation and achieve independence. The Independence Movement, which began on 1 March 1919 and lasted for several months throughout the country, is one of the consequences of the leaders' attempt to find the Korean "spirit" that had been oppressed under Japanese colonization. The search for a just and righteous wisdom for life is one of the basic religious attitudes of human beings. This may be the commonality between religions, as almost all religions recommend searching sincerely for the way to wisdom.

It is not easy to find the way to wisdom, however, and the Bible emphasizes this fact. As Job 28 stresses, and Baruch also says,

"No one knows the way to her, or is concerned about the path to her [wisdom]" (Bar 3:31). The rich, the leaders and rulers, the young, the giants, the brave, the Canaanites, the Temanites, or sons of Hagar do not know where the way to wisdom is found. Thus, one should search faithfully and persevere to find the way to wisdom. That is the message of this poem. Wisdom is not in the hands of rulers and imperialists or on the side of the powerful. Wisdom can be attained and known only when one believes in God and becomes one with the divine, and only when God teaches it. This is far from being an easy way. Therefore, it is extremely undesirable and regretful that there have been increasing segments of Christianity in Asia announcing that the way to gain the wisdom of God is easy and readily available to all.

Kyung-Sook Lee

Powerful rulers (and inspired craftsmen) are supposed to be close to wisdom—but Bar 3:19 has a counterargument: they died leaving no trace and were superseded by new generations. The contrast between life and death, a traditional sapiential opposition referring to a life with or without wisdom, is taken literally here as opposition between real life and real death, and combined with the notion of light for those living on earth opposed to the netherworld with her darkness. Baruch 3:19a might allude to a motif in Job 28:22 according to which "abyss and death" have heard a rumor of wisdom who, of course, is not found there. Moreover, Bar 3:19-21 seems to recall the thoughts of the ultra-rich ruler Qoheleth who, after having enlarged on his successful life, asks in disillusion: "How can the wise die just like fools?" (Eccl 2:16), casting doubt on the validity of traditional concepts of wisdom. As can be seen, at the end of their life, when dying, those powerful rulers are made equal to every human being—what, then, about their wisdom? If Qoheleth would disqualify his efforts as "vanity" without denying that he has been wiser than others (Eccl 2:17), the voice of Bar 3:19-21 goes one step further, questioning in principle whether the rulers mentioned possessed wisdom at all, especially as they could not even transmit it to the generations after them.[11]

11. Baruch 3:19 has another interesting intertextual reference: Ps 48:2 LXX/49:2 MT. This psalm is very similar to Qoheleth in insisting that everybody, wise and fool alike, will die, but it goes one step further to proclaim that God "will ransom my soul from the power of Sheol/Hades," a formula not far from a belief in life after death. For the book of Baruch, this seems not (yet) thinkable.

With the first stanza it becomes clear already that the question of who gained access to the place or storehouses of wisdom (3:15) will not find a quick answer.

Israel's Neighbor Cultures—Without Wisdom (3:22-23)

Powerful and wealthy rulers of nations and beasts supposed to be equipped with wisdom, prudence, and knowledge are mortals and unable to ensure that their descendants follow their direction. This reasoning questions their wisdom, as they do not have "life"; it questions their power, as they have no domination over generations to come. As a side effect, the god-like nimbus of those rulers is destroyed; the argument functions as demystification of power, hence, as a criticism of power. The audience of "Baruch's" speech could think of the wise and god-like prince of Tyre who became proud in his wealth and was killed by his enemies, losing his likeness to God and becoming like a mere human being (Ezek 28:1-10). They could remember Nebuchadnezzar and his dominion over all the territories, including the animals (Jer 27:6 MT; 34:6 LXX), but perhaps also Nebuchadnezzar's dream where he appeared first as a mighty tree and protector of animals and was then transformed into a wild animal himself (Dan 4). These biblical texts use mythical images and language that seem also to appear in Bar 3:16-21.

Baruch 3:22-23 takes a closer look at the people surrounding Israel that are known as experts of wisdom. In biblical times, Teman was known as a region of wise people: one of Job's friends, Eliphaz, is a Temanite (Job 2:11; 4:1); and Jer 49:7 as well as Obad 8–9 mention Teman (Edom) as a country of wisdom, but both already show this wisdom perishing. The biblical text does not refer to a specific sapiential knowledge in Canaan, although Bar 3:22 seems to presuppose such a tradition[12]—but only to negate it: Canaan and Teman are not places or spaces where wisdom is taught or practiced.

If the "descendants of Hagar" with their zeal for "understanding" or "power of comprehension" (σύνεσις; Bar 3:23) are connected to Ishmael, Hagar's son (Gen 16:11-16), one can trace a line to Lemuel, king of Massa,[13] and his mother's pedagogical admonitions as found in Prov 31.

---

12. Some commentators think of Phoenicia; Steck, *Das apokryphe Baruchbuch*, 146; Isabelle Assan-Dhote and Jacqueline Moatti-Fine, *Baruch, Lamentations, Lettre de Jérémie*, La Bible d Alexandrie 25.2 (Paris: Cerf, 2008), 107.

13. See Gen 25:14 for Massa as a son of Ishmael.

Bar 3:22-23	
22She has not been heard of in Canaan, or seen in Teman; 23the descendants of Hagar, who seek for understanding on the earth,	the merchants of Merran and Teman, the story-tellers and the seekers for understanding, have not learned the way to wisdom, or given thought to her paths.

TRANSLATION MATTERS

3:22 *seen in Teman*: ὤφθη, literally: "appeared" in Teman; see 3:37.

Hence, there is a remarkable line of female wisdom from Hagar to the queen mother of Massa and her song about the capable woman (Prov 31:10-31)[14]—one could add the Queen of Sheba—accepted by other biblical writers. Baruch 3:23, however, denies the wisdom of their descendants and even their efforts to "give thought" to her. Besides them, "the merchants of Merran and Teman," widely travelled persons who enriched their experience and can be expected to be wise, come into the focus. Maybe these same persons are also considered "storytellers" (μυθολόγοι, "mythologists"), persons who have a lot to say and who know how to relate their experiences, who heard a lot during their travels to distant places and bring back new and exciting tales. Again, and with formulae referring back to the first stanza (3:20), these persons and their experiences are not considered as being close to wisdom.

Denying in such a rigorous way the wisdom of those who are expected to be wise is a new and surprising emphasis compared to other biblical statements. Job, a non-Israelite, argues with his friends—among them Eliphas the Temanite—about whether it makes sense any longer to trust in a world governed by God in wisdom and justice, and it is true that finally their arguments are shown to fall short. But the fact that Job argues with his friends is itself a sign of respecting their experience, knowledge, and prudence. The Queen of Sheba comes to meet Solomon and "to test

---

14. One has to admit that the "king of Massa" in Prov 31:1 is a corrected reading of the MT, in which an Atnach separates מֶלֶךְ ("king") from מַשָּׂא (understood as "oracle"). The NRSV, for example, does not accept this correction.

him with hard questions" (1 Kgs 10:1), hence to enter with him into a wisdom combat. Although Solomon's wisdom wins against her, her visit to Jerusalem is described with much sympathy and admiration for her. Even Ben Sira, who in his great wisdom poem has Lady Wisdom rove the world to find a dwelling place (Sir 24:1-7), sees her gaining influence among the peoples of the world before she settles in Jerusalem. Baruch's speech, however, introduces, so to say, a distinction between being and semblance, seeing all those who usually are considered to be wise on the side of semblance. Who, then, might be able to find her paths?

The Giants of the Land—Without Wisdom (3:24-28)

A third attempt is made to propose candidates of wisdom: the "giants" (γίγαντες; Bar 3:26). In the Septuagint, the first occurrence of the term refers to the mythical offspring of the "sons of God"[15] and the "daughters of humans" in primordial times (Gen 6:1-4). In its present context of Gen 1–9, this note serves to show how chaos and corruption permeated the world created by God and how God had to intervene by sending the flood. The (Ethiopic) book of Enoch expands on this (see esp. 1 En. 6–11): the giants were taught divine or angelic mysteries (or wisdom) by their heavenly fathers, including warfare, but then started to devour the humans and to devastate the world. Sirach 16:7 and Wis 14:6 might allude to this. Baruch 3:26-28 might reflect a somewhat different tradition about these exceptional beings, without decisively negative connotations. The characteristic "famous of old" recalls Gen 6:4 and expresses admiration; "expert in war" would rather refer to 1 En. 8:1 and 10:7 but again without apparent devaluation. Moreover, Bar 3:26-28 seems to merge the primordial giants as experts of war with the giants of Canaan the Israelites met when they decided to explore or to spy out the country (Num 13:32-33) and whom they saw again when conquering the land (Josh 12:4 LXX; 13:12 LXX).[16] The reference to the giants, however, does not have the shape of a historical reminiscence of these events; Baruch's wisdom poem is interested in neither Israel's conquest of the land nor the land's original inhabitants. Could one speak of typological interest?

---

15. The Septuagint of Gen 6:1-4 considers the giants as being "sons of God" (υἱοὶ τοῦ Θεοῦ), while the reading of the Hebrew text, בני אלהים, "sons of Elohim," can also be translated as "sons of the gods."

16. See also Gen 14:5 LXX.

Bar 3:24-28

²⁴O Israel, how great is the house of God,
how vast the territory that he possesses!
²⁵It is great and has no bounds;
it is high and immeasurable.
²⁶The giants were born there, who were famous of old,

great in stature, expert in war.
²⁷God did not choose them,
or give them the way to knowledge;
²⁸so they perished because they had no wisdom,
they perished through their folly.

TRANSLATION MATTERS

3:24 *the territory that he possesses*: κτῆσις, literally: "the place of his possession" (see 3:17).

3:26 *experts*: ἐπιστάμενοι, better: "having know-how," to underline the common root of ἐπίσταμαι (3:26) and ἐπιστήμη (3:27).

3:28 *wisdom*: φρόνεσις, better: "prudence" see 3:9, 14.

3:28 *folly*: ἀβουλία, better: "want of counselling; thoughtlessness." This word occurs only here and Prov 14:17 LXX.

These giants are said to be born in the "house of God" (3:24), making the primordial space between heaven and earth before the Flood, still without territorial boundaries, God's possession and dwelling place.[17] God's "house," God's possession (κτῆσις; 3:24), has no bounds, thus comparable to the mighty rulers of old with their possessions (κτῆσις; 3:17). Moreover, by the huge measures in its three dimensions, God's domain becomes an apt place for beings beyond human measure, or,

---

17. Steck, *Das apokryphe Baruchbuch*, 147–48, understands the expression "house of God" to mean the whole "world of creation" (*Schöpfungswelt*). This might be a too rational description of a much more mythical meaning. Anthony J. Saldarini, "The Book of Baruch. Introduction, Commentary, and Reflections," in *Introduction to Prophetic Literature, Isaiah, Jeremiah, Baruch, the Letter of Jeremiah, Lamentations, Ezekiel*, ed. Leander E. Keck, NIB 6 (Nashville, TN: Abingdon Press, 2001), 929–82, at 966, recalls Philo, *De aeternitate mundi* § 112. David G. Burke, *The Poetry of Baruch: A Reconstruction and Analysis of the Original Hebrew Text of Baruch 3:9–5:9*, SBL Septuagint and Cognate Studies 10 (Chico, CA: Scholars Press, 1982), 127 n. 76, adds Philo's *De Cherubim* § 52 and his *De opificio mundi* § 21. Some older commentators use the formula to find traces of Alexandrian erudition in the Greek text of Baruch.

conversely, the giants, beings of celestial and human origin, live close to God and seem to be privileged to learn wisdom (or: "prudence"; 3:28).

But now, the text takes a new turn: wisdom cannot be found by one's own efforts. Different from traditional sapiential logic according to which wisdom is an art of living open to all who are willing to learn from teachers or to observe natural phenomena, another line of thought is developed here: wisdom can be learned, but she has to be made accessible first. According to Prov 8, Lady Wisdom is a powerful counsellor of kings (8:14-21) connected to the realm of God where she was present when God created the world (8:22-31), but she was not sent by God; those who decide to do so can approach her (8:32-36). By contrast, the book of Job breaks with this concept: wisdom cannot be found in and through the structures of the world; wisdom is hidden (Job 28:20-22) and therefore accessible through revelation by God only (Job 38:1–42:6). But there is a man, Job, who struggles with God and who provokes such a divine revelation; there is a very strong effort by a human to understand and in this sense to "find" wisdom. Baruch 3:27 seems to conceive things in an even more radical way: wisdom depends totally on God's disclosure. There was no disclosure to the primordial inhabitants of the world, and therefore their death reveals that "they had no wisdom" (ἀβουλία; 3:28).

Negative Summary (3:29-31)

A new set of questions takes up the rhetorical moment and the general movement of Bar 3:15 ("Who has found her place? And who has entered her storehouses?") but gives that movement a much more sophisticated structure. The "place" of wisdom is elaborated as "heaven" and "clouds," "finding" her presupposes long journeys overseas, to "enter" her realm signifies reaching the ends of the universe, her "storehouse" is transformed into the gold someone needs to obtain her. In the same breath Bar 3:29-30 is in conversation with Job 28:12-19, knowing that wisdom is not with the sea (28:14b), that she cannot be compared to gold or jewels (28:15-19), and that she has been hidden from the birds of the sky (28:21b).

It comes as no surprise, then, that the answer given to these questions is similar to Job 28:13 LXX: "Mortals do not know the way to it." Note that the Greek βροτός, "mortal," unlike the Hebrew אנוש, "human," used in Job 28:13 MT, may include the "mortal" giants too. The synonymous pair of "way" and "path" links Baruch's conclusion to the three preceding stanzas (3:20-21, 23, 27): between heaven and earth there is no one who has access to wisdom.

Bar 3:29-31	
²⁹Who has gone up into heaven, and taken her, and brought her down from the clouds? ³⁰Who has gone over the sea, and	found her, and will buy her for pure gold? ³¹No one knows the way to her, or is concerned about the path to her.

Wisdom with God Alone: Wisdom Given to Israel (3:32–4:4)

After this large tour d'horizon with a purely negative outcome, the speech now moves on to the positive answer, indicating this switch by the adversative "but," in the context of Bar 3:9–4:4 used only here. The only one close to wisdom is identified indirectly (3:32-34), then directly, "This is our God" (Bar 3:35), and is connected to Israel by translating wisdom (3:36-37), which, in turn, becomes identified with the book of the Torah Israel is invited to accept (4:1-4).

Close to wisdom is but one, characterized by "perceiving" (εἰδώς), a form—and the corresponding verb—used only here in the book of Baruch, underlining the specificity of such "knowing" and distinguishing its bearer.[18] His understanding (σύνεσις; 3:14, 23) grammatically surrounds her; he found her and holds her, his "finding" (ἐξευρίσκω;[19] 3:32) being different from all the attempts of human "findings" (3:15). The audience or the readers will without doubt think of their God, but rhetorically this is left open in order to give room for an indirect characterization.

To explain God's all-encompassing perception and power, reference is made to the two dimensions of the cosmos, earth and heaven, paying more attention to celestial phenomena. Already Job 28:23-27 shows God as all-knowing and focuses on wind, water, rain, and thunder. The "light" of Bar 3:33 could then be the lightning preceding thunderclaps, under God's command with its "trembling" or twitching appearance, as the stars are with their shining (3:34). In contrast to Job 28, where meteorological phenomena are in the foreground, reminiscent of the God of Israel as a Weather God, the focus of Bar 3:34 is on the astral sphere, a predominant concern of Babylonian, Persian, and Hellenistic times and cultures. Whereas

18. The formula εἰδὼς τὰ πάντα, "who knows all (things)," is found only here and in Susanna's prayer (Sus 35 LXX/42 TH).

19. This verb is used only once more in the LXX, in the prayer of the mother of seven, 2 Macc 7:23, to give hope to her sons.

Bar 3:32–4:4

[32]But the one who knows all things knows her,
he found her by his understanding.
The one who prepared the earth for all time
filled it with four-footed creatures;
[33]the one who sends forth the light, and it goes;
he called it, and it obeyed him, trembling;
[34]the stars shone in their watches, and were glad;[20]
he called them, and they said, "Here we are!"
They shone with gladness for him who made them.
[35]This is our God;
no other can be compared to him.
[36]He found the whole way to knowledge,
and gave her to his servant Jacob
and to Israel, whom he loved.
[37]Afterward she appeared on earth
and lived with humankind.
[4:1]She is the book of the commandments of God,
the law that endures forever.
All who hold her fast will live,
and those who forsake her will die.
[2]Turn, O Jacob, and take her;
walk toward the shining of her light.
[3]Do not give your glory to another,
or your advantages to an alien people.
[4]Happy are we, O Israel,
for we know what is pleasing to God.

according to Job 28 the meteorological phenomena as ordered by God are named to compare them to wisdom, in Bar 3:33-34 they seem rather to serve to praise God. Similar to Job 28, the figure of wisdom continues to remain hidden, opaque, with no clear personal contours.

Another biblical tradition comes to mind: the creation account of Gen 1. The four-footed creatures (Bar 3:32) recall the sixth day of creation where the earth is filled with them, before humans appeared (Gen 1:24); the stars (Bar 3:34) belong to the fourth day (Gen 1:16) whereas the "light" refers back to the very first day when God called the primordial light to allow for the difference between darkness and brightness (Gen 1:3-5).

20. NRSV has vv. 34-37; other translations count v. 34b-c as v. 35 and have NRSV's vv. 35-37 as vv. 36-38, according to the critical edition of Joseph Ziegler, ed., *Ieremias, Baruch, Threni, Epistula Ieremiae*, Septuaginta: Vetus Testamentum Graecum, auctoritate Academiae Scientiarum Gottingensis editum 15 (Göttingen, Vandenhoeck & Ruprecht, 1957; 2013).

TRANSLATION MATTERS

3:35 *no other can be compared to him*: οὐ λογισθήσεται ἕτερος πρὸς αὐτόν, literally: "no other counts besides him."

3:37 *lived with*: συνανεστράφη, literally: "associated with."

4:1 *She is the book . . .*: αὕτη ἡ βίβλος, literally with more emphasis: "It is her, the book . . ."

4:2b *walk toward the shining of her light*: διόδευσον πρὸς τήν λάμψιν κατέναντι τοῦ φωτὸς αὐτῆς, also possible: "walk toward the shining in the sight of her light."

4:4 *we know what is pleasing to God*: τὰ ἀρεστὰ τῷ Θεῷ ἡμῖν γνωστά ἐστι, literally (as NJB): "what pleases God has been revealed to us."

Interestingly, Bar 3:33 does not insist on God as creator in the sense of turning, by his call, nonbeing into being[21] but underlines God's royal power before which the light as servant trembles.[22] In contrast to this trembling, the stars are rejoicing, another form of recognizing their ruler and creator. Emphasis is on their shining, their usefulness to illuminate the night, and their regulated order, a motif strongly developed in the Ethiopic book of Enoch, especially chapters 72–82, showing this world of celestial "beings" under God's control.

Baruch 3:32-34 is singing the praise of the One ruling over earth and firmament, and the following passage explicitly identifies this creator-king with the God of Israel. Simultaneously, the voice of the wisdom teacher, using imperatives to address Israel or descriptive mode to demonstrate the failure of any attempt to search for wisdom, now changes to a confessional-style statement, bringing the speaker and the addressed community into one collective unity. This confession to the one and only God emphasizing that "no other counts besides him" (Bar 3:35b) uses a phrase unique in the Greek Bible but thematically in line with most of the monotheistic statements declaring other gods not simply nonexistent but rather irrelevant for Israel. In the present case only the God of Israel is able to find and explore what Israel needs (ἐξευρίσκω; 3:32, 36), hence the only one who counts. "Knowledge" (ἐπιστήμη) as *pars pro toto* for

21. See 2 Macc 7:28 with its formulation open to understand it as referring to a *creatio ex nihilo*, which is not yet at stake in Baruch.
22. Some commentators think of meteorological lightning, which trembles. Maybe the appearance of the first light is considered here in analogy to such meteorological lightning.

"wisdom" is always, in Baruch's speech, connected to the "way" (ὅδος): neither the rulers with their descendants (3:20) nor the giants in God's domain (3:27) had this "way to knowledge." Only God did. Like a wisdom teacher or a father/mother figure teaching wisdom to children, God did not hold this knowledge back but passed it on. Grammatically both feminine, "knowledge" and the "way" to it can be the object; maybe both are aimed at. The recipient is Israel, mentioned by the double name "Israel" and "Jacob," connecting present Israel to her ancestor who received that name (Gen 32:29), and by the designation παῖς, bearing the nuance of "child" but also "servant,"[23] reflecting the legal status of children under the authority of their parents as comparable to the status of servants and slaves under their masters and mistresses.[24] The child/servant Jacob/Israel, however, is ἠγαπημένος, "beloved," and this might be the explanation for why he was privileged to get access to wisdom.

The suspense between the introductory imperatives with the following extensive survey of beings without wisdom is finally released: Israel is able to learn wisdom because God chose Israel to do so. Just as there was no explanation for why God refused wisdom to the giants of old, now no explanation is given for God's choice.[25] Instead, wisdom/knowledge receives a specific shape: she is identified by a solemn and complex formula with God's Torah, the multiplicity of single commandments, resumed as "law" (νόμος), in the written form of a book, ensuring, as her divine provenience does, accessibility, validity, endurance. Compared to Ben Sirach's wisdom poem similarly identifying wisdom with a divine book (Sir 24:23), Baruch insists on its purely divine origin, while Sirach has it as the "book of the covenant of the Most High God, the law that Moses commanded us." At the same time Baruch solves, for his audience between Babylonia and Jerusalem, the problem of transmitting wisdom to coming generations: if there is a book containing that wisdom it can be taught, transmitted, seized, studied.

Life and death, the two fundamental opponents in sapiential thinking, reappear in Bar 4:1 to be connected to "the book of the commandments of God." The connection motivates the imperative in 4:2, "turn, O Jacob, and take her," addressed to Israel as Jacob like Ben Sirach does when

---

23. See Bar 1:20; 2:28 for Moses as παῖς and 2:20, 24, the prophets as παῖδες.

24. Baruch 4:13 will talk about the "paths of education" on which mother Jerusalem and father God tried to keep their children.

25. The following verse (Bar 3:37) is often considered to be a Christian addition. It shall be passed over here as it requires an extensive commentary and will be treated below.

campaigning for wisdom as a book in Sir 24:23. Like the shining of the stars (λάμπω; Bar 3:34) is her—the book's, the Torah's—"shining" or, more accurately, "radiance" (λάμψις; 4:2), and, like the "light" (φῶς; 3:33), God is sending out her "light" (φῶς; 4:2) toward which Jacob/Israel is called to walk, corresponding to the expected "light for the eyes" in the introductory passage (3:14).

Which Wisdom? Whose Wisdom? Part 3

Many Asian religions say that to obtain wisdom, the way (Tao), is a process of extremely difficult training and adherence. The only difference between them is where and how to find it. For example, Chun-Do-Gyo encourages finding and developing god's personality within "me" (the thought is that being human is being divine, In-Nae-Chun). Confucianism looks for the Tao (Way) in nature and human relations, and Buddhism in the "nothingness," that is, the "emptiness." Even with these differences, they all suggest ethical perspectives and promote just and harmonious relations with nature or other human beings. They reject modern materialism and search for *via negativa*, through which a new ethical order to liberate others from suffering can be found. This is the Asian way to find the "path of wisdom." In this sense, the Bible, including the Apocrypha, and Asian religions agree that only "wisdom" is important in order to live anew in God's way.

According to this poem, however, the only One who knows the path to wisdom is God, who alone has insight and wisdom. Defining and disentangling the relationship between God and wisdom is a complex process. Originally, they are likely to have been separate entities; however, this text reveals the intention to connect them into one. The God of Israel discovered wisdom and gave it to Jacob and to Israel. This gift of wisdom was contained in a book of his commandments and law. Israel must now follow the laws and commandments in order to walk in the path of wisdom.

Almost all Asian religions, including Confucianism, agree that wisdom can only be acquired from the heavens. However, in Asian religions, gods are not personified beings, telling human beings how to live their lives. In other words, heaven is simply the essence of the universe, the origin of finite things, which governs everything on earth. Heaven also represents a moral system of the universe, and so helps the good, while guarding and punishing the evil. This may make it appear to have characteristics of a personified being, even though it does not. Thus in Asian religions, human beings have to seek the way to heaven, the Tao, and to realize and adhere to the moral system of the universe. The way to heaven can be gained through becoming aware of it.

As for Israel, wisdom is in the law, while for Asian religions such as Confucianism, wisdom, the way to heaven, is in nature and human beings. Even though such differences exist between the religions, the ultimate aim that is sought is much the same. That aim is to become aware of heaven and the Way (Tao), to live it out in practice on earth. This commonality could be a valuable resource to help facilitate mutual and respectful communication between religions.

Kyung-Sook Lee

On one level, the comparison of commandments and Torah to light (Prov 6:23) comes to mind.[26] But there might be more: while according to Job 28 wisdom is put into the context of meteorological phenomena but does not get a specific shape, Baruch brings her into the sphere of shining stars, insists on her astral-like appearance, and might even compare her to the primordial light of the first day of creation, thus reinterpreting Lady Wisdom's appearance "at the beginning of God's work, the first of his acts of long ago" (Prov 8:22).[27] Wisdom has lost her anthropomorphic/gyno-morphic personification and her "erotic appeal" for young men that she has in the book of Proverbs; she has also lost her fascination as a fragrant tree, as in Ben Sirach's writing; she enters the realm of philosophy—in a speculative sense, but at the same time in the sense of practical philosophy or "way of life," as the book of God's commandments.[28]

26. Carey A. Moore, "1 Baruch," in *Daniel, Esther and Jeremiah: The Additions*, AB 44 (Garden City, NY: Doubleday, 1977), 302.

27. This resembles strongly the way that Aristobulus, a Jewish-Alexandrian philosopher writing around 170 BCE conceives wisdom, trying to reconcile Jewish scriptures and Greek philosophy. For Aristobulus, quoted in Eusebius, *Praeparatio Evangelica* 13.12, from wisdom all light proceeds, and he recalls Peripatetics who speak of wisdom as *lampter* (lantern); Bar 4:2 has λάμψις = "radiance." A reference to Aristobulus is found in J. Cornelis de Vos, "'You Have Forsaken the Fountain of Wisdom': The Function of Law in Baruch 3:9–4:4," *ZABR* 13 (2007): 176–86, but only to discuss the concept of "alien wisdom," not with reference to the light metaphor of Bar 4:2.

28. Thus, I am less optimistic than is Patricia Tull, who argues for the femininity of wisdom in Bar 3:9–4:4, although not fully personified. Patricia K. Tull, "Baruch," in *Women's Bible Commentary*, 3rd ed., ed. Carol A. Newsom, Sharon H. Ringe, and Jacqueline E. Lapsley (Louisville, KY: Westminster John Knox, 2012), 418–22.

If wisdom has to be identified with God's νόμος, "Torah," a rereading of Baruch's tour d'horizon (3:15-31) brings in new dimensions; indeed, God's Torah was given neither to the rulers of the people nor to Israel's neighbors nor to the primordial inhabitants of "God's house," but only to Israel, the "beloved child." Torah becomes the instrument of Israel's education exercised by God as teacher or father/mother. At the same time Torah becomes something very precious and reserved for Israel. Baruch's wisdom poem culminates in showing the very special relationship between Israel and God that is established through the gift of Torah. In a way, the poem describes a search for wisdom as Torah in the world, a search that comes to an end in Israel. In a way, the poem creates a compelling notion of wisdom connecting to only Israel's Torah in order to motivate the audience to follow wisdom.

The imperative in Bar 4:3 takes up the metaphor of light, speaking of the Torah as glory, with the Greek δόξα oscillating between glory, honor, and splendor. In addition to the move toward wisdom as Torah, there seems to be a move of separation or isolation from others who are conceived as foreigners or aliens, especially when the "alien" (ἀλλότριος) recalls the "foreign country" or "foreign soil" (γῆ ἀλλότρια) of the introductory passage (3:10). Does the imperative "do not give your glory to another" require that Torah-wisdom be reserved only for Israel and refused to non-Israelites? A different reading is possible. Indeed, the admonition uses the difference between Israel and "the others," but by this they appeal to the audience's feeling of honor and shame to encourage them to put all their energy in searching for Torah-wisdom. Perhaps one could identify the stylistic device of a *litotes*, an ironic device using the negative opposite of a superlative or formulating negatively what is meant all the more positively. "Do not give your glory to another" could then be translated: "Do make the most of what you've got." Accordingly, the last line of the poem affirms by way of a macarism, again including the speaker in the community addressed, that to Israel "has been revealed what is pleasing to God" (4:4). The end of the speech comes back to its beginning: reproach turns into encouragement; the speech direction is turned entirely ad intra.

What remains problematic is the language of the whole poem excluding others from true wisdom and the ironic device at the expense of non-Israelites. Other biblical wisdom texts, like the book of Proverbs, see wisdom as virtue or capacity shared with surrounding cultures. Even Deut 4:5-8, with its focus on Torah-wisdom, has other people admire that wisdom since, because of their own wisdom, they understand Israel's specific wisdom. Wisdom in Bar 3:9–4:4, however, has turned to a *specificum isracliticum* in difference to others. When such conviction is uttered by a strong group, it might sound demeaning and arrogant to others around them. But this same claim sounds different coming from a minority group who tries to find a new self-esteem in the face of a strong majority and to affirm their own values as precious.

It is true that in our times even the structure of such a self-understanding becomes suspicious: where groups construct themselves as minoritarian, suppressed, but elected by God, with God on their side, the result can be military aggression, suppression of others, and making their own values absolute. Perhaps some hints in Baruch hamper such reception. It could be that the speech does not so much claim that wisdom was not given to a specific non-Israelite group but rather that it emphasizes a focus on abilities or qualities for or within Israel itself: true wisdom does not materialize herself in riches or power, neither in success in business, nor in beautiful stories, nor in the art of war. Life with and in accordance to God's "Law" is wise and does not need these verifications. Even stronger: such materializations of wisdom are suspect.

A similar result occurs when the characterizations of those excluded from wisdom are understood as typological: mighty rulers, successful businessmen, superhuman beings, all kinds of "heroes" do not have access to wisdom. This reading would promote a life in modesty, far from politics and power games. Another line of argumentation is possible: instead of finding in the three stanzas a reference to concrete people in Israel's surroundings, one could stress the mythical elements in their characterization. Perhaps the wisdom teacher is a μυθολόγος ("storyteller") himself (Bar 3:23), evoking mythical rather than historical or different contemporary cultural traditions.[29] The point, then, would not be to deny wisdom to people living around Israel but to show that, for Israel, wisdom is not found in mythical pasts or distant lands but close by and very concrete. As the wisdom poem is addressed to both communities, the one living in Babylonia, the other in Jerusalem, it sends the message that God's will can be done—and should be done—everywhere. Torah is becoming a "portative homeland," as the German-Jewish writer Heinrich Heine puts it in his memoirs.

This explanation, then, matches the perspective of Deut 4:5-8: other people around the people of Israel look at Israel's "wisdom," God's

---

29. Schökel seems to read in a similar direction, saying about the giants that they constitute a legendary reminiscence of a heroic age. Luis Alonso Schökel, "Baruc," in *Daniel—Baruc—Carta de Jeremias—Lamentaciones*, Los Libros Sagrados 18 (Madrid: Ediciones Cristiandad, 1976), 154.

Torah, and are full of admiration. Other people have their own wisdom that puts them in the position to compare, to assess according to their own criteria, and to acknowledge Israel's particularity in the double sense of this notion. In contrast to Deut 4:5-8, however, Baruch's wisdom poem appears not to be interested in recognition or admiration by others but keeps an inside perspective.

Israel's Wisdom—Christian Wisdom? (3:37)

Knowledge/wisdom is given to Israel and must be identified with the book of God's law—this is the message of Bar 3:35–4:1. One verse, however, seems to stand out from this straight line of thought:

> Afterward she appeared on earth
> and lived with humankind. (Bar 3:37)

"Afterward," after having been given to Israel, wisdom is to be found "on the earth" or "in the land" and in company of "the human beings."[30] The textual perspective appears strongly extended on a spatial and social scale but also unspecific.

From the beginning of historical-critical research on Baruch until recently, Bar 3:37 has sometimes been considered a Christian interpolation. Indeed, since Irenaeus of Lyon, it was taken to refer to the incarnation of Christ.[31] It is possible, however, to understand this verse within its pre-Christian, Early Jewish context. One very simple explanation would see the verse as a narrative extension of what was said before:[32] God gave wisdom to Israel, and now she was visible on earth and among humans; she left the hiddenness of the divine sphere and entered the realm of humans (Prov 8:31). The history of Israel can be re-narrated as story of Israel in company of wisdom walking among them, as the book of Wisdom tries to do (Wis 9:18–11:1).

---

30. See NJB: "only then did she appear on earth and live among human beings."

31. See the extensive and diligent research on the Christian reception of Bar 3:36-38 during patristic times by Rüdiger Feuerstein, *Das Buch Baruch*, Studien zur Textgestalt und Auslegungsgeschichte, Europäische Hochschul-Schriften XXIII/614 (Frankfurt: Peter Lang, 1997), 125–61.

32. This explanation is given, e.g., by Franz Heinrich Reusch, *Erklärung des Buchs Baruch* (Freiburg i. Br.: Herder, 1853), 200–202.

Which Wisdom?
Whose Wisdom? Part 4

As has already been discussed, the message of this poem is one that Israel in torment and trial is sending to themselves. The poem is an internal message of comfort, encouraging Israel to overcome the oppression. When Christianity inherited the religion of Israel and tried to be a worldwide religion, however, this text was turned into one of violence; the lamentation of the oppression turned into a song of victory for the oppressor, which led to persecution and oppression of other nations and religions. The song of the oppressed Israel was distorted into a statement of domination by the Roman Empire.

At an evangelical level, it may be suggested that Christianity is the one unique, revealed religion. If Christianity continues to repeatedly insist that it is the one true religion, however, it cannot help but provoke conflict with other religions. This is especially the case in a multireligious society like Korea; the result is then the deterrence of the gospel itself. It can also be seen as a violent religion to others, due to its extreme focus on itself to the exclusion of all others.

In the Bible, God unconditionally and inclusively loves everyone and commands that people love one another, even their enemies. Throughout history, Christianity has followed the path of human violence, however, putting the name of religion on mass slaughters. It is a great tragedy that there have been the Crusades, misogyny, witch-hunts, the Inquisition, religious wars, anti-Semitism and Jewish genocide, slave trade, and colonialism in the Third World, all in the name of Jesus. Such violence has transformed the nonviolent Jesus, who suffered and died by Roman imperialism, into a violent and triumphant Christ, on a foundation of misunderstandings and misinterpretations of the message in the Bible. Now the time has come to rediscover the wisdom, to find the solidarity, of the self-emptied Messiah, Jesus Christ, in the Bible and the theology of Asian religions, in order to respect each other and live together in harmony.

Kyung-Sook Lee

Another attempt to understand the verse without a reference to Christ would point to the wisdom poem of Ben Sira (Sir 24): wisdom has come a long way, wandering around in the cosmic spheres, descending to earth and visiting many people before taking root in Jerusalem, becoming there the tree of life and the book of the law. Baruch seems to reverse this order: first, wisdom was given to Israel; then, she visited other people (Bar 3:36-37). This is why Bar 3:22 had to state that wisdom had not appeared (ὤφθη) in Teman—not before she appeared (ὤφθη; 3:37) in Israel.

Wisdom is not restricted to Israel, although that people was a privileged recipient. The following verse would specify: wisdom identical with the book of God's commandments is open to "all who hold her fast" (4:1). Through Israel, God's Torah as wisdom or wisdom as Torah came down to earth, and other people might live according to her. Israel is no longer defined only by genealogical ties but by associating with Israel's Torah. Read from a non-Christian Jewish perspective, the verse would affirm and complete the long wisdom poem (3:9-37), showing that wisdom was found nowhere: indeed, before God offered wisdom-Torah to Israel, in the times of mythical rulers, mythical giants, mythical traders, and story-tellers, she was not found on earth. But afterward times have changed; she can be found among the peoples of the world.

In spite of these attempts to read Bar 3:37 without a Christian focus, the verse cannot be ruled out as a Christian interpolation. Its place in the narrative chronology of Bar 3:15–4:4 is somewhat difficult, and its perspective puts wisdom into the center as agent of her association with humans, not humans striving for wisdom. Baruch 3:37, then, might be an early trace for Christian appropriation of a Jewish writing.[33]

Indeed, Baruch's wisdom poem, 3:9-15 and 3:32–4:4, forms part of the Roman Catholic Lectionary as a reading of Easter Vigil. In the sequence of the numerous Old Testament readings from Genesis, Exodus, and the Prophets, it has its place among the prophetical texts, after Isa 54:5-14 and 55:1-11 and before Ezek 36:16-17a, 18-28 and Ezek 37:1-14. A closer look at the choice of these texts shows that the Old Testament is used in an allegorical or typological sense: the figures and motifs all prefigure Christ. This typological use might explain why and how Baruch's wisdom poem was shortened: after the questions for the place of wisdom, the answer follows immediately; wisdom is with God who made her accessible to Israel; she appeared on earth (3:37), and the new Israel, the church, is happy to know what pleases God (4:4). Together with the surrounding texts from Isaiah announcing the living word of God and from Ezekiel proclaiming a new covenant, Baruch's wisdom-

---

33. Walther Harrelson discusses the Ge'ez translation of the verse ("and was/became like a human"; *wa-kona kama sab'e*) and seems ready to understand it in a non-Christian way as referring to a semi-divine being now among mortals. At least Christians among the Ethiopians, however, were able to read this verse like their Latin-speaking counterparts as allusion to Christ. Walther Harrelson, "Wisdom Hidden and Revealed According to Baruch (Baruch 3.9–4.4)," in *Priests, Prophets and Scribes: Essays on the Formation and Heritage of Second Temple Judaism in Honor of J. Blenkinsopp*, ed. Eugene Ulrich et al., JSOTSup 194 (Sheffield: Sheffield Academic Press, 1992), 158–71, at 165.

Torah serves to reveal the christological message of the Old Testament. After a long history of Christian supersession over against Judaism, with the "new covenant" in Christ, the word of God, putting an end to the "old covenant" of Moses, it seems difficult to continue with such an order of readings as though nothing were wrong. Instead of affirming Christ as "true wisdom" or "new law," Christians could emphasize what is common in Christian and Jewish faith and ethics, in Torah-wisdom and Christ-wisdom. Maybe a new hybrid reading of Bar 3:37 could emerge that would make deciding between a Jewish or Christian understanding obsolete.

Baruch 4:5–5:9

Jerusalem, Woman-City and Mother of Israel

With the imperative "Take courage, my people" (Bar 4:5), the final section of Baruch begins. It brings the audience back to the mood of the initial prayer but opens up a perspective of hope right at the outset.

Again—and a third time after the prayer and the wisdom speech—it seems necessary as a first step to work through the guilt of the past, its consequences extending well into the present era. This is done in such a way that the personified city of Jerusalem sings her song of lament and confidence. A voice responding to her brings a message of consolation and promises of a bright future, such positive visions seeming to be possible only after repeatedly dealing critically with the past. For the final section as a whole, this leads to a structure of three units: an address to the people (4:5-9a), Jerusalem's song (4:9b-29), and words for Jerusalem (4:30–5:9).

According to the narrative introduction (Bar 1:3-14), those who listened to Baruch's book reacted with mourning rites and the decision to ask for offerings, prayers, and the reading of the book in Jerusalem. The last part of the book of Baruch reveals the deepest reason for this reaction as it explicitly brings into the center of distress and hope the city of

Jerusalem. Even more, it is in Jerusalem that distress turns into hope and even into rejoicing. Again it seems evident that the book read out in Babylonia is intended to link the community of exiles to Jerusalem as their point of orientation and identity.

Jerusalem: City and Woman

The city of Jerusalem[1] does not have a central role in every biblical book or tradition. The Pentateuch does not mention the name of Jerusalem at all; neither do the two extensive sapiential books of Job and Proverbs. Jerusalem as city of the temple and the only legitimate house of God becomes a central subject for deuteronomistic theology, especially the books of Kings, building on Deuteronomy, and even more in the books of Chronicles. A personification of Jerusalem, however, occurs above all in the prophetical books of Isaiah, Jeremiah, Ezekiel, and the Dodekapropheton, or Book of the Twelve Prophets. Jerusalem is a female character corresponding to a widespread ancient Near Eastern/West Asian notion of cities as female.

The roles of Jerusalem as city-woman or woman-city are diverse and seem to be related to a girl's or a woman's biography in traditional societies, including the typical social roles and good and bad experiences or expectations related to them. Jerusalem is daughter Zion, a young and attractive woman dependent on her father, God, in her case. Jerusalem is also the wife of her divine husband; she is unfaithful and adulteress, gets her divorce letter, and becomes a woman abandoned by her lovers. In addition, she is a widow, and she experienced rape. With these metaphors, the prophetic writings paint Jerusalem's (his-/her-)story and blame her as guilty of her own destruction. She is also the woman accepted again as wife by her husband and the woman who regains her honor—metaphors for a new beginning of the destroyed city. Likewise, Jerusalem is mother of her children, the inhabitants of the city; she is the mother who loses her children by death and deportation but also the mother who, in the impending new era, gets back her children, brought

---

1. Groundbreaking works include Christl M. Maier, *Daughter Zion, Mother Zion: Gender, Space, and the Sacred in Ancient Israel* (Minneapolis: Fortress Press, 2008); Maria Häusl, "Künderin und Königin. Jerusalem in Bar 4:5–5:9," in *Tochter Zion auf dem Weg zum himmlischen Jerusalem. Rezeptionslinie der "Stadtfrau Jerusalem" von den späten alttestamentlichen Texten bis zu den Werken der Kirchenväter*, ed. Maria Häusl (Leipzig: Leipziger Universitätsverlag, 2011), 103–24; and Othmar Keel, *Jerusalem und der eine Gott. Eine Religionsgeschichte* (Göttingen: Vandenhoek & Ruprecht, 2011; 2nd ed., 2014).

back from afar. The metaphor of Zion-mother mirrors in a specific way the story of the city moving from splendor to destruction, and on to new beginnings. All those metaphors are inspired by concrete women's lives and play on the roles of women in patriarchal societies. Many feminist studies have shown the risks and dangers of such metaphors for women and men. These metaphors use reality and distort it poetically, but poetical distortion might lead to negative perspectives on realities. It is true that the metaphors in question use *female* reality to criticize mainly *male* auditors/readers, but by doing so they actually reaffirm dichotomous images of gender relations.

Patriarchy, Punishment, and Power, Part 1

Reading Bar 4:5–5:9 as a trained biblical scholar, one is first of all struck by the banality of the text. It consists, like so many other biblical texts, of a lament over the destruction of Jerusalem, followed by a prophetic consolation about the turn of fortune in store for the city and her children; they will return from exile and their enemies will be punished. As a trained feminist scholar, one notes the female imagery of the mother/widow Jerusalem, who is grieved and then consoled. Here I would like to take stock of this image, which is at the same time as banal as it is revealing.

Biblical cities are often described as women. I quote some examples: The beloved in the Song of Songs is compared in her beauty to the cities of Tirzah and Jerusalem (6:4). The cities of Samaria and Jerusalem are compared to two wanton women by the prophet Ezekiel (23:3-4). The prophet Nahum describes the great city of Nineveh as a harlot (3:4-7). Isaiah describes Babylon as a ravished maiden (47:1-3). The book of Lamentations describes Jerusalem continuously as a bereaved widow and mother (1:1, 16; 4:2). The metaphor is obvious and unsurprising. It does, though, already in this partial list, show the types of women that come to the biblical author's mind when contemplating the fates of cities in war: the harlot who should be punished, for which purpose war is conceived; the innocent virgin who is ravished as a victim of war; and the bereaved mother whose children are enslaved and murdered, all war victims as well. These images are very patriarchal—men wage war, and women are its objects, the prizes and the victims thereof. Baruch uses these metaphors as well, building on them to create a more complete patriarchal image of society.

Tal Ilan

Perhaps the character of Jerusalem as a woman-city has mythical roots. The image of a city as a woman mourning and singing laments can be made plausible by pointing to the genre of city laments in Mesopotamian literature, liturgical texts going back deeply into the second millennium and copied in a somewhat different genre and style until Seleucid times.[2] Mesopotamian city laments are responses to the destruction of a city, personifying the affected city and lamenting about her destruction but also showing the divine patroness interceding for her city. The mythological background seems to be the following: a city provoked the wrath of one or several gods who decide to destroy her; the divine patroness of the city tries to prevent the destruction, but in vain. The deity's lament, then, has a double dimension: she is affected by the destruction of her city and the sorrows of the inhabitants; she herself is humiliated and expresses her sufferings. At the same time, as the city goddess receives the laments of her children in the city, she would be directly addressed and be expected to intercede for her city before the other gods. After the destruction is carried out, she can intercede only through rites of self-humiliation, as humans would do to moderate divine anger. The Mesopotamian city laments seem to express this twofold dimension of lament, possibly as parts of liturgies around reconstruction of a destroyed temple, and their annual reciting would serve to prevent the renewed outburst of divine wrath.

Read against this background, the biblical figure of Jerusalem the woman-city receives exciting contours. Of particular interest is the book of Lamentations, part of the Jeremian tradition. Jerusalem the woman laments about her destruction. Her lament can be heard as cry to stop the divine anger. Perhaps this is more than a literary analogy to Mesopotamian traditions; perhaps ancient Israel had its own similar Jerusalem mythology. One of its elements, probably reaching back historically into preexilic times, is the special election theology concerning Jerusalem:[3] this city is beloved by YHWH, and yet it is YHWH who pours out his anger on her. The main theological problem with this conviction in its present literary context within the Tanak springs from Israel's belief in only one God: the same God who poured out anger is the one to be addressed by the lament—there is no other savior and helper. The figure of Jerusalem in Bar 4–5 gets her specific profile in this particular theological context.

---

2. See Marc Wischnowsky, *Tochter Zion. Aufnahme und Überwindung der Stadtklage in den Prophetenschriften des Alten Testaments*, WMANT 89 (Neukirchen-Vluyn: Neukirchener Verlag, 2001), for more background.

3. Keel, *Jerusalem und der eine Gott*.

Another background has to be considered: "The depiction of the city as a woman is also frequent in Greek culture."[4] One line of sources points to personified cities, represented as women with mural crowns, and to the so-called *tyche poleos*, the "personified fortune of the city,"[5] another connection, as already mentioned before,[6] to the concept of *metropolis* as the mother city with her dependent colonies.[7] A Greek-speaking Jewish audience could have been familiar with these personifications of cities and might have had them in mind when listening to Bar 4:5–5:9.

Take Courage by Looking Back! (Bar 4:5-8)

"Take courage" (θαρσεῖτε) is the way the Septuagint usually translates the Hebrew אל־תיראו, a speech element often opening prophetical messages. After the sapiential sphere of the wisdom speech (Bar 3:9–4:4), the audience enters into the prophetic realm with both of its components, accusation (4:6-8) and words of salvation (4:30–5:9), preceded by a formula radiating confidence (4:5). The address "my people" is a familiar prophetical way to express God's relation to Israel; the voice speaking here shows intense connectedness with the audience, but might also subtly claim high authority. "Perpetuate Israel's name" is a good rendering for the somewhat difficult image of Israel as a "memorial" (μνημόσυνον) keeping alive Israel's memory against all calamities experienced and thus another expression of confidence and hope.

The image belongs to one of several allusions in Bar 4:5-8 to Moses' retrospective song before his death (Deut 32). According to Deut 32:26, Moses has to announce God's decision "to blot out the memory of them [Israel] from humankind." Baruch 4:5 would correct this threat. Those who are listening already experienced what was announced in Deut 32; they are a remnant to whom different words can be said. But first they have to understand why they were sold like slaves or delivered like prisoners (Bar 4:6; allusion to Deut 32:30[8]): they provoked God's anger

---

4. Nuria Calduch-Benages, "Jerusalem as Widow (Baruch 4:5–5:9)," in *Biblical Figures in Deuterocanonical and Cognate Literature*, ed. Hermann Lichtenberger and Ulrike Mittmann-Richert, Deuterocanonical and Cognate Literature Yearbook 2008 (Berlin and New York: Walter de Gruyter, 2009), 149.

5. See Maier, *Daughter Zion, Mother Zion*, 68, with rich documentation (64–69) of both types of personifications.

6. See commentary on Bar 1:9.

7. Calduch-Benages, "Jerusalem as Widow," 149.

8. In Deut 32:30 LXX the verbs ἀποδίδωμι ("to sell") and παραδίδωμι ("to deliver") both come from the same root. In contrast Deut 32:30 MT and Bar 4:6 use two distinct verbs for "to sell" and "to deliver": מכר and סגר (*hiph.*) in Deut 32:30 MT, and πιπράσκω

Bar 4:5-8

⁵Take courage, my people,
who perpetuate Israel's name!
⁶It was not for destruction
that you were sold to the nations,
but you were handed over to your
enemies
because you angered God.

⁷For you provoked the one who
made you
by sacrificing to demons and
not to God.
⁸You forgot the everlasting God,
who brought you up,
and you grieved Jerusalem,
who reared you.

or wrath, a motif also prominent in Bar 1–3. The reasons for God's anger are given with another reference to Deut 32: Israel practiced idolatry, more precisely and in literal quotation of Deut 32:17 LXX, "sacrificing to demons, not to God" (Bar 4:7). "Demons" is a term emphasizing other nonhuman powers besides the God of Israel but at the same time show-ing contempt for them without reducing them to images/idols as the Letter of Jeremiah will do.

As the reverse of such a cult for "demons," Bar 4:7 identifies turning away from God as creator. Again, the connection of motives comes from the song of Moses (Deut 32:17-18 LXX). There is, however, a shift of terminology from Deut 32:18 LXX evoking God as creator who "begot" Israel (γεννάω) to Bar 4:7 where God is the one who "made you" (ποιέω), thus referring rather to Deut 32:6 or 32:15. It seems that while Moses's song has no problem mixing genealogical-mythical and techno-poetical language for God as creator, in Bar 4, at least in its extant Greek text,⁹ genealogical conceptions of God's relation to Israel are avoided. Instead,

---

and παραδίδωμι in Bar 4:6. This similarity in verb patterns in Bar 4:6 and Deut 32:30 MT is another indication that the Greek text of Baruch was inspired by the Hebrew Bible as we know it, to say the least.

9. In his reconstruction of the Hebrew *Vorlage*, Johann Jacob Kneucker corrects to "God who begot you [*meholel*]" and "your mother [*yoledet*] Jerusalem." See Johann Jacob Kneucker, *Das Buch Baruch. Geschichte und Kritik, Übersetzung und Erklärung auf Grund des wiederhergestellten hebräischen Urtextes* (Leipzig: Brockhaus, 1879), 320, 357. Similarly, but more open to gender flexibility, Johann W. Rothstein suggests the conjecture "who gave birth to you." See Johann W. Rothstein, "Das Buch Baruch," in *Die Apokryphen und Pseudepigraphen des Alten Testaments*, vol. 1, ed. Emil Kautzsch (Tübingen: Mohr, 1900 [repr. 1921]), 213–25, at 222.

TRANSLATION MATTERS

4:8 *who brought you up*: τροφεύσαντα ὑμᾶς, better: "who nourished you" or "who breastfed you."

another motif comes into focus: God as nourisher.[10] The verb τροφεύω ("to serve as a nurse"), used in Bar 4:8, appears only once more in the Septuagint; in Exod 2:7 the word "nurse" describes the woman who will breastfeed the baby rescued by Pharaoh's daughter. God as Israel's nourisher receives traits of a *dea lactans*![11]

The shift goes even further. According to Deut 32:18 God alone is the one who "begot" and "gave birth" to Israel; God alone is named "father" (but not "mother"; see Deut 32:6), whereas Bar 4:8 brings in a second parental figure besides God. In an elaborate play of word order and sounds, God and Jerusalem are juxtaposed as parents, confirming that the Greek text is not a mere one-to-one translation but a creation in itself.

> You have forgotten the one who nourished you, the everlasting God
> You haved grieved the one who brought you up, Jerusalem.

Spontaneously one might be ready to see Jerusalem as "mother" beside God the "father." Certainly, Bar 4:8 assumes that the prophetical traditions of Jerusalem as woman-city and as mother of her children are well-known. Given the background of such prophetic texts and, in addition, the penitential prayer, one could think of God as "father" who punishes, and Jerusalem as "mother" who compassionately weeps for her children and admonishes them. The gender roles associated with God and Jerusalem seem clear-cut and very traditional.[12] But already in Isa 66:10-13, one of the prophetic texts bringing together God and

10. See Juliana M. Claassens, *The God Who Provides: Biblical Images of Divine Nourishment* (Nashville, TN: Abingdon Press, 2004), on the motif; see also Juliana M. Claassens, *Mourner, Mother, Midwife: Reimagining God's Delivering Presence in the Old Testament* (Louisville, KY: Westminster John Knox Press, 2012), 41–63.

11. Moore remarks: "Given the strong patriarchal character of Yahwism, one might argue that 'nursing' was an inappropriate activity for a male deity like Yahweh; but see Hos 11:4, where Yahweh seems to refer, quite literally, to nursing." Moore does not expand further on this subject. Carey A. Moore, "1 Baruch," in *Daniel, Esther, and Jeremiah: The Additions*, AB 44 (Garden City, NY: Doubleday, 1977), 309.

12. This is how Schökel conceives and describes them. Luis Alonso Schökel, "Baruc," in *Daniel – Baruc – Carta de Jeremias – Lamentaciones*, Los Libros Sagrados 18 (Madrid: Ediciones Cristiandad 1976), 157.

Jerusalem, the metaphors are complex:[13] Jerusalem with her nourishing breasts and God explicitly compared to a mother comforting her son are two maternal figures, while a father is missing. Likewise, the metaphors in Bar 4:8 hide a surprise. God's care is clearly connected to a female body; Jerusalem's activity is described in a less precise way. The Greek verb ἐκτρέφω, covering a broader range of rearing, is used in Prov 23:24 LXX to characterize a good father's care for his son. The apparent gender-crossing or gender-troubling in Bar 4:8 might serve as a further means to avoid mythical speech in a straightforward way. The focus is on rearing and nourishing,[14] in premodern times connected to the female body, but fundamentally a social task and not restricted to mothers only: Bar 4:8 has its focus on social parenthood of God and Jerusalem.

In a way, Bar 4:8 is nevertheless mythologizing: Jerusalem becomes parent of all Israel, not her former inhabitants only; by juxtaposing her to God, the radiance of divinity is given to her. Jerusalem is and has to become foundational and fundamental for the identity of those promoting Baruch's book, and they want to extend this to all Israel. A further trait is new: in contrast to the prophetical writings that describe Jerusalem the woman as guilty and responsible for her disaster, Baruch places Jerusalem beside God as likewise grieved by the deeds of her children. Jerusalem is "innocent";[15] Jerusalem has to be distinguished from her children and becomes a foundational (in this sense, a mythical) entity. At the same time, a profound difference between "mother" Jerusalem and "mother" God remains, as God alone is "everlasting" (4:8), and in her song, Jerusalem will repeatedly refer to God as "the Everlasting" (4:10, 14, 20, 22, 24).

Jerusalem's Sorrow and Hope (4:9-29)

In an extensive and impressive manner, Jerusalem's song shows her sorrow and grief. The woman-city addresses her female neighbors in the

---

13. See Maier, *Daughter Zion, Mother Zion,* 201–5 for details.

14. Saldarini realizes that "the author uses female imagery associated with nurture to characterize the relationship of both Jerusalem and God to the people," but he does not explore this thought further. Anthony J. Saldarini, "The Book of Baruch: Introduction, Commentary, and Reflections," in *Introduction to Prophetic Literature, Isaiah, Jeremiah, Baruch, the Letter of Jeremiah, Lamentations, Ezekiel,* ed. Leander E. Keck, NIB 6 (Nashville, TN: Abingdon Press, 2001), 929–82, at 974.

15. See Schökel, "Baruc." Luis Alonso Schökel, "Jerusalén inocente intercede: Baruc 4:9-19," in *Salvación en la Palabra: Targum, Derash, Berith; en memoria del profesor Alejandro Diez Macho,* ed. Domingo Muñoz León (Madrid: Ediciones Christiandad, 1986), 39–51.

first part (4:9b-16) and, after an intermediary section (4:17-20),[16] her children in the second part (4:21-29).

Jerusalem's lament can be interpreted as a text put in the mouth of a female figure by a male redactor of the book in its present form or as a text embracing experiences of women in distress—and perhaps both perspectives do justice to this poetical song, as laments are a genre connected to women mourners in Ancient Israel.[17]

Women Neighbors in Solidarity (Bar 4:9b-16)

Jerusalem opens her song by a call to listen to her and creates an audience for her words. Invited to listen are, literally, the "women living nearby," personified cities in the surrounding areas. They are not regarded as equally marked for destruction or as guilty as Jerusalem—a perspective developed in Jer 25 for Samaria and also for all the small neighbor kingdoms and their capitals. Neither are they regarded as malicious and gloating enemies or as those who participate in Jerusalem's destruction—like the image of the Philistine cities developed in Ezek 16:27. Jerusalem's neighbors, the cities around her,[18] considered as females, come into view as cohabitants of the common land responsive to solidarity, and there is no explicit distinction between Judean cities and "foreign" neighbors—a remarkable shift of perception!

Jerusalem explains her sorrow as loss of her children (Bar 4:10). In the book of Lamentations, her grief concerns the death of her inhabitants, but

16. I agree with Odil Hannes Steck, *Das apokryphe Baruchbuch*, FRLANT 160 (Göttingen: Vandenhoeck & Ruprecht, 1993), 181, 183. ("Übergang.")

17. See Claassens, *Mourner, Mother, Midwife*, 18–40, for this female tradition. Athalya Brenner and Fokkelien van Dijk-Hemmes, *On Gendering Texts: Female and Male Voices in the Hebrew Bible*, BibInt 1 (Leiden: Brill, 1993), were groundbreaking for detecting "female voices" in "male texts" and to connect them with concrete realities of women in ancient Israel. As they worked with genres this might be a real possibility. My approach is more modest, keeping my observation restricted to the world within the text. Differences between the perspectives of the lament and those of the surrounding speech might not necessarily point to a female "author" of the lament, as the lament in itself appears already to be "constructed" according to the overall theology of the book of Baruch.

18. Kneucker, *Das Buch Baruch*, 321–22, 357, seems to misunderstand the metaphor when he suggests a Hebrew masculine noun for the surrounding peoples at the base of the Greek "women neighbors." He does not take into consideration the capital cities of these surrounding peoples as referents *sui generis*. Wambacq, on the other hand has no problem associating the feminine noun with surrounding "lands." See Benjamin N. Wambacq, "Baruch," in *Jeremias – Klaagliederen – Baruch – Brief van Jeremias*, De Boeken van het Oude Testament (Roermond and Maaseik: J. J. Romen & Zonen, 1957), 380.

Bar 4:9b-16

⁹For she saw the wrath that came
    upon you from God,
  and she said:
Listen, you neighbors of Zion,
    God has brought great sorrow
      upon me;
¹⁰for I have seen the exile of my
      sons and daughters,
  which the Everlasting brought
      upon them.
¹¹With joy I nurtured them,
    but I sent them away with
      weeping and sorrow.
¹²Let no one rejoice over me, a
      widow
  and bereaved of many;
I was left desolate because of the
    sins of my children,
  because they turned away
      from the law of God.
¹³They had no regard for his
    statutes;

they did not walk in the ways
    of God's command-
      ments,
  or tread the paths his righ-
      teousness showed
        them.
¹⁴Let the neighbors of Zion come;
  remember the capture of my
      sons and daughters,
  which the Everlasting brought
      upon them.
¹⁵For he brought a distant nation
      against them,
  a nation ruthless and of a
      strange language,
which had no respect for the aged
    and no pity for a child.
¹⁶They led away the widow's be-
      loved sons,
  and bereaved the lonely
      woman of her
        daughters.

in the book of Baruch, it is their deportation into exile, according to the overall perspective of the book. Baruch 4:11 explores the same motif of loss, bringing into the foreground the emotional aspects. The audience is invited to sympathize with mother Jerusalem made childless. A certain distance from real experiences can be felt, however, in contrast to the second lament in the book of Lamentations, with its gloomy reality. Baruch is similar to Lamentations in the inclusive way he mentions the "children": they are "sons" and "daughters" (4:11, 14), and with the Greek τέκνα, "children" (4:12; 4:19, 21, 25, 27), use is made of an inclusive noun to designate both. This specific sensitivity to both sexes might relate to the extreme situation of violence and death affecting even children, comparable to the penitential prayer that relates the horrible fate of the little sons and daughters (2:3).

Jerusalem describes Israel's exile in a twofold way: as expression of God's wrath upon her children (4:10) and as sorrow God brought upon her (4:9b). By this she places herself in an intermediary position, as the song's narra-tive introduction did in 4:9a—thereby coming strikingly close to the Meso-potamian city-goddess who expresses her own humiliation and her grief

TRANSLATION MATTERS

4:9, 14, 24 *neighbors*: αἱ πάροικοι, literally: "women living nearby."

4:10 *exile*: αἰχμαλωσίαν, better: "captivity" or "capture," as in 4:14.

4:13 *tread the paths his righteousness showed them*: τρίβους παιδείας ἐν δικαιοσύνῃ αὐτοῦ ἐπέβησαν, more precisely: "tread the paths of education in his righteousness."

4:15 *ruthless*: ἀναιδὲς, better: "shameless."

4:15 *children*: παιδίον, better: "little children."

4:16 *beloved sons*: τοὺς ἀγαπητούς, literally: "beloved"; the form is masculine plural and can be used to include both genders.

concerning the inhabitants of her city. Jerusalem's intermediary position makes her a mediator, again comparable to the Mesopotamian model: she is affected by the city's destruction, but she is not guilty, and this is why her lamenting intercession or her intercessory lament can be effective.

Jerusalem asks her women neighbors not to laugh at her harm, as they, in a social context of honor and shame, are expected to do regarding her miserable situation; she asks for compassion instead of humiliation by accumulating a variety of terms to express her desolation (4:12). These terms are reminiscent of Jerusalem traditions in line with Jeremiah and Isaiah: she is called a widow in Lam 1:1; she is shown as a deserted place in Isa 64:10. Isaiah 49:21, as the closest reference to Bar 4:12, brings together childlessness, widowhood, and desolation as a past experience for Jerusalem; for those who read or listen to Jerusalem's song incorporated in Baruch's book, the notion of hope would be present here already. On the narrative level of her song, Jerusalem proceeds to explain the reason for her misery. Again, accumulating many terms is her stylistic means of describing or confessing the guilt of her "children" in four parallel lines (4:12c-13). Their fault is disrespect of God's prescriptions and, by this, disrespect for God as their "pedagogue" who tried to give them orientation in their life; the literal translation of 4:13c is "they did not . . . tread the paths [of pedagogy] in his righteousness." For sons who do not respect their parents and their pedagogy—that is, their disciplining, including beatings—the deuteronomic law provides that they are put to death (Deut 21:18-21). Jerusalem tries to justify God's wrath by sketching her children as rebellious, creating a distorted family picture without problematizing, as modern readers would do, the "poisonous pedagogy" exercised by the divine educator. For readers who still have Baruch's wisdom speech in their mind, however, another connotation would suggest itself: God's law is not the arbitrary prescription of an authoritarian patriarch but the source of life for Israel (Bar 3:9–4:4); leaving this source of life leads to death.

With Bar 4:14 a new stanza begins, focusing again on Jerusalem's neighbor cities and asking them to help her remember what she remembers now: mother Jerusalem now brings into the foreground not the sins of her children but the horrible destiny they had to undergo. Again, she would not hide that it was God who acted upon them. If in the first stanza Israel's transgression and God's righteousness were underlined, now it is Israel's suffering that is focused on, making this stanza a cry for compassion addressed not only to the women neighbors of Jerusalem but also indirectly to the divine originator.

Patriarchy, Punishment, and Power, Part 2

The text of the final section of Baruch begins in 4:5 with a description (probably suggested by Baruch himself) of the familial relationships among Israel, Jerusalem, and God. Israel consists of the children of a marriage between God the father and Jerusalem the mother. Baruch chides Israel, the children, with the words "You forgot the everlasting God, who brought you up, and you grieved Jerusalem, who reared you" (4:8). Then the text changes in 4:9b from second to first person, and it is now Jerusalem herself who is speaking. She describes herself as "a widow and bereaved of many" (4:12). Being a widow suggests her husband is dead, but immediately in the next line we learn that this is not quite so, for Jerusalem exclaims: "I was left desolate because of the sins of my children, because they turned away from the law of God" (4:12). God the husband is not dead. He has merely deserted his wife, Jerusalem, because of the sins of their common children. He is the patriarch of the family and his law is the law all should follow. His children's rejection of his law results in the breaking up of the patriarchal family. God punishes the children by exiling them and torturing them (4:14), without consulting the mother (4:16), and deserts her too (4:19).

God the father, in this text, has the power to punish wife and children. He punishes the children because of what he perceives as disrespect, and he believes that this punishment will bring repentance. When this repentance comes, he will forgive his children. This is, indeed, what Jerusalem tells her children: "cry to God, and he will deliver you from the power and hand of the enemy" (4:21). She promises them that when this happens, God will bring his children back to their mother (4:29). He will restore his wife to her previous exalted position (5:2-3) and even reward his children by allowing them to punish those who had oppressed them (4:25).

Tal Ilan

The words recalling Israel's misery (Bar 4:14) recall also the beginning of Jerusalem's lament including the mention of "sons and daughters" (4:10) and move toward giving concrete contours to what was merely alluded to as "exile" there. The image drawn depends on contrasts: on one hand, the woman is already left alone and her children taken away from her, with the sons emphasized as "beloved" (4:16), revealing the patriarchal perspective of this mother-city;[19] on the other hand are those who executed the deportation. The characterization of that nation takes up elements from Deut 28:49-50, a reference text already important for the community's prayer (Bar 1:15b–3:8). The characterization given is fourfold, drawing on real experiences, but also generalizing, expressing distance, disgust, and rhetorical humiliation: the invaders come from far away, are not neighbors but are strangers and foreigners; they speak a language different from Israel's language, which is also an expression of a different mentality and culture; they are, in one word, "shameless" in all they do and behave against Israel's norms of honor and shame. As a telling example, their conduct toward the weakest in a society is described as having "no respect for the aged and no pity for a [little] child [παιδίον]" (Bar 4:15). Such distanced and distancing speech, also used in the wisdom speech (3:10; 4:3), relies on the otherness of foreigners and on the presumed "naturalness" of the subject group's—Israel's—own behaviors and values. It is an effective means of rhetorically degrading or disdaining another group. It is interesting, however, that the nation referred to is left anonymous. On the level of the book, Babylonia, the invading power involved, is now for the exiles the context of "Baruch's" community and the object of prayers for the sovereign (1:11-12).

Between Lament and Hope (Bar 4:17-20)

In the first part of her lament, Jerusalem had her neighbor cities as audience, while her children were the object of her thoughts. Now in Bar 4:17, she addresses her children directly and portrays a scene involving three agents: her inhabitants, herself, and God. Her inhabitants are about to leave her; she cannot prevent them and calls on them to go (4:19). She herself is ready to sing her lament song, hence to perform the rites of self-humiliation, including a change of clothing (4:20); the finely woven στολή, "robe," gives way to a coarse tissue, the σάκκος, "sackcloth." For those familiar with Hellenistic Jewish writings, two other female figures

---

19. Wambacq, "Baruch," 380, is sensitive to the androcentric perspective of this phrase.

Bar 4:17-20

¹⁷But I, how can I help you?	for I have been left desolate.
¹⁸For he who brought these ca-	²⁰I have taken off the robe of peace
lamities upon you	and put on sackcloth for my
will deliver you from the hand	supplication;
of your enemies.	I will cry to the Everlasting all
¹⁹Go, my children, go;	my days.

come to mind: Queen Esther in solidarity with her people threatened by Haman's edict of annihilation (Add Esth C and D), and Judith before leaving her city to meet Holofernes (Jdt 9:1; 10:1-3).[20] "Taking off the robe of peace" might be an allusion to Jeru*salem*'s name, city of *shalom*, of peace, of well-being, although, in this moment, there is no *shalom*. The third agent she evokes is God, who will be addressed by her lament as the one who can turn the situation around. Again, Jerusalem appears in the colors of the Mesopotamian city goddess, but now she takes over her role as intercessor; she acts like the goddess supplicating for the people under her protection, and here it becomes clear that there is no other God to rescue them but the one who brought about their destruction.

In her announcement to "cry to the Everlasting" (Bar 4:20), Jerusalem is similar to Susanna, the beautiful woman accused of adultery by two men of her community. Because they were elders and respected, the assembly believed them and condemned her to death. "Then Susanna cried out with a loud voice, and said, 'O eternal God, you know what is secret and are aware of all things before they come to be; you know that these men have given false evidence against me . . .'. The Lord heard her cry" (Sus 42-44 TH[21]). Susanna puts her trust in the "everlasting God," and likewise mother Jerusalem turns to the "Eternal One" whose "understanding is unsearchable" (Isa 40:28; another occurrence of the rare formula θεός αἰώνιος, "eternal God"), so that there might be hope for her children.

Jerusalem and Her Children (Bar 4:21-29)

From Bar 4:21 onward, Jerusalem abandons her role as woman mourner asking her neighbors for assistance. From now on the surrounding women

20. This intertextual reference has been highlighted by Franz Heinrich Reusch, *Erklärung des Buchs Baruch* (Freiburg i. Br.: Herder, 1853), 219; and Joseph Knabenbauer, "Commentarius in Baruch," in *Commentarius in Danielem prophetam, Lamentationes et Baruch*, Cursus Scripturae Sacrae III/2 (Paris: Lethielleux, 1889), 493.

21. Sus 42-44 TH corresponds to Sus 35 LXX, but in LXX she does not "cry out" but "weep and speak in herself."

Bar 4:21-29

²¹Take courage, my children, cry
to God,
and he will deliver you from the
power and hand of the
enemy.
²²For I have put my hope in the
Everlasting to save you,
and joy has come to me from
the Holy One,
because of the mercy that will
soon come to you
from your everlasting savior.
²³For I sent you out with sorrow
and weeping,
but God will give you back to
me with joy and glad-
ness forever.
²⁴For as the neighbors of Zion
have now seen your cap-
ture,
so they soon will see your salvation by God,
which will come to you with great
glory
and with the splendor of the
Everlasting.

²⁵My children, endure with pa-
tience the wrath that has
come upon you from God.
Your enemy has overtaken you,
but you will soon see their destruction
and will tread upon their necks.
²⁶My pampered children have
traveled rough roads;
they were taken away like a
flock carried off by the
enemy.

²⁷Take courage, my children, and
cry to God,
for you will be remembered by
the one who brought
this upon you.
²⁸For just as you were disposed to
go astray from God,
return with tenfold zeal to seek
him.
²⁹For the one who brought these
calamities upon you
will bring you everlasting joy
with your salvation.

cities are only spectators of what happens with her "children." Pointing to
a better future, the role she assumes now is a prophetic one; for her part
she uses the call "take courage" (θαρσεῖτε; 4:21; see also 4:5) and she utters
a kind of oracle of salvation. She can do this not because of prophetic inspiration but because of her close proximity to God as presupposed by the
voice introducing her song (4:5-9a) and actualized by her intercession.

Throughout the second part of her song, Jerusalem addresses her
"children" by direct speech. Following her imperatives three stanzas
emerge, vv. 21-24, 25-26, and 27-29.

The first of these starts with contrasts: besides mourning, there is already joy (4:22-23); instead of capture, there is hope for salvation (4:24)—
and above all there is brightness shining from the Divine, a motif also
present in the wisdom poem (3:14; 4:2). But Jerusalem does not yet take
off her sackcloth, and her "children" are still far away.

Patriarchy, Punishment, and Power, Part 3

The basic concept of this patriarchal worldview is that children's (=Israel's) misbehavior should be punished by inflicting violence and suffering on them. The wife, Jerusalem, fully identifies in this chapter with the father who punishes her children, and she urges them to placate their father (4:25), and she herself acknowledges and accepts her own lot (4:22), much like a beaten woman often attempts to appease her husband, in the hope that his violence will subside.

The consolation that God's children (and his wife) should take in this social structure is that the tool God used to punish them (in this case the Babylonians, who destroyed Jerusalem) will in turn be punished by the victims seeking revenge. The city of Babylon, again perceived metaphorically as a woman, will be ravished by the revenging Israelites (4:32-33). This creates a cycle of perpetual violence and revenge, which is hard if not impossible to break.

Tal Ilan

As a complementary image Bar 4:25-26 is about the destiny of the enemies. Using a very old ancient Near Eastern/West Asian motif of victory,[22] the Israelites are shown trampling down their former suppressors. A kind of supplementary remark or parenthesis follows, remembering again Israel's deportation as compared to an animal transport as they "were taken away like a flock" (4:26). Perhaps this remark can be read as an attempt to justify the image of retributive justice by simple reversion. As such, it would be an indication of a tradition that has already become difficult at the time the Jerusalem poem was composed but cannot (yet?) be dismissed.[23]

The last stanza, 4:27-29, with its repeated call to "take courage," comes back to the first one in the way of compositional inclusion. Jerusalem admonishes her children to turn back to God and to do this with a maximum of effort. Interestingly it is not stated clearly that returning to God is conditional for obtaining a reversal of destiny; Jerusalem's admonitions can also be interpreted in the sense of correspondence between a new beginning provided by God and a new orientation of Israel toward her God.

22. That motif is represented on the so-called Narmer palette from the very beginnings of dynastic Egypt; as biblical evidence, see Deut 33:29; Josh 10:24-25.

23. For Reusch, *Erklärung des Buchs Baruch*, 224, there is no problem extending this prophetical announcement to "the submission of the peoples under the Church" ("die Unterwerfung der Völker unter die Kirche").

The reversal of Jerusalem's and Israel's destiny is expected to begin in a near future; the threefold recurrence of "soon" (Bar 4:22, 24, 25) creates an atmosphere of imminent expectation. Within the song, "soon" is part of Jerusalem's admonition and encouragement; within the book of Baruch, it is not completely in accordance with a prayer for the Babylonian rulers and the affirmation that "we will serve them many days" (1:12). Perhaps the actual book reflects a discussion within the community of readers between those who would like to force a return to Jerusalem and others who prefer to stay in their diaspora contexts.[24]

Prophetical Answer (4:30–5:9)

The last words of Jerusalem's song announce "everlasting joy with your salvation" for Israel (Bar 4:29). What follows in Bar 4:30–5:9 is a response to her song, perhaps by the same voice who introduces her words. The introduction (4:5-9a) was addressed to Israel, then Jerusalem continued the song beginning in 4:9b, ending with Jerusalem addressing her "children" in the second part of her song (4:17-29). Now in 4:30, Jerusalem herself is the center of attention, addressed directly by the text. Again, it becomes clear that she is not simply a free poetical variable for the city's population or for a Jerusalem-centered Israel but an entity *sui generis* with mythical qualities. Focusing on the rhetorical formula consisting of an imperative followed by the title "Jerusalem," four units can be defined: 4:30-35; 4:36-37; 5:1-4; 5:5-9. These units correspond roughly to four thematic emphases.

The voice responding to the woman-city's speech takes up her introductory words of courage (Bar 4:5) to give fresh heart to Jerusalem who herself had encouraged her audience (4:21, 27). Also articulated is the motif of consolation, prominent in the so-called deuteroisaianic passages and related to the people about to leave the Babylonian exile (Isa 40:1-2; 49:13; 51:12; 52:9) and also to the restored city of Jerusalem (Isa 51:3; 54:11). God "named" her as an expression of God's deep relationship with the city. Maybe such naming confirms, in a more concrete way, that her name, alluding to שׁלוֹם, "peace/well-being," will be a sign of coming times. Moreover, Jerusalem's renaming (Bar 5:4) is prepared.

---

24. Erich S. Gruen's historical study on Jews and Diaspora (*Diaspora: Jews amidst Greeks and Romans* [Cambridge, MA: Harvard University Press, 2002]) is valuable but does not consider Baruch.

Bar 4:30–5:9

³⁰Take courage, O Jerusalem,
  for the one who named you will
    comfort you.
³¹Wretched will be those who mis-
    treated you
  and who rejoiced at your fall.
³²Wretched will be the cities that
    your children served as
    slaves;
  wretched will be the city that
    received your offspring.
³³For just as she rejoiced at your
    fall
  and was glad for your ruin,
  so she will be grieved at her
    own desolation.
³⁴I will take away her pride in her
    great population,
  and her insolence will be
    turned to grief.
³⁵For fire will come upon her from
    the Everlasting for many
    days,

and for a long time she will be
    inhabited by demons.

³⁶Look toward the east, O Jeru-
    salem,
  and see the joy that is coming
    to you from God.
³⁷Look, your children are coming,
    whom you sent away;
  they are coming, gathered
    from east and west,
at the word of the Holy One,
  rejoicing in the glory of God.

⁵:¹Take off the garment of your
    sorrow and affliction, O Je-
    rusalem,
  and put on forever the beauty
    of the glory from God.
²Put on the robe of the righteous-
    ness that comes from God;
  put on your head the diadem
    of the glory of the Ever-
    lasting;

In harsh contrast to this passage of promise comes an oracle of doom and destruction, addressed to those cities who have been involved in Jerusalem's misery and who have profited from her fall, hence to those women neighbors who were not ready to show compassion. Jerusalem in her lament already touched briefly on the destiny of her children's enemies (4:25). It seems that, in what follows, the voice comforting Jerusalem refers in a chiastic and hence quite systematic way back to the lament, affirming its wishes and hopes and turning them into promises.

Besides the more general motif of reversed gloating (Bar 4:31; 4:25), there is the concrete allusion to enslavement of children (4:32a). Again, crimes against children as the weakest members of a society and at the same time a society's future are considered the ugliest (4:26). Enslavement of children by selling them abroad is also a subject of accusation

³for God will show your splendor
 everywhere under heaven.
⁴For God will give you evermore
 the name,
 "Righteous Peace, Godly Glory."

⁵Arise, O Jerusalem, stand upon
 the height;
look toward the east,
and see your children gathered
 from west and east
 at the word of the Holy One,
 rejoicing that God has remembered them.
⁶For they went out from you on
 foot,
 led away by their enemies;
but God will bring them back to
 you,
carried in glory, as on a royal
 throne.
⁷For God has ordered that every
 high mountain and the everlasting hills be made low
and the valleys filled up, to
 make level ground,
so that Israel may walk safely
 in the glory of God.
⁸The woods and every fragrant
 tree
 have shaded Israel at God's
 command.
⁹For God will lead Israel with joy,
 in the light of his glory,
 with the mercy and righteousness that come from
 him.

in Joel 3:6-8, here perhaps linked to experiences of slave trade between the Philistine cities and Greece in late Persian and Hellenistic times. Powers that support trafficking of children are cursed by this oracle. It is true that modern readers cannot accept this type of conflict management, but they might be able to agree on the criterion given for intolerable inhuman actions and understand the urgency of political measures in such cases.

Different is the case of the single city the oracular voice turns to now with a whole cascade of threats (Bar 4:32b-35). In accordance with the notion of retributive justice, Jerusalem's destiny is to recoil back on that city where her "children served as slaves" (4:32). That city will lose her population, be humiliated by gloat, and even burn with a fire sent by God, like Sodom in the days of Lot (Gen 19). The mention of "demons" living in her ruins might be due to a translation of different sorts of "spirits" thought to frequent uninhabited places as in Isa 34:14, but "demons" definitely refers back to the reproach directed at Israel who was "sacrificing to demons and not God" (4:7). The enemy city will be dominated by those false gods Israel is accused of having turned to but has now abandoned. According to the setting of Jerusalem's song,

TRANSLATION MATTERS

4:36 *toward the east*: πρὸς ἀνατολάς, literally: "toward the rising" (of the sun).

4:37 *from east and west*: ἀπ' ἀνατολῶν ἕως δυσμῶν, better: "from east to west."

5:4 *Righteous Peace, Godly Glory*: εἰρήνη δικαιοσύνης, καὶ δόξα θεοσεβείας, more literally: "Peace of Righteousness; Glory of Respect of God."

Babylon is aimed at by these dire predictions, but again it is not named. Indeed, the prophetical voice of Bar 4:30-35 merges traditional oracles against Babylon with those against Nineveh (e.g., Nah 3:1-7). The passage reads like a compulsory rhetorical exercise with its accumulation of formulae, or it could be heard as a last outburst of frustration to draw a final line and look into a different future. There is, however, "a lapse into the divine first person in 4:34," communicating the "intensity of the prophetic poet's feeling about Jerusalem's enemies."[25]

Going back one step further to the motifs of Jerusalem's song, Bar 4:36-37 refers to her joy in 4:21-24 and combines it with a first image of the exiles returning. Looking toward the rising of the sun means, on a practical level, looking from Jerusalem toward the east, into the direction where Israel was deported. On a symbolic level, the rising of the sun mirrors the radiance of the divine alluded to several times already (3:14; 4:2; 4:24). The concrete direction of (eastern) exile combines quickly with a look all around into the different regions of a diaspora since Persian times, "from sunrise to sunset," i.e., "from east to west" (4:37). Again, these two verses call to mind Isaian passages, especially Isa 60 with its vision of Israel's return to Jerusalem.

With a new imperative for Jerusalem, Bar 5:1-4 goes back to the motif of changing garments in times of sorrow (4:20). While Jerusalem was speaking, she was imagined as being dressed in her sackcloth. Now the prophetical voice asks her to bring her bodily appearance into accord with the new situation. The parallel to Queen Esther and to Judith is again evident; they wear garments of mourning during their preparation for their dangerous mission but dress sumptuously to meet the imperator. Unlike these women's garment changes, Jerusalem's changing of garments is marked as a metaphorical one; in fact, it is about the restitution of the city still destroyed or at least in poor condition.

25. Saldarini, "The Book of Baruch," 980.

Patriarchy, Punishment, and Power, Part 4

It seems that to this day, this cycle of violence and revenge has not been broken. Jerusalem, as the bride of God, has been wed by the God of three monotheistic religions, who, like jealous lovers, continuously vie for her favors and punish her when she shows preference for one over the other. They continuously punish her children, each banishing and killing those of her other lover. They continuously clothe her in glory and crown her with beauty, these only to be torn and disheveled by the other. There is hardly a city in the world that has endured so much violence or that has had so much emotion invested in its conquest and occupation. There is no other city that has so often been designated "city of peace" (as in 5:4: "For God will give you evermore the name: Righteous Peace, Godly Glory") while perpetuating so much war. Living in Jerusalem makes one daily aware of the rhetorical use of peace alongside the jingoism of war that is ever present in it.

It seems to me that this text of Baruch is a typical example of a patriarchal war song, the likes of which have contributed much to perpetuate the lot of Jerusalem, the metaphoric woman ravaged by war, and the lot of real women who are ravaged by war. Its author is deeply aware of the suffering that war has in store for women, who are not its perpetrators, but it never criticizes the social norms that inflict such suffering; instead it seems to perceive a usefulness for this suffering—a tool with which to punish the guilty.

Tal Ilan

Righteousness (δικαιοσύνη) is again a term most frequent in the Isaian tradition and in the psalms; the book of Baruch attributes righteousness to God alone, as could be seen in the penitential prayer (1:15; 2:6, 18) and also in Jerusalem's lament (4:13). Jerusalem's righteousness, which her children refused to adopt by discipline, is given to her by God, together with glory, radiance, and honor (5:2). Adorned with this garment and diadem, she will be presented to the world (5:3). Her splendor and glory recall the splendor and glory of God's salvation promised to Israel (4:24), but also, like a mirror, the shining light of the Torah-Wisdom (4:1-2). Since Jerusalem is not God's bride but, together with God, nourisher of their children, the diadem should not be imagined as a bride's jewelry. Instead, think of a queen's coronation with God as her king.[26] It is this motif of

---

26. I agree with Häusl, "Künderin und Königin," 118–24, who works this out.

coronation that brings her into a certain analogy with a *tyche poleos* and her mural crown, so that it might have been possible for readers familiar with this tradition to perceive personified Jerusalem as their genuine symbol of the fortune, the newly gained splendor of the city.

Jerusalem's coronation comes into a consistent image with the names she receives from God, throne names expressing the new government's program. Her first name, "Peace of Righteousness," recalls a component of her actual name, city of *shalom*, of peace/well-being, and also literally the "robe of peace" she changed for her sackcloth (4:20). She had already received a new "robe of . . . righteousness," which is now confirmed by the other component of her first throne name. Righteousness (δικαιοσύνη) is more than justice; it encompasses, according to the Hebrew צדק or צדקה, the whole order of the cosmos. Jerusalem's second name refers to the splendor as a sign of God's divinity, but it also has the meaning of "honor" and hence provides her with esteem in the eyes of those who look at her. Combined with this splendorous honor is θεοσέβεια, an expression covering "fear of God" in the sense of "respect of God," but also the corresponding activity or attitude of piety. θεοσέβεια is one of the translations of the Hebrew יראת אלהים (e.g., in Job 28:28), a sapiential formula comprising what is appropriate in the relationship between God and humans and, in the book of Baruch, might encompass acceptance of God's Torah.[27]

The last passage of Baruch, 5:5-9, calls to mind Isaian articulation (Isa 60) in which Jerusalem's grief about the loss of her children turns positive. Jerusalem is called to arise, to stand up from her sitting position as a person in grief. Jerusalem's children receive their own portion of her royal dignity as they are carried back "as on a royal throne" (5:6) and need not walk. Another Isaian motif describing how God prepares a way for the people back to Jerusalem (Isa 40:3-5) is modified and refers to Israel's undisturbed ways with her God (Bar 5:7). Even trees are transformed into helpers; they provide shade on the roads and no longer seduce Israel to sacrifice to other gods, as deuteronomistic voices would criticize. God is in control; nature obeys God's commandments (5:8) and does what the voice of the wisdom teacher told Israel to do with the "book of the commandments of God" (4:1-2). The final sentence (5:9)

---

27. Steck, *Das apokryphe Baruchbuch*, 231, with reference to Kneucker, *Das Buch Baruch*, 345–46, thinks that a wordplay can be assumed with "Jerusalem" so that both components of her actual name, שלם (peace) and יראה (respect), would resonate in her new names.

seems to summarize the whole book: out of God's mercy arises salvation for Israel, announced by the prophetic voice for Jerusalem (4:5–5:9) hoped for in the penitential prayer (1:15–3:8) and substantiated by offering the book of Torah-Wisdom (3:9–4:4). There can be confidence that, finally, Israel will accept God's righteousness for herself (5:9).

In the context of the book of Baruch, the images of exiled Israel returning to mother Jerusalem appear to underline the idea of a finally empty diaspora. An alternative possibility of giving meaning to the last part of Baruch's book would be to understand Israel's return in terms of regular pilgrimages to Jerusalem.[28] In fact, this became a common way that Jews living in the diaspora expressed their relation to their mother-city: "Next year in Jerusalem."

28. See Maier, *Daughter Zion, Mother Zion*, 189–210, for (Isaian) Jerusalem texts referring to pilgrimage. In Bar 5:1-9, however, there is no pilgrimage of the nations but of Israelites only.

Baruch 1–5

Looking Back as a Feminist Reader

Does the book of Baruch stand up to its assertion to heal a distorted community? Whose healing is considered? Who is excluded? What are the remedies? And who is offered as the healer?

Looking back at the narrative of the book, a clear movement is detectable. It runs from a collective prayer expressing shame, repentance, and willingness to subject oneself to God's prescriptions; to a teaching on wisdom, identified with the book of God's prescriptions given to Israel; and to a prophetical voice disclosing the reason of present misery by quoting personified Jerusalem, who brings to mind, for her part, Israel's rejection of God's prescriptions, and raising hopes for renewal. Liturgical forms, wisdom teaching, and prophetical speech are used to underline the fundamental significance of God's Torah for Israel's existence. The Torah thus ascends to the status of the one and only remedy to heal the community.

The lack of concrete prescriptions alluded to is, however, striking. There is, for example, no insistence on keeping the Sabbath, a concern important for Priestly circles but also found in the book of Jeremiah (17:19-27). There is no mention of the four commandments of the Decalogue Jeremiah alludes to in his temple speech: stealing, murdering, committing adultery, swearing falsely (Jer 7:9). This is all the more astonishing as the Jeremian speech continues with blaming his audience

for venerating other Gods, and idolatry is the only transgression mentioned in Bar 1–5. The book of Baruch does not measure Israel's apostasy
by social parameters and is not interested in regulations for the social
life of the community. In particular and in contrast to the Deuteronomistic History, the book of Baruch does not blame foreign women for
Israel's cultic apostasy. In contrast to the books of Ezra and Nehemiah,
neither does it demand the divorce of a mixed marriage of Israelite men
to non-Israelite women.

Baruch 1–5, therefore, is open to divergent interpretations between
the two poles: for the social life of Israel, regulations can be developed
according to circumstances, if only Israel adheres strictly to her God
alone; or Israel's social life is precisely regulated by the Book of Commandments so that there is no need to repeat particular norms. In the
latter case—more probable within the overall context of Bar 1–5—there
is, of course, the necessity of further interpretation of what is written in
the Book of Commandments, but the general frame would be circum-
scribed to a considerable degree. Non-Israelite wo/men and wo/men
longing for gender equality have a much longer way to walk through a
book claiming divine authority and at the same time shaped by patriarchal structures as well as androcentric and ethnocentric perspectives.

The book of Baruch, with its narrative move from confession of guilt,
to admonition to adhere to the Book of Law, and to its prophetical reference to Jerusalem, has as its implicit audience an Israel with specific
contours. It is a community with common roots in Judaea or more precisely in Jerusalem, one part still living there, the other part uprooted
from there. It is a community who considers Jerusalem as their center
where cultic acts have to be performed, but at the same time the members
of that community know that God can be invoked anywhere. The community recognizes the political structures in Jerusalem consisting of a
Priestly group of leaders but at the same time does not rule out the possibility of a renewed monarchy, since descendants of the royal family
are still among the living. The members of the community are willing
to accept foreign rulers for some time but hope to reach political independence or national sovereignty, the "national" being defined in a
classical sense of common genealogical ties. This might be one of the
reasons why Baruch gets his rather extensive genealogy at the beginning
of his book.

In contrast to older codes of prescriptions that reflect on foreigners or
strangers in the midst of Israel and try to develop a modus vivendi, the
book of Baruch makes no mention of them. Again this can be interpreted

as obvious inclusion but also as a blind spot, so that the book of Baruch can be used to construct a community open to foreigners—or opposed to anybody (and anything) of another provenience or "an alien people" (ἀλλότριος; Bar 4:3) in a land where foreigners have a difficult life. A further blind spot concerns women. One cannot be sure about their implied presence among those who pray, listen to the wisdom teacher, or hear the prophetical announcements.

The narrative move of the book of Baruch is equally enlightening for a characterization of the implied authors. They are the "sons" distancing themselves from the transgressions of their "fathers," knowing that adherence to God's prescriptions will be the path to go. They are speaking through the voice of a wisdom teacher who diminishes wisdom as a female personification and transforms her into an ethical-theological enlightenment, who cuts off the tradition of Israelite wisdom shared with other people and identifies true wisdom with God's commandments. The implied authors finally rise to put forward the view of the prophetic voice: that mother Jerusalem will get back her children. They are a new generation compared to their "fathers," constructing a new "ground zero" from where new visions now have to come and new structures will emerge. They are claiming power, not in cultic affairs, not in a straightforward political realm, but as those who understand the Scriptures and know how to interpret them for the present and future. They distance themselves from their "fathers"; they do not need the erotic appeal of Lady Wisdom, but they long for a return to their mother, Jerusalem.

Jerusalem, for them, is a mother, not in terms of origins or mythical genealogy, and not in terms of nourishing breasts. She is a mother repeating the admonitions of the wisdom teacher, hence a pedagogue, and here she resembles the mother of seven (2 Macc 7), encouraging her sons to adhere to God's commandments and to not fear death. Moreover, Jerusalem is the space to go and to live a new life under the protection of God, who is not identified as father but to whom mother Jerusalem is clearly subordinate. At the same time, the implied authors themselves construct their mother Jerusalem, quote her lament, and grant her a joyful future. With these learned sons, a new type of masculinity emerges, not a warrior or a king-ruler claiming hegemony by physical power or power transmitted by political structures, not a prophet-type of masculinity or a priest-type, not an ancestor-type, but a masculinity characterized by intellectual power. If or how these learned "sons" have relations with concrete women is not spelled out: neither wives nor daughters are mentioned—but at the same time no sons. The hope that Israel will never be expelled from their land implies, one would say, ongoing procreations and births. In contrast to a vision like 1 En. 10:17, though, where the future life in happiness includes thousands of children begotten by men—who gives birth to them is not mentioned—the book of Baruch is not interested in these details.

Jerusalem does not explicitly receive the designation "mother" in Bar 1–5, but her lament when speaking of her children allows for such a conclusion. Isaiah 1:26 LXX uses the term μητρόπολις ("mother-city") along with πόλις ("city") to introduce the names for Jerusalem: "City of Righteousness" (cf. "Righteous Peace, Godly Glory" in Bar 5:4) and "Faithful Mother-City [μητρόπολις] of Zion." The term μητρόπολις has no occurrence in Bar 1–5, but Bar 3:7-8 speaks of Israel's present state in Babylonia as ἀποικία, a term used in classical Greek for a "colony." In the book of Baruch, however, ἀποικία is not considered a colony where new economic possibilities for the mother city are disclosed but as a site of colonized life—even though, according to the fictitious situation, the impetus for a renewed relation to God comes out of the ἀποικία. Coming home to mother Jerusalem and hoping for political sovereignty in a context where empires exploit their colonies (see Neh 9:36-37) appears to be an understandable demand. To people from former colonies whose ancestors were deported as slaves, this will ring familiar.

The implied authors of Bar 1–5, however, would not enter into an armed battle to achieve this goal—they are not at the side of the Maccabean fighters; they do not prepare a revolution—but they hope for God's intervention. In the meantime, they pray for their oppressors but also imagine their oppressors' destruction. Are different voices in the community speaking up here? Or can this be interpreted as expression of mixed feelings in a colonized situation?

God-talk in the book of Baruch is connected to various designations God receives. In the narrative introduction and the prayer only (1:10–3:8), God is called κύριος, "Lord," extended by παντοκράτωρ, "Almighty One" (3:1, 4), in accordance with the prayer's general scheme to subject to God's power and acknowledge God's justice. At nearly every occurrence κύριος is connected with ὁ θεός ἡμῶν, "our God," thus affirming the indissoluble relation between the community in prayer and their God, possibly a translation of the Hebrew יהוה אלהינו, "YHWH, our God."

Throughout the wisdom speech, no other designation than θεός, "God," is used, in line with the cosmic dimensions paced out by the text, but also with the confession to the one and only God underlying the whole book. The last part of the book, in particular the Jerusalem poem, has another specific naming for God, ὁ αἰώνιος, "The Eternal One," or "the Everlasting." Expressed by this name is hope for Jerusalem's restoration. The book of Baruch as a whole is monotheistic in that there is but one God with infinite power in the cosmic as well as the political realm. It is not monotheistic in a strict philosophical sense of denying the existence of other deities besides YHWH. Rather, as the book tries to show, such other deities have been a temptation for Israel (Bar 1:22), although they can be reduced to demons (4:7) and cannot be a serious alternative to the one and only God. This is true all the more since the one and only God is close to Israel as pedagogue, as nourisher, and as savior. In an enlightened future (4:2; 5:9), the hope of those who composed and transmitted the book is that other gods will fade away. Ultimately, the one and only healer is God, revealing a face of "mercy and righteousness" (Bar 5:9).

The Letter (Epistle) of Jeremiah (Bar 6:1-73)

A Deconstruction of Images

Introduction

The Epistle of Jeremiah is, by genre, not a typical letter, in spite of the indication given in v. 1 (EpJer 1 = Bar 6:1), reminiscent of Jeremiah's letter in Jer 29 MT/36 LXX. Maybe its title—ἐπιστολή, "epistle"—does not so much refer to the genre of letter but to the more general written form of communication, a writing sent out, as the Greek can be rendered literally.[1] Indeed, the (fictitious) situation sketched in the first verse is the preparation of the Jerusalemites for deportation to Babylon. To these people the prophet Jeremiah wants to communicate a divine message; he wants them to take this message with them on their way to Babylonia, because its content addresses the situation they will experience there. Since, according to the last chapters of the Greek book of Jeremiah, the prophet is not in Judaea but in Egypt (Jer 44–45 MT/51 LXX), there is no other way to communicate with those in Jerusalem but by a writing sent to them.

---

1. See Lutz Doering, "Jeremiah and the 'Diaspora Letters' in Ancient Judaism: Epistolary Communication with the Golah as Medium for Dealing with the Present," in *Reading the Present in the Qumran Library: The Perception of the Contemporary by Means of Scriptural Interpretation*, ed. Kristin De Troyer and Armin Lange (Atlanta, GA: SBL Press, 2005), 48–54.

Subalterns Speak Up: Dalit Women, Part 1

The Deuterocanonical book of Baruch is closely linked to the Letter of Jeremiah. It was written to those who will soon be deported to Babylon. According to this, the exile is imperative but limited. It also asks the people to resist the worship of the gods of Babylonians. While giving reasons for such a resistance and mocking these gods and religious practices, it uses some images, analogies, and parallels relating to or referring to women, such as their love for ornaments (v. 9), their acting as prostitutes (v. 11), their involvement in cultic practice during the time of their menstruation (vv. 29-30), selfishness in preserving the sacrificial meat without giving to the poor and helpless (v. 28), sitting in the streets and performing dubious rites (vv. 42-44). So in the text, the Babylonian gods, religion, and women are constructed as "the other" to be mocked and derided.

Now, the above is the perspective of the Jewish religion and its prophet. We can also make an attempt to see the religion of the others from their own perspective and to understand how the religious beliefs and practices of the other religions work for their believers. Instead of trying to find out how the Babylonians perceived their gods, religion, and cultic practices, I would like to substitute their religious beliefs and practices by those of Dalits and Dalit women, "Dalit" designating the "untouchable"

The verses following the heading (vv. 2-7) switch immediately to the style of an exhortation speech imbued with deuteronomistic theology similar to the book of Jeremiah. From v. 8 onward the text develops as a satirical poem on the idols of Babylonia, connected to the exhortation style of the introduction only by the repeated formula "do not fear them." Its one and only subject is the futility of venerating images as gods, idolatry in the genuine sense of the word. Three passages end with a very similar line: "From this it is evident that they are not gods; so do not fear them" (v. 16; see also vv. 23, 29). These three passages can be bound together as a first part and distinguished from a second part comprising vv. 30-65.[2] Refrain-like formulae appear here again, with slight modifications and rather as rhetorical questions, thus allowing for

2. Kratz, in his fine contributions to Ep Jer, has shown this convincingly; see Reinhard G. Kratz, "Die Rezeption von Jeremia 10 und 29 im pseudepigraphen Brief des Jeremia," *JSJ* 26 (April 1995): 1–31, esp. 4–7, and Reinhard G. Kratz, "Der Brief des Jeremia," in *ATD Apokryphen*, vol. 5, ed. Otto Kaiser and Lothar Perlitt (Göttingen: Vandenhoeck & Ruprecht, 1998), 75–77.

population of India. Dalit women constitute 47.96 percent of the total Dalit population and 16.3 percent of India's total female population. So, about one out of every twelve Indians is a Dalit woman. In the Indian context of caste oppression, religion and religious practices of the Dalits are signs of hope, solace, and comfort. Their cult and myths are ways of expressing their cherished values and aspirations. Even some of the occurrences that happen in women, such as menstruation and childbirth, for which women often are treated as secondary and as low-graded, have a different perspective and understanding in the eyes of the Dalits and Dalit women.

It is not my point to make the Babylonian religion a religion of oppressed people but to reveal structures of "othering" and counter-perspectives. Maybe some of my points might help to make differences within Babylonian religion and within the religion behind the Letter of Jeremiah too. I will deal with three areas and portray how Dalits and Dalit women perceive them. The voices are drawn from so called testimonios of Dalit women,[3] especially from two women named Viramma and Bebī Kāmbale.[4] Although the Dalit and Dalit women can be considered "subalterns,"[5] these testimonios show that they speak up.

Anthony John Baptist

detecting seven more strophes. Verse 65 takes up again the refrain similar to v. 16 and sets an end to the second part of the speech. Verses 66-69 and 70-72 seem to form a double conclusion, while the last verse (v. 73) sums up everything with a practical consequence.

The "spirit" of this poem is not specifically deuteronomistic, but, as will be shown, has strong signs of a Priestly/Levitical worldview. Its most obvious structure consists in sets of similar lines used as refrains. At some instances, though, the refrains seem to interrupt a continuous reflection linked by catchwords or similar motifs. It might be, therefore,

3. See Anthony John Baptist, "Testimonios as Representation of Dalit Women Reality and Their Use in Researches," in *Theology for a New Community: Dalit Consciousness with a Symbolic Universe and Meaning Systems*, ed. T. K. John and James Massey (New Delhi: Centre for Dalit/Subaltern Studies, 2013), 173–87.

4. Viramma, Josiane Racine, and Jean-Luc Racine, *Viramma: Life of a Dalit*, trans. Will Hobson (New Delhi: Social Science Press, 2000); Baby Kamble, *The Prisons We Broke*, trans. Maya Pandit (Hyderabad: Orient Longman, 2008).

5. See Gayatri Chakravorti Spivak, "Can the Subaltern Speak?," in *Marxism and the Interpretation of Culture*, ed. Cary Nelson and Lawrence Grossberg (Chicago: University of Illinois Press, 1988), 271–313.

that an original mockery speech on idols stemming from Priestly circles—who could have had the knowledge or education, and the authority, at least in the eyes of their recipients, to present insights into Babylonian cult practices—was reworked and transformed into an exhortation in the Jeremian style.[6]

At any rate, Jeremiah's letter (Ep Jer) is hybrid in terms of genre, Israelite traditions used, confrontation with non-Jewish cults, and linguistic complexity. The textual hybridity might be seen as reflecting hybrid contexts of origin in Hellenistic times[7] as well as of reception from those times onward.

Heading: A Message for the Exiles (6:1)

In the heading to the Letter, a complex process of communication and authorization is initiated: Jeremiah, the prophet in times of crisis, addresses himself to those who are about to be deported as captives to Babylon. This group is not specified here; according to Jer 52:15, we see among them the rest of the people who were left in the city of Jerusalem, a formula including women and children.

His address is delivered as the written copy of a written document. For Hellenistic-Jewish writings in the Greek language,[8] this duplication of a writing was a specific way of giving authority to what had to be transmitted. This form includes oral deliverance, as the Letter might be read out to the addressees. The Letter comes under the authority of Jeremiah; his message has an even stronger authorization as its origin is assured to come from God.

---

6. I believe that this hypothesis does not run counter to the diligent study of Kratz, "Die Rezeption von Jeremia 10 und 29," who seeks to explain the whole structure of the Letter as a combination of elements and structures coming from Jer 10 and 29. Kratz's observations can be used to affirm that Jeremian influence is clearly detectable in Bar 6:1-6, from v. 65 onward, and in the refrains structuring the text as a whole. These exactly would be the "redactional" parts reworking a piece of satirical polemics.

7. For an attempt to date the Letter more precisely to the years around 300 BCE, see Kratz, "Der Brief des Jeremia," 81–84. Also interesting is the argument by the Italian-Jewish scholar and Rabbi of Florence (1926–1934), Elia Samuele Artom, "L'Origine, la data e gli scopi dell'Epistola de Geremia," *Annuario di studi ebraici* 1 (1934), 49–74, who thinks the Letter was dated to the period between 350 and 335 BCE and has a Hebrew-speaking author warning his too-much-assimilated community of Persian idolatry.

8. See 1 Esd 6:7; Add Esth E, 1; 1 Macc 8:22; 11:31; 12:5, 19-20.

Bar 6:1

⁶:¹A copy of a letter that Jeremiah sent to those who were to be taken to Babylon as exiles by the king of the Babylonians, to give them the message that God had commanded him.

TRANSLATION MATTERS

6:1 *as exiles*: αἰχμαλώτους, literally: "as captives."

The singular of the noun "God" seems to indicate that the God of Jeremiah, the God of Israel, is the one and only God for the implied authors as well as for their implied readers or listeners. God's uniqueness is presupposed, not explicitly mentioned or even affirmed emphatically. But in a subtle way, a conflict of powers is alluded to: the syntactical construction puts into parallels "God" as sender of a message to the exiles and "the king of the Babylonians" as the one who is going to execute deportation. Two powers stand one against the other, and within that logic of a power battle the question arises: why does God allow the Babylonian king to send Israel into exile; what about God's power?

Exhortation: Beware of Worshiping Images of Gods! (6:2-7)

Jeremiah's pseudepigraphic epistle begins with an explanation of the imminent exile as a consequence of Israel's sins (v. 2)—a better rendering could be "missing the mark" of what God wanted Israel to do. A similar interpretive figure marks the book of Jeremiah where the coming destruction of Jerusalem is mentioned over and over again. The Babylonian king was able to conquer Jerusalem because God withdrew protection and delivered the city, or even because this king became God's instrument of wrath (Jer 25:9). Israel's sins provoking Jerusalem's downfall is a motif characterizing the book of Baruch as well and is a *basso continuo* in the book of Lamentations.

One of Israel's principal sins, according to the book of Jeremiah is the worship of other gods besides the God of Israel, practiced by everybody, young and old, high and low, women, men, and children (Jer 7–8; 44). From a historical-critical point of view, the book of Jeremiah owes this motif of fighting against the worship of other gods to deuteronomistic reshapings of an older tradition about the prophet. The Letter of Jeremiah

Bar 6:2-7

²Because of the sins that you have committed before God, you will be taken to Babylon as exiles by Nebuchadnezzar, king of the Babylonians. ³Therefore when you have come to Babylon you will remain there for many years, for a long time, up to seven generations; after that I will bring you away from there in peace. ⁴Now in Babylon you will see gods made of silver and gold and wood, which people carry on their shoulders, and which cause the heathen to fear. ⁵So beware of becoming at all like the foreigners or of letting fear for these gods possess you ⁶when you see the multitude before and behind them worshiping them. But say in your heart, "It is you, O Lord, whom we must worship." ⁷For my angel is with you, and he is watching over your lives.

presupposes the deuteronomistic image of Jeremiah as a prophet blaming Israel for her worship of other gods and develops it: now that the population of Jerusalem and Judah has to live through life in exile for up to seven generations (v. 3)—probably modifying the seventy years in Jer 29:10—they will meet a new but similar challenge in their new context in Babylon. Hence, exile is seen not only as the logical consequence of Israel's failure but also as a time of probation.

Baruch 6:4-6 evoke a solemn public procession of richly adorned cult images, more precisely: cult statues of gods and goddesses carried on shoulders, with people looking at them and worshiping them.

In ancient West Asia, processions with cult statues would have been rare events at special holy days; during the year the statues would have their place within a temple far away or even hidden from ordinary worshipers, visible only for their priests who had to provide their daily service.⁹ Today, the fascination of such events can be imagined when participating in the liturgies of Holy Week in Spain, in a Mexican feast of the Virgin of Guadalupe, or in the so-called Chariot Festival (Rath Yatra) in the south Indian city of Puri.

From the outset, the Letter of Jeremiah leaves no doubt that it contests any meaning or relevance of this cult. The images' very first characteristic mentioned is their material: gold, silver, and wood (v. 4). This seems to be an apt description, as cult statues might consist of a wooden figure

9. See Angelika Berlejung, "Geheimnis und Ereignis: Zur Funktion und Aufgabe der Kultbilder in Mesopotamien," in *Die Macht der Bilder*, ed. Günter Sternberger and Marie-Theres Wacker, Jahrbuch für Biblische Theologie 13 (Neukirchen-Vluyn: Neukirchener Verlag, 1998).

TRANSLATION MATTERS

6:2 *sins*: ἀμαρτίας, The Greek verb ἁμαρτάνω has the meaning of "missing the mark"; hence "fail"; the noun ἁμαρτία corresponds to "failure" or "fault."

6:4 *heathen*: ἀλλοφύλοις, literally: "the foreign peoples" (see v. 51). "Heathen" might too narrowly focus on the religious difference.

6:4 *fear*: φόβος, can also refer to "awe."

6:6 *them*: αὐτά, The Greek text refers to the "gods" with a pronoun not in the masculine or feminine but in the neuter, thus degrading the gods (and their images) to mere objects. This rhetorical strategy is also used in vv. 8, 23, 26, 40-41, 45-46, 48, and 72. Where the Greek text has adjectives or participles in the neuter referring to the gods, the NRSV translates appropriately by "things"; see vv. 29, 39, 47.

6:6 *O Lord*: δέσποτα; the Greek δέσποτης is used here, not the more frequent κύριος. In the LXX, this word sometimes translates the Hebrew אדון or אדני besides the Tetragrammaton. Hence, in this prayer God is not called by name but by a title underlining power.

6:7 *my angel*: ἄγγελός μου, NETS suggests "my messenger" as alternative rendering. Thus the analogy with Jeremiah as someone who "brings/gives a message" (ἀναγγέλλω; v. 1) becomes visible.

coated with gold and/or silver and jewels used to mark eyes or as supplementary ornaments. But when one considers that in ancient Mesopotamia cult statues were regarded as the visible presence of a god or a goddess,[10] it becomes clear that v. 4 focuses on the material in order to reduce the images to their material provenance. Furthermore, the verse insists that the icons are "fabricated." A strong tradition of idol polemics in prophetical writings denigrates images of Gods for being made by the hands of humans (esp. Isa 40–48; Jer 2:28; 10:1-16). A pronominal reference to the gods using the neuter form of "them" (αὐτά; v. 6) underlines their status as mere objects. Those who react in "fear" or "awe," bowing before the images in a rite of veneration and recognizing in them the presence of their gods, are labeled "the peoples" (v. 4; better than NRSV "heathen") and "foreigners" (v. 5), setting a clear boundary between "the others" and those addressed by the Letter.

10. For a reconstruction of Assyrian/Babylonian theology of cult images, see the groundbreaking contribution by Angelika Berlejung, *Die Theologie der Bilder. Herstellung und Einweihung von Kultbildern in Mesopotamien und die alttestamentliche Bilderpolemik*, OBO 162 (Freiburg and Göttingen: Universitäts-Verlag, 1998).

Subalterns Speak Up:
Dalit Women, Part 2

The Letter of Jeremiah mocks Babylonian cultic practices outside and inside the temples, like carrying gods of silver and gold and wood on their shoulders during feasts (vv. 4, 26), decking gods out with garments (v. 11), lighting up lamps (v. 19), howling and shouting before gods (v. 32), the statue being brought before someone who cannot speak and pray so that they may speak (v. 40b), women responsible for sacrificial meals (v. 30), women offering incense in the streets (v. 42).

The religious practices of the subaltern can be considered to be means to express their value system, aspirations, self-affirmation, and self-dignity. The festivals are cultic situations where the Dalit men and women try to subvert normal, usual practices of discrimination. One such discrimination regards the place of inhabitation. In normal circumstances the Dalit men and women are not allowed to enter ur, the living place of people of high castes. In the context or pretext of a feast it is broken. Viramma, one of the Dalit women, narrates it thus: "We go to the ur very neatly dressed in new yellow cloth, with a pot of turmeric water mixed with cow urine in our hand. We buy tiny little needles in front of the temple which the priests put in us. We prostrate ourselves and go round the ur shouting, 'Govinda! Govinda!'" [invocation of the deity]. This can be interpreted as the utopia of the Dalits to be equal to and

At the same time, the text seems to admit that a procession of cult images has its own fascination and charm. Those who become eyewitnesses have to distance themselves by at least six means: first, they have to set spoken words—a kind of spell?—against the visual impression (v. 6); second, the sumptuous public rite has to be countered by a modest ritual of personal or private piety, a prayer; third, the procession outside, in the streets, has its counterpart inside, in the mental sphere, the prayer being said "in your heart" (v. 6); fourth, against the plurality of gods, the One Lord has to be recognized explicitly; fifth, the identity of those addressed is different from those from other tribes, the "foreigners," and there is a twofold warning not to assimilate (v. 5); and sixth, the peoples worshiping their gods can be regarded as a "crowd" or "throng" while the addressees are strongly individualized because everybody has to pray in his or her heart (v. 6). Again, the construction of the "other" to affirm one's own identity is more than palpable.

Verse 7 mentions an angel, a sign of divine presence in a situation where power and splendor of other gods seem to prevail. An angel was

be part of the high castes. But it can be also interpreted as a kind of safety valve. The dominant groups co-opt the revolt of the subordinates by allowing them to walk through their streets in a controlled cultic ambient.

During the festival times, the subaltern group experiences what we can call the god-experience. In the words of Viramma, "The smell of camphor and incense filled the ceri [=the place of inhabitation reserved for Dalits] and we felt like we were in a heavenly world! In this joyful atmosphere, with all the shouting and noise."[11]

Unlike the dominant religious trends of Hinduism, in the subaltern religions the women do perform some cultic practices and they are accepted as normal. These practices give them a sense of self-dignity, self-affirmation, and self-worth. Viramma narrates how she offered food to god Periyandavan, the god of her line: "I took a big banana leaf, a very wide one, and put in it a good helping of pongal [a rice dish], some condiments, three bananas, seven coconuts and some camphor I'd lit. I offered the whole thing to Periyandavan. Everyone prostrated themselves in silence."[12] Thus the Dalit women see the religious practices as means to express their idea of subversion, god-experience, and sense of self-dignity.

Anthony John Baptist

promised during Israel's way in the desert to protect and guide the people, but that angel would not pardon transgression, especially in regard to idolatry (Exod 23:20-23). Similarly, the Letter's angel watching over the people's life in Babylonia might require their life in case they do not resist temptation.[13]

Addressed are all those who will be exiled: men and women, nobles, craftsmen, and ordinary people, adults and children (Jer 52:15[14]). It is presupposed that all have transgressed the commandment not to worship other gods. If we can assume that not only men but women and children alike are allowed or maybe even obliged to stand in the streets when the sumptuous processions with the divine images take place,

11. Viramma, Racine, and Racine, *Viramma*, 174.
12. Ibid.
13. See Panc C. Beentjes, "Satirical Polemics against Idols and Idolatry in the Letter of Jeremiah (Baruch chap. 6)," in *Aspects of Religious Contact and Conflict in the Ancient World*, ed. Pieter W. van der Horst, Utrechtse Theologische Reeks 31 (Utrecht: Universiteit Utrecht, 1995), 121–33, at 122, for this double face of the angel in Bar 6:7.
14. Jer 29:1 MT/36:1 LXX has a specified list of addressees, but this Letter is directed to the first Golah eleven years before the destruction of Jerusalem.

every person among the exiles is addressed as a person able to resist and as a person belonging to a minority different from the world outside.

Verses 2-6 develop a sharp difference, even a dichotomy, between the Judeans who will be exiled and the world they will meet in their exile. They will be subjected to the power of the Babylonian Empire, but they have a reference outside these structures: their God, who, as a superpower, has everything under control but demands loyalty to him alone. They will meet a world reflecting the power of the empire, but they have the means to resist the fascination and temptation of that world. The gender of the addressees is not specified; women as addressees are not visible on the literary level but seem to be "included" as exiles and also among those who have transgressed God's commandments. The gender of the Babylonian gods is not specified either; they all represent the wrong concept of the divine visible in their images.

Mockery, First Part: The Images, Their Houses, Their Inanimateness (6:8-29)

Verses 8-29 consist of three sub-passages: 8-16; 17-23; and 24-29. Each one concludes with the nearly identical line "From this it is evident that they are not gods; so do not fear them." The subject of "fear" or "awe" introduced in v. 4 reappears here; the observations given intend to remove any fear of the foreign gods, or, more precisely, want to prevent awe of the foreign deities or their images among those in the audience. At the same time, the length and intensity of the speech mirrors the *tremendum et fascinosum* experienced by the implied authors when confronted with these images.

The first sub-passage, vv. 8-16, deals with the appearance of the images and demystifies them by a rhetorical strategy that could be labelled "semiotic unmasking." The second sub-passage, vv. 17-23, takes a view of the alleged sacred spaces where the images are to be found and uses the strategy of rhetorical desacralization. And the third sub-passage, vv. 24-29, focuses on the images' inanimateness and rejects as illusive the idea that animation might be in them.

Sub-Passage 1: Splendid Appearances Are Deceiving (6:8-16)

What catches the eye of a reader in the first sub-passage is the repeated notion of gold and silver as part of the appearance of the gods or their images. Gold and silver strike the eye of someone who looks at such images; it fascinates, suggests power—and has to be demystified. Again the argumentation focuses on visibility, presupposes the impressive

Bar 6:8-16

⁸Their tongues are smoothed by the carpenter, and they themselves are overlaid with gold and silver; but they are false and cannot speak. ⁹People take gold and make crowns for the heads of their gods, as they might for a girl who loves ornaments. ¹⁰Sometimes the priests secretly take gold and silver from their gods and spend it on themselves, ¹¹or even give some of it to the prostitutes on the terrace. They deck their gods out with garments like human beings—these gods of silver and gold and wood ¹²that cannot save themselves from rust and corrosion.[15] When they have been dressed in purple robes, ¹³their faces are wiped because of the dust from the temple, which is thick upon them. ¹⁴One of them holds a scepter, like a district judge, but is unable to destroy anyone who offends it. ¹⁵Another has a dagger in its right hand, and an ax, but cannot defend itself from war and robbers. ¹⁶From this it is evident that they are not gods; so do not fear them.

TRANSLATION MATTERS

6:8 *they themselves*: αὐτὰ is neuter gender: "those things."

6:11 *terrace*: τέγος, literally: "roof." See discussion below.

power of the visible, and seeks to uncover as deceiving what has been seen: never rely upon your eye (alone)!

Three observations implying demystification are set forth in vv. 8-11. First, contrary to being covered with gold and silver and thus appearing powerful, those images "cannot speak" (v. 8). Their finely modeled tongue pretends what is not the case; these images are false and deceitful—a catchword to reappear often in the whole speech. Here it might, on the one hand, refer to the images themselves, ridiculing the notion that a ritual of mouth-opening would bestow divine power on the idol with its carved tongue.[16] On the other hand, their priests are

---

15. Text-critical matters: v. 12 "corrosion": Greek literally, βρῶμα, "that which is eaten" = food. This might go back to a different vocalization of the Hebrew אכל; not "what is eaten" (*'akhul*) but "the eater" (*'okhel*), i.e., a moth or a worm. In this case a better translation would be "woodworm" instead of "corrosion." The Greek translator might have thought of impure food served to the gods; see vv. 29, 30.

16. See Angelika Berlejung, "Washing the Mouth: The Consecration of Divine Images in Mesopotamia," in *The Image and the Book: Iconic Cults, Aniconism, and the Rise of the Book Religion in Israel and the Ancient Near East*, ed. Karel van der Toorn, CBET 21 (Leuven: Peeters, 1997).

deceiving because their words, mediated through the images, cannot have a divine origin. Second, the golden crowns are just ornaments the gods are thought to be fond of, like "a girl who loves ornaments" (v. 9). What seems tolerable for a girl is ridiculous for gods. Third, the precious material used for the images serves dubious aims when priests enrich themselves with it[17] or give it away to "prostitutes on the terrace" (v. 11a).

The exact meaning of "prostitutes on the terrace" is controversial. That priests give gold to prostitutes suggests that they go to these women to use them. The matter offensive to the early Jewish readers might have been a mingling of the sphere of the divine and the sphere of prostitution, be it through sexual contact between priests and whores—although Levitical prescriptions prohibit only marriage of priests to whores, not sex (Lev 21:7)—or rather through a transfer of gold for the deity to these women.[18] But why is prostitution described as taking place "on the terrace" (or, more literally, τέγος, the "roof")? Could this be a secondary Greek interpretation of an originally Aramaic text pointing to the hire of a prostitute?[19] Is "roof" simply a general designation for a brothel?[20] Could the allusion be to a brothel in the temple precinct, or to a brothel organized by cult officials?[21] From a Jewish perspective, both types of institutions would have been unthinkable, given the prescription that a prostitute's wage should not come into the temple (Deut 23:18; Mic 1:7), as well as the detestation behind the remark that the Greek invaders of Jerusalem

---

17. A similar deceiving activity, priests secretly taking the food offerings of the deity, is a motif in Bel and the Dragon (Dan 14).

18. T. Levi 14:5 has another problem, priests eating sacrificial food together with whores.

19. Dieter Kellermann, "Apokryphes Obst. Bemerkungen zur Epistula Jeremiae (Baruch Kap. 6), insbesondere zu Vers 42," ZDMG 129 (1979): 23–42, at 27–28.

20. Thus Wolfgang Kraus and Georg Gäbel, trans., "Epistole Jeremiu/Der Brief des Jeremia," in *Septuaginta deutsch. Das griechische Alte Testament in deutscher* Übersetzung, ed. Martin Karrer and Wolfgang Kraus (Stuttgart: Deutsche Bibelgesellschaft, 2009), 1358–61, at 1359. Heinrich Reusch, *Erklärung des Buchs Baruch* (Freiburg i. Br.: Herder, 1853), 242, compares the different translations of the *qubbah*, the place where the Israelite man and the non-Israelite women meet according to Num 25:8: Aquila translates as *tegos*, Symmachos as *porneion*, and the Vulgate as *lupanar*; all of these interpreting the *qubbah* as a brothel. Knabenbauer provides similar explanations in "Commentarius in Baruch," in *Commentarius in Danielem prophetam, Lamentationes et Baruch. Cursus Scripturae Sacrae* III/2 (Paris: Lethielleux, 1889), 505–6. The Nova Vulgata edition 1979 accepts this translation for Bar 6:10.

21. See Tanja S. Scheer and Martin Lindner, eds., *Tempelprostitution im Altertum. Fakten und Fiktionen* (Berlin: Verlag Antike e.K., 2009), 10, which covers the whole ancient Eastern Mediterranean world for these necessary differentiations.

had intercourse with women in the temple area (2 Macc 6:4). An even further-reaching explanation considers that the term "whore" is part of a rhetorical defamation sensible in the whole speech.[22] The women labeled "whores" might have been, from a Babylonian perspective, women serving in or for a temple and practicing specific rites, with or even without sexuality being involved.[23] The common denominator behind all these possibilities to explain the passage is the Priestly-Levitical concept of separation between cult and sexuality, a concept Jeremiah's letter seems to take for granted for its implied audience.

On the whole, this little example shows how difficult it is to draw historical information from a highly polemical text. With certainty, one can affirm its defamatory implications for the priests mentioned. And definitely the text's rhetorical use of women figures who are dubious in the eyes of the implied addressees of the Letter constructs Babylonian reality as detestable and monstrous in order to shame the gods' priests and cults of the "other." More precisely, the case of the young woman who loves her jewels brings in a certain well-known cliché associated with women[24] in order to ridicule the idols. And the case of the "whores" either distorts women's lived reality in a cultic context or blames the priests of the "other" for detesting practices involving women, with no regard for these women themselves. In both cases the argument works because, for the implied authors of Jeremiah's letter, such reality and practice has negative connotations, and the implied readers—or auditors—accept this kind of boundary marking. We do not know anything about the reaction to the Letter of the primary real readers or listeners, but there is no reason to assume that women would have been resistant or more resistant than men to this message.

22. See Luis Alonso Schökel, "Carta de Jeremias," in *Daniel – Baruc – Carta de Jeremias – Lamentaciones*, Los Libros Sagrados 18 (Madrid: Ediciones Cristiandad, 1976), 171.

23. Kratz, "Brief des Jeremia," 93, mentions scholars referring to Herodotus, *Histories* 1.181. Herodotus describes a huge tower with a cell on top where a women would pass the night to wait for the god who chooses her, a passage often interpreted as referring to a "sacred marriage rite." Saldarini sees Herodotus referring to "ritual prostitution." See Anthony J. Saldarini, "The Letter of Jeremiah: Introduction, Commentary, and Reflections," in *Introduction to Prophetic Literature, Isaiah, Jeremiah, Baruch, the Letter of Jeremiah, Lamentations, Ezekiel*, ed. Leander E. Keck, NIB 6 (Nashville, TN: Abingdon Press, 2001), 983–1010, at 995. The scholarly literature is permeated by similar terms combined with manifold and sometimes voyeuristic or at least orientalizing attitudes. For a differentiated approach to the subject of so-called sacred prostitution, see the contributions in Scheer and Lindner, *Tempelprostitution*.

24. This is a cliché on which the first Letter to Timothy seems to play too; see 1 Tim 2:9-13; see also 1 En. 8:1 (women [and men?] are taught by fallen angels to use jewels).

Subalterns Speak Up: Dalit Women, Part 3

The Letter of Jeremiah is in its entirety a polemic against the Babylonian gods. Hinduism, unlike the monotheistic religions of Islam, Judaism, and Christianity, but like the Babylonian religions, is polytheistic. From a Dalit perspective, one has to be clear which gods we are talking about: are we talking about the gods of the subaltern or about the gods of the oppressors who keep the structures of caste and power going? The Dalits and Dalit women do find hope, solace, liberation, support, relief, and consolation when they worship and offer sacrifice to "their" gods; some even think "that dalits do have their own separate religion, belief systems, and rituals" and are not "part of the Hindu fold."[25] However, entering into the temple of the great Hindu traditions can be a privilege and honor for them. Viramma narrates her entry into the famous Tirupati temple: "It was the first time in my life that I'd travelled so far! When we arrived at the foot of the mountain, we started climbing the steps that lead to the temple. Just before we got there, our priest started singing about [the deity] Perumal. When he stopped, we shouted, 'Govinda! Govinda!' and we did so very reverently because it was the first time that we people of the ceri had gone into a temple."[26]

In addition to the gold and silver coating the wooden figure, cult im-ages can be clothed with precious garments, underlining their powerful divine splendor or splendid divine power, and invested with special equipment (paraphernalia), indicating their specific abilities or qualities. Jeremiah's letter affirms that the beautiful garments just cover corruption and dirt underneath, corrosion of the metallic coat, and probably rot in the wooden figure (vv. 11-12). Again the text invites the audience to imagine what the eye cannot perceive and to think of deceit. Dirt or dust, as in the next observation, can also be detected on the visible surface of the statues and has to be wiped away to help them keep their faces shin-ing (v. 13). The argument shows the impotence of the alleged powerful ones. Along this line, scepter, dagger, and ax are paraphernalia express-ing royal or juridical authority and success in fighting or war (vv. 14-15).

25. Shalini Mulackal, "Dalit Belief Systems and Rituals," in John and Massey, *The-ology for a New Community*, 144.

26. Viramma, Racine, and Racine, *Viramma*, 102.

Gods can turn into gods of the oppressors when they are used as tools to oppress the subalterns. Dalits and Dalit women mock them and ridicule them. While narrating the ritual called Pachvi, Baby Kamble criticizes and brings out well how the ideology of a religion is used to oppress people. She says, "It was believed that the goddess Satwai and the god Barama visited the house at midnight to write the baby's future on its forehead. Barama, it was believed, had a pen with which he made Satwai write the fate of the baby. There is a saying that Barama's words and Satwai's writing are indelible and can never be wiped off. . . . But didn't all the babies in the Mahar community [one of the lower castes in North India] share the same fate? So what was there to write on the forehead of each baby? . . . Or they must have made one common stamp for all the Mahar children! . . . Today, if we come across Barama and Satwai, we would like to give them both a sound thrashing and ask, 'Barama and Satwai, you ruined the lives of generation after generation of the Mahars!' "[27]

Anthony John Baptist

Again, these signs do not fulfill what they promise; they only reveal the pseudo-power of those who keep them. For the (implied) Jewish readers, the mockery of the statues of Bel and Nebo, packed on "beasts and cattle" so that the people of Babylon can take them away on their flight (Isa 46:1-2), might come to mind. A specific turn of irony can be seen in the fact that Jeremiah's letter dares a satiric mockery, and no God takes up arms to requite the offence.

The passage in vv. 8-15 makes use of a rhetorical strategy I want to label "semiotic unmasking" or, more precisely, "unmasking by semiotic means": a sign—here taken not as letters of a word, but as a real object with significance—is separated from its ordinary significance or meaning and from its expected reference. The Letter of Jeremiah presupposes the idea that the (real) signs of gold, silver, crown, or scepter point to or signify royal, even divine dignity and power. Hence, images invested with these signs suggest that they are or represent gods. To suspend that plausibility, the text starts at two possible points. A first approach focuses on the precious materials of the signs and shows that it can be used for dubious purposes. By this new reference—gold being given to prostitutes, jewels

27. Kamble, *The Prisons We Broke*, 62.

used by girls fond of them—the meaning of the signs (divine dignity or power) becomes dubious. A second approach focuses on the signs the images are invested with and appeals to the audience's experience that the meaning of those signs is not unequivocal: clothes might cover mere dirt; weapons do not prevent a statue being stolen or burned. These signs do not necessarily refer to the divine; on the contrary, they might refer to shameful realities. Hence it follows that they cannot be considered as proof of divinity. To summarize: the strategy detectible in vv. 8-15 could be labeled deconstructive in the sense that it seeks to delegitimize hegemonic constructions of reality by multiplying meanings and references of signs. The consequence of this rhetoric is obvious: fear or awe of gods who are unveiled as mere constructions is nonsense.

The strategy detected here refuses to think only about concrete evidence; it mocks such thinking. Could this be linked to the observation that, in the Letter of Jeremiah, no direct statement about the God of Israel is made? Jeremiah 10:1-16 is supposed to have inspired Jeremiah's letter, yet it spells out explicitly and repeatedly the contrast between the idols and the true God. The silence of the Letter, in this regard, is all the more striking.

Sub-Passage 2: The Space/Place of the Gods and Its Desacralization (6:17-23)

The second sub-passage (vv. 17-23) addresses the cult statues' place in a temple.[28] A temple is the holy space hosting the divine images, and the images, representations, even incarnations of the deities, contribute to the holiness of such a place. Uncompromisingly, Jeremiah's letter aims at the nimbus of holiness surrounding the place or space of the cult statues.

The stated uselessness of the images (vv. 17-18a) could be a conclusion drawn from the last lines in the first passage, linking this second passage to the first and introducing the new focus on the statues standing in their temples. Again, the dust on the images was already mentioned (v. 13), but now the source of this dust is specified: it comes from those who have the intention or the duty of worshiping or fulfilling necessary services for the images. The text seems to pace out what can be observed in a temple and denigrates it. Two lines of argument emerge: the first reveals that the images cannot use their senses; they neither see what happens (v. 19) nor feel it (vv. 20-22). A splendid, bright illumination of the temple is useless; the oil lamps and torches produce only smoke,

28. See how proudly the scribe of the Ephesians reports about the temple of his city with the famous image of Artemis, Acts 19:21-40.

¹⁷For just as someone's dish is useless when it is broken, ¹⁸so are their gods when they have been set up in the temples. Their eyes are full of the dust raised by the feet of those who enter. And just as the gates are shut on every side against anyone who has offended a king, as though under sentence of death, so the priests make their temples secure with doors and locks and bars, in order that they may not be plundered by robbers. ¹⁹They light more lamps for them than they light for themselves, though their gods can see none of them. ²⁰They are just like a beam of the temple, but their hearts, it is said, are eaten away when crawling creatures from the earth devour them and their robes. They do not notice ²¹when their faces have been blackened by the smoke of the temple. ²²Bats, swallows, and birds alight on their bodies and heads; and so do cats.[29] ²³From this you will know that they are not gods; so do not fear them.

TRANSLATION MATTERS

6:23 *do not fear them*: μὴ φοβεῖσθε αὐτά, Greek, neuter: "do not fear those things."

---

which turns the golden faces of the images dark. These images are without senses or sense-less.

Along the second line, the temples seem to be seen as a site of death, as a tomb, and, consequently, as a site of impurity, hence, in the extreme, even the opposite of holiness: temples are "full of dust" like tombs (v. 18); the images are imprisoned in their temples like criminals who await their "sentence of death" (v. 18); the garments and wooden figure of the statues are "eaten away" by worms, like corpses in their tombs (v. 20); the birds fluttering around the images (v. 22) might bring to mind ruins or tombs. If this line is intentional, it is an extreme example of rhetorical desacralization or profanation, as priests, according to the Levitical purity law (Lev 21:1-4; 22:4-8), are not allowed to come close to corpses or to spaces of death. Again, the gods of the "others" and their priests are blamed according to the logics of one's own in-group rules. Again, there

---

29. Text-critical matter: v. 22 "cats": αἴλουροι. The Greek verb used in this phrase (ἐφίπταμαι) is a *hapax legomenon* in the LXX, meaning "to fly" (toward, onto, or over). It fits for the flying creatures mentioned but not for the cats. By the way, this is the only instance in the whole Bible where cats are mentioned. Could it be that these cats are a later (Greek?) addition? See the discussion in Kellermann, *Apokryphes Obst*, 28–29.

is no reason to believe that women in this group would resist such rhetoric.

Sub-Passage 3: Illusive Animateness (6:24-29)

In the last sequence of part 1 (vv. 24-29), the red thread seems to be the animation or, more accurately, the inanimateness of the images. Before stating this explicitly (v. 25) and developing it, the first observation links the passage to the preceding one: they do not shine without human assistance (v. 24; cf. v. 21); their radiance, though, would be a sign of their divine life. Readers of or listeners to Jeremiah's letter might think, in contrast, of the God of Israel living in splendid glory. A first proof of the images' inanimateness is that they did not realize their own coming into being (v. 24b). Another argument: they have to be carried, as they have no feet (v. 26). To be carried in sedan-chairs or sitting on a throne is, in many cultures, the privilege of rulers. (One might think of the papal *sedia gestatoria*, which was still in use at the Second Vatican Council.) While such treatment could be considered a sign of the divinity of the images, the Letter of Jeremiah turns it against them, pointing to their lack of feet, a defect which is better remaining shamefully hidden. The grammar of honor and shame is extremely meaningful for at least some groups in early Judaism (see particularly the writing of Ben Sira and also Baruch). That grammar is brought in here in a twofold expression of "worthlessness" (better, "dishonor") and "put to shame" (v. 26). And furthermore, adapting an argument from prophetical idol polemics (Isa 40:18-19; 41:7), the Letter points out that the images cannot change their position without help (v. 27).

A last set of observations concerns offerings to the deities with respect to their images. The Letter distinguishes between gifts (δῶρα; v. 27) and sacrifices (θυσίαι; v. 29). The former are related to a form of cult of the dead, hence again denigrated by semiotic shifting, accompanied by the repeated affirmation that these images are like the dead. As to the sacrifices, the reproach is that the images do not prevent misuse of the food reserved for them. Were they alive, they would stand up against it with anger (vv. 28-29)!

The passage (vv. 28-29) has in mind a threefold misuse, given the accepted Levitical practice that sacrificial meat offered by worshipers will not be served completely for the deities; parts of it can be kept for the maintenance of the priesthood, and parts might be sold to the public. A first misuse mentioned regards the proceeds of the meat sold. Again, as in v. 10, the priests are characterized as greedy, using the proceeds

Bar 6:24-29

²⁴As for the gold that they wear for beauty—it will not shine unless someone wipes off the tarnish; for even when they were being cast, they did not feel it. ²⁵They are bought without regard to cost, but there is no breath in them. ²⁶Having no feet, they are carried on the shoulders of others, revealing to humankind their worthlessness. And those who serve them are put to shame ²⁷because, if any of these gods fall to the ground, they themselves must pick it up. If anyone sets it upright, it cannot move itself; and if it is tipped over, it cannot straighten itself. Gifts are placed before them just as before the dead. ²⁸The priests sell the sacrifices that are offered to these gods and use the money themselves. Likewise their wives preserve some of the meat with salt, but give none to the poor or helpless. ²⁹Sacrifices to them may even be touched by women in their periods or at childbirth. Since you know by these things that they are not gods, do not fear them.

TRANSLATION MATTERS

6:26 *worthlessness*: ἀτιμίαν, better: "dishonor."

6:26 *those who serve them*: θεραπεύοντες αὐτὰ, Greek, neuter pronoun: "who serve those things."

6:28 *helpless*: ἀδύνατος, literally: "those without power." See Lev 19:15 LXX, where the poor and the powerful stand together. The choice of vocabulary in v. 28 might stem from this Levitical perspective. Lev 19:15 MT has דל and גדול, hence clearly social differences of low and high.

6:29 *women in their periods*: ἀποκαθημένη, literally: a woman "who sits apart," i.e., a woman who has her menstruation and takes care not to come close to people or objects.

for themselves instead of returning them to the temple. In the second and third misuse, again, women in their company are involved. This time, the priests' wives are focused on as members of the Priestly family, engaging in a cultural technique well-known since ancient times, which they pass on to the next generation: preserving meat by salting. The critical point is their refusal to share this highly precious and costly food with others who do not have access to meat. In the eyes of the implied authors and readers, the women in the Priestly families of the "others" do not respect a fundamental principle of Torah—care for the poor—and thus demean their Priestly class. Another critical point regards inappropriate periods for women to touch sacrificial material. Evidently the reference principles are again those of Torah, here the way to deal with discharges of body liquids, in particular female blood (Lev 12; 15). The sacrifices appointed for a deity of the Babylonians do not conform to the Levitical prescriptions, making these sacrifices "impure," the opposite of "holy." What seems to be a horror for the implied authors (and recipients) of the Letter is projected onto the "others."

Subalterns Speak Up: Dalit Women, Part 4

Verse 29 of the Letter of Jeremiah speaks of the women in their menstrual periods or after childbirth. In patriarchal thinking, menstruation and childbirth are considered as a time of impurity. The Greek word used to refer to the women in their periods is ἀποκαθημένη, literally meaning "a woman who sits apart." This implicitly means that they should not come close to people or objects. Then one can imagine how much more it is with gods and things related to idols and cult. In the same line of thought one must take v. 30b, where women are mentioned who serve meals for gods. The implicit reason for such prohibition seems to be that they are impure because of their menstruation. While Lev 15 speaks of impurity of both men and women, this text speaks only of the impurity of women.

In many societies women are relegated to a lower level because of their menstruation. The same thing is applicable to Dalit women too. In the caste ideology, even natural menstruation and childbirth are seen as impure. Thus, even the high-caste women are seen as impure while their men are pure. The duration of seclusion at puberty differs according to castes. It is longer in the case of higher-caste women, while it is shorter for lower-caste women. For the former, celebration of puberty ritual is associated with their social status. Since the Dalit women have less to lose in terms of power and status, and are needed for agricultural work, it is shorter for them. The Dalit women do not have any solemn celebration during their first menstruation time. In a novel by Imaiyam, the Dalit girl assists herself without any ceremony attached to it by taking a bath and carrying on the routine work. She helps her mother during her menstrual days.[30] Fulfilling her duty as daughter, that is, taking care of her mother, is more important to her than the purity laws.

Anthony John Baptist

30. Imaiyam (V. Annamalai), *Koveru Kazhudaigal* (Chennai: Crea, 1994), 16.

Levitical purity prescriptions on bodily liquids apply to men and women alike. Both can have regular or irregular emissions, as the well-balanced composition of Lev 15:1-32 underlines and discusses.[31] Therefore it is conspicuous that only women are taken as a test case in this passage. Their "impurity" is considered a more complex issue than that of men; women have to spend longer uninterrupted periods apart from people and objects they would contaminate. Therefore, they might have been more plausible candidates for the implied authors as well as for their readers to illustrate the abomination of the "others" regarding purity and holiness. On the other hand, what emerges as the profile of a "good" wife in a Priestly family is her taking care of the poor and powerless and her paying attention to cultic purity, as far as her body is concerned. Before criticizing this from a Christian or a modern secular point of view, one should take seriously that within this Levitical/Priestly concept, bodily purity cannot be separated from social sensibility, as both are aspects of respecting God's holiness.

Mockery, Second Part: The Illusive Power of the Images (6:30-65)

The rhetorical question, "For how can they be called gods?" (v. 30a), can be understood as an introduction or even a motto to the second part of the speech, since expectations one would direct toward "true" gods are tested for correlation with reality, all ending in negative results. Quite a number of motifs used in the first part appear again under new perspectives. While the first part developed the discrepancy between visible appearance and the reality behind the visible, the second part focuses on power and effectiveness (or, rather, ineffectiveness) of the deities.

The structure, here less clear, has refrain-type formulae of greater variation than in part 1 and section breaks that are sometimes difficult to explain. One possible way to break down vv. 30-65 is to recognize seven

---

31. See the analysis by Dorothea Erbele-Küster, *Körper und Geschlecht. Studien zur Anthropologie von Leviticus 12 und 15*, WMANT 121 (Neukirchen-Vluyn: Neukirchener Verlag, 2008), 531–38; see also Dorothea Erbele-Küster, "Gender and Cult: 'Pure' and 'Impure' as Gender-Relevant Categories," in *Torah: The Bible and the Women*, vol. 1, ed. Irmtraud Fischer and Mercedes Navarro Puerto (Atlanta, GA: SBL Press, 2011), 375–406.

Bar 6:30a

[30a]For how can they be called gods?

sub-passages.[32] Those who wish to do so can find two suggestive numerical patterns: the structure of 3+7=10 units in the two principal parts of the speech; the structure of 3+7+2=12, including the two final sections vv. 66-69+70-72.

Sub-Passage 1: Cults without Dignity, Images without Power (6:30b-40a)

In this first sub-passage of the second mockery, two sets of reproaches are bound together: the Priestly class in its entirety is involved in cultic practices unworthy of true gods (vv. 30b-34a), and these gods do not fulfill their beneficial roles for humans (vv. 35-38). The bridging idea seems to be the incapacity of the statues to prevent shameful treatment or to act like deities; v. 34b forms a transitory statement between the two units. As in vv. 28-29a, the two areas of cult and of political-ethical action are again kept together, typical for a Levitical/Priestly approach.

The first part of the speech (vv. 10-11; 28-29) paints everyday practices in the Priestly families as abominable in the eyes of the implied Jewish readers and listeners. Now the shift is actually to cultic acts. Verses 31-32 focus on a ritual performed by the (male) priests. The description of what can be seen (torn garments, shaved heads) and heard (shouting and howling) resembles a lament, and indeed the text compares the ritual to a funeral meal. Whereas in part 1 the references to the world of the dead remained rather indirect, here the insinuation is made plain, and for the implied early Jewish audience the message is unmistakable: such a cult does not respect the rules of Priestly purity and runs counter to God's holiness. The Greek text of v. 31, taken literally, adds to this scene the element of a chariot driven by the priests. The idea could be that, similar to the major public processions, there are minor ones within the temple compounds in which the statues are placed on chariots and led around. Combined with the funeral meal, the picture is that

---

32. In this I modify my analysis in Marie-Theres Wacker, "Baruch: Mail from Distant Shores," in *Feminist Biblical Interpretation: A Compendium of Critical Commentary on the Books of the Bible and Related Literature,* ed. Luise Schottroff and Marie-Theres Wacker (Grand Rapids, MI: Eerdmans, 2012), 31–38.

Bar 6:30b-40a

30bWomen serve meals for gods of silver and gold and wood; 31and in their temples the priests sit[33] with their clothes torn, their heads and beards shaved, and their heads uncovered. 32They howl and shout before their gods as some do at a funeral banquet. 33The priests take some of the clothing of their gods to clothe their wives and children. 34Whether one does evil to them or good, they will not be able to repay it. They cannot set up a king or depose one. 35Likewise they are not able to give either wealth or money; if one makes a vow to them and does not keep it, they will not require it. 36They cannot save anyone from death or rescue the weak from the strong. 37They cannot restore sight to the blind; they cannot rescue one who is in distress. 38They cannot take pity on a widow or do good to an orphan. 39These things that are made of wood and overlaid with gold and silver are like stones from the mountain, and those who serve them will be put to shame. 40aWhy then must anyone think that they are gods, or call them gods?

of an extensive ritual for the dead, hence further ridiculing the statues and their priests.

That these priests themselves are unworthy of true gods can be proven by their not respecting the distinction between sacred and profane. They take some of the clothing manufactured for the gods or given as votive offering by worshipers and bring it home for their families, their wives and children (v. 33). As in vv. 10-11, personal enrichment is at stake,[34] combined with a transgression of boundaries.[35]

Sub-passage 1 opens with a glimpse of women, this time not introduced as wives of priests but in a role of their own: they are active in the service of their gods (v. 30b). They serve drink and food offerings, which means that they fulfill a Priestly task, part of the complex sacrificial cult.

33. Text-critical matter: v. 31; the Greek verb διφρεύω, translated by NRSV as "the priests sit," literally means "to drive a chariot." Possibly the Semitic (Hebrew) verb נהג, which has two meanings, to drive and to groan, is at the base of the Greek translation. The idea might be that the priests, in their temples, perform processions and lead the chariots with the statues. NRSV "sit" corresponds to the Latin text of the Vulgate, not to the Greek of the LXX.

34. The story of Bel is even more radical, showing the Priestly families, the priests, their wives and children, entering the temple of Bel by night and consuming the offerings dedicated to the deity—an early case of Priestly fraud! This story can be found in the NRSV as "Bel and the Dragon" and in other editions of the Bible as Daniel 14.

35. The motif is not strictly in line with the perspective on ritual in vv. 30b-32; it might have been attracted by the keyword "clothes" and developed like an implication.

Subalterns Speak Up: Dalit Women, Part 5

Dalit women express their view on menstruation in their lifecycle rituals like puberty rituals. They affirm the girl as a sexual being, calling for restrained behavior on her part and the need for protection and vigilance on the part of the parents. In other words, these rituals affirm the personhood of the girl. Viramma narrates her experience when she had her first periods: "We had only just left the ceri when I felt something running down my thigh. . . . I lifted my underskirt and found, to my horror, blood, fresh blood. . . . Seeing what was happening, Grandmother Subbu didn't panic at all. Quite the opposite: she told me that it was a happy event and that she was proud to witness."[36] When the girls attain puberty, they are confined to a secluded place in the house or in a tent made outside of the house. They have to be there without touching anything in the house and doing nothing. Special food items are prepared and served to them and special attention is given to them. Viramma explains the reason, "It was a strange moment in my life: on the one hand, I was rejected and confined because I was unclean; on the other I was constantly surrounded. I felt that the reason I was being cared for so well was to tear me away from childhood and throw me into the real life of an adult. A woman had to be made out of me in those eleven days."[37]

Though the prophet Jeremiah may be justified in taking an apologetic stance against the religion and deities of Babylonians, given the fear of Israelites being carried away to other religions during their exile, today in our multireligious context of India and South Asia one cannot be heavily critical of these religions. While we, the Christians, are deeply rooted in our faith, we also make an attempt to understand other religions, their beliefs and religious practices. Though the oppressors use religions as tools to oppress people, for the subalterns these religions are means of hope, solace, and consolation. This gives added reason to understand or at least attempt to understand the religion of the other positively.

Anthony John Baptist

36. Viramma, Racine, and Racine, *Viramma*, 29.
37. Ibid., 34.

The problem in the eyes of the implied authors cannot be the type of offering, since drink and food offerings (cereals and meat) also belong to the cultic service in the temple of Jerusalem even in the time of the Second Temple. The problem is the activity of female personnel in the sacrificial cult. The Letter of Jeremiah seems to presuppose that in the temple of Jerusalem only male priests are involved in the maintenance of the God of Israel. Indeed, as far as we know, the sacrificial cult during the time of the Second Temple was in the hands of male priests only, even though in preexilic times the so-called קדשות ("holy women," often misunderstood as "cultic prostitutes") might have been part of temple practices (see Hos 4:12-14).[38] In the Letter of Jeremiah, a sacrificial cult without women becomes a distinctive difference between Israel and the nations and thereby an important normative rule for the correct attitude to the holiness of God and the temple. The reason why women should not serve meals to God, why women should not act as priests, remains unexplained. If one assumes a catchword style as a characteristic of the text, a link can be seen between v. 29, women touching the offerings during menstruation and after childbirth, and v. 30b, women serving meals to their gods. Note that the text denies the title of "priests" to these women in contrast to their male colleagues, thus linguistically underlining the conviction that women cannot be priests.

While in Judaism after the destruction of the Second Temple in 70 CE there was no need for discussion of women priests, it became a topic in emerging Christianity. Reasons given in official documents of the Catholic Church for the exclusion of women from the priesthood are theologically questionable. The cultural argument that many societies in the Southern Hemisphere are not ready to accept women priests seems to point to the problem of ongoing patriarchy in these societies instead of providing guidance on how to solve it.

Verse 34b, read as a conclusion to what precedes it, describes the incapacity of the gods to react to all the practices of their female and male servants that dishonor them. The verse also might function as an introduction to what follows: these Gods cannot requite the good or evil deeds of their followers; nor are they able to act on their own for the sake of

---

38. See Marie-Theres Wacker, " 'Kultprostitution' im Alten Israel? Forschungsmythen, Spuren, Thesen," in Scheer and Lindner, *Tempelprostitution im Altertum*, 55–84, and Christine Stark, *"Kultprostitution" im Alten Testament? Die Qedeschen der Hebräischen Bibel und das Motiv der Hurerei*, OBO 221 (Göttingen: Vandenhoeck & Ruprecht, 2006).

those who are in need. If v. 34b aims at the very foundations of a society with its legitimate ruler, the text would call into question the political foundations of Babylon altogether. Verses 36-37 refer to desperate situations and severe handicaps. The explicit mention of blindness is very concrete; it mirrors a very common problem in antiquity and also in many regions of our contemporary world. In the context of Jeremiah's letter, it highlights the incapacity of gods whose eyes are full of dust (v. 18). Implied listeners to the Letter are invited to think of the psalms in their tradition with their expressions of despair, hope in salvific interventions by God, and thanks and praise for being heard. The Letter ignores the fact that the Babylonian religion uses very similar prayers of distress, hope, and thanksgiving and that the religious experience of the people might have much in common with the early Jewish community addressed. The implied authors do not give an accounting for their own convictions and do not reflect on the philosophical reach of their arguments; they are interested not in comparative studies of religions but in delineating boundaries.

Verse 38 (see also v. 33) mentions women with their children again, but here as a group of needy persons. Widows and orphans, according to the Torah, are under the special protection of Israel's God, while, following Jeremiah's letter, the gods of Babylon do not care for the weakest of society. On the contrary, they allow their priests to have in mind only their own interests. A statement of this kind is convincing and would disqualify those to whom it refers.

The closing lines (vv. 39-40) come back to the rhetorical technique of reducing the gods to mere objects and to their material elements, adding a comparison that underlines their fragmentary, ridiculous state. As a consequence, those who adhere to these gods lose face according to the grammar of honor and shame. Given all this, the final question must be a rhetorical one: why would anybody think that they are gods?

Sub-Passage 2: Self-Deception and Derision in the Cult of the Images (6:40b-44)

The second sub-passage is clearly demarcated: it opens with an adverb introducing an additional observation ("besides" or "furthermore"); its conclusion is a rhetorical question nearly identical to v. 40a. Again, two apparently very different subjects are bound together, one of them once more linked to women. The motif of "speaking" seems to form a thematic bridge. As a catchword from the preceding section (v. 39), "dishonor"

Bar 6:40b-44

40bBesides, even the Chaldeans themselves dishonor them; for when they see someone who cannot speak, they bring Bel and pray that the mute may speak, as though Bel were able to understand! 41Yet they themselves cannot perceive this and abandon them, for they have no sense. 42And the women, with cords around them, sit along the passageways, burning bran for incense. 43When one of them is led off by one of the passers-by and is taken to bed by him, she derides the woman next to her, because she was not as attractive as herself and her cord was not broken. 44Whatever is done for these idols is false. Why then must anyone think that they are gods, or call them gods?

(v. 40b) is the link between the two examples given, and the (dis)quali-fication of "falseness" connects this passage to the very beginning of the mockery (v. 8).

The first example concerns a person unable to speak. According to the translation of the NRSV, the Letter alludes to a ritual with a (smaller) cult statue set before the mute person and a prayer recited. An alternative interpretation of the grammar suggests that the mute was brought before the statue, waiting for an oracle. In biblical and early Jewish writings, the name of Bel ("Master") refers to a Babylonian deity, in most cases Marduk. Perhaps the concrete naming of the deity here seeks to evoke other shame-ful memories as alluded to in Isa 46:1-2; Jer 50:2; 51:44; and the whole story of Bel and the Dragon (Dan 14). As, for the implied authors, it is clear that a statue has no sensory or intellectual perception, so they can ridicule this ceremony. The mockery is specifically ironic as it is again (v. 8) directed against the "other's" basic conviction that deities represented by statues are able to communicate with humans after the ritual of mouth opening was exercised on them. Verse 41 is difficult to interpret; the pronoun used in the verse seems to extend the sense-less-ness of the im-ages to their servants or worshipers.

The second example in vv. 42-43 concerns a scene about which there is much speculation in scholarly research.[39] Again, women are the center of attention. The picture painted is concrete and vague at the same time: "the women, with cords around them, sit along the passageways, burning bran for incense" (v. 42). Someone listening to this description could imagine that the women of the "Chaldeans" (= the Babylonians) used to sit at any street and that the streets in Babylonian cities were thronged

---

39. For a summary, see Stark, *"Kultprostitution" im Alten Testament*, 19–21.

TRANSLATION MATTERS

6:40 *dishonor them*: ἀτιμαζόντων αὐτά, Greek, neuter pronoun: "dishonor those things."

6:40 *they bring Bel and pray that the mute may speak*: προσενεγκάμενοι τὸν Βῆλον ἀξιοῦσιν φωνῆσαι, alternative rendering: "they bring the mute, expecting that Bel may speak."

6:41 *abandon them*: καταλιπεῖν αὐτά, Greek, neuter: "abandon those things."

6:44 *these idols*: αὐτοῖς; the Greek has the demonstrative pronoun only: αὐτοῖς, "these." As throughout the Letter, the statues are called "gods" (except the very last verse, where the Greek word εἴδωλον, "idol," appears); an insertion of the word "idol" into the text should be avoided.

with women in a strange outfit and offering incense, an activity evoking a cultic atmosphere. The verb used alludes to the incense offerings of the Judeans for other gods in all the streets of Jerusalem incriminated by Jeremiah (Jer 44 MT /51:1-30 LXX), as well as to the revolt against the prophet that was led by women (Jer 44:15, 20, 24). This intertextual link to a prominent speech of reprimand in the book of Jeremiah underlines the polemical subtext of the grossly biased picture. These women are, according to the information given, waiting for strangers passing by and sleeping with them. The broken cord indicates that the woman found a partner; moreover, it could be taken as symbol of defloration. Commentators usually quote Herodotus's *Histories* 1.199 where the ancient Greek historian mentions a ritual intercourse performed by Babylonian women once in their life to serve the goddess Ishtar-Mylitta. Whether vv. 42-44 know of such practices actually performed or if the passage refers to Herodotus's notes is open. What seems clear is the highly polemical tendency of the passage. In a Priestly-Levitical framework of thinking as it appears to underlie the Letter, sex and cult are incompatible; what the women do and what is done to them is, to the implied authors, abominable from the outset.

More precisely, the point is the act of dishonoring the deities, not so much because of the sexual rite, but because of the behavior of the women involved: they laugh scornfully at one another; they dishonor one another.[40] Deities who tolerate such shameful behavior are false deities. Well-informed male and female Jewish readers of and listeners to

---

40. For Schökel, "Carta de Jeremias," 175, the focus for the implied readers is on the perversity of the woman who prides herself on being violated.

that passage might read it together with Peninnah humiliating Hannah (1 Sam 1) and Leah humiliating Rachel (Gen 30:1-24), two stories in which a woman stands against another woman. A gender stereotype arises: when women fight against one another, they will not do it with weapons; they do it with words, and they humiliate one another by derision. These connections might also confirm the hypothesis that the women in cords must be seen as waiting for their first intercourse as initiation into what they are supposed to do: bear children.

Sub-Passage 3: Subjected to Their Artisans (6:45-47a)

Bar 6:45-47a

⁴⁵They are made by carpenters and goldsmiths; they can be nothing but what the artisans wish them to be. ⁴⁶Those who make them will certainly not live very long themselves; ⁴⁷ᵃhow then can the things that are made by them be gods?

Sub-Passage 4: Protectors, Subjected to Protection (6:47b-49)

Bar 6:47b-49

⁴⁷ᵇThey have left only lies and reproach for those who come after. ⁴⁸For when war or calamity comes upon them, the priests consult together as to where they can hide themselves and their gods. ⁴⁹How then can one fail to see that these are not gods, for they cannot save themselves from war or calamity?

Sub-Passage 5: Mere Work of Human Hands (6:50-52)

Bar 6:50-52

⁵⁰Since they are made of wood and overlaid with gold and silver, it will afterward be known that they are false. ⁵¹It will be manifest to all the nations and kings that they are not gods but the work of human hands, and that there is no work of God in them. ⁵²Who then can fail to know that they are not gods?

Verses 45-52 consist of three small units, each concluded by a similar rhetorical question (vv. 47a, 49, 52) but interwoven in their motifs and formulae. The rather general observations and admonitions put together in this passage do not distinguish groups or persons in terms of sex or gender.

TRANSLATION MATTERS

6:45 *them*: αὐτὰ, Greek, neuter: "those things."

6:45-47 *made/make*: κατασκευάζω, the Greek verb could also be translated as "constructed/construct" or "built/build."

6:46 *those who make them*: αὐτοί τε οἱ κατασκευάζοντες αὐτὰ, Greek, neuter: "who make those things."

6:47 *only lies and reproach*: ψεύδη καὶ ὄνειδος, more literally: "only falseness and disgrace."

6:48 *comes upon them*: ἐπέλθη ἐπ᾽ αὐτὰ, Greek, neuter: "comes upon those things."

The affirmation that the gods are "constructed" (vv. 45-47) seems to correspond to their reduction to a mere "work of human hands" (v. 51), the most frequent motif of prophetical critique of idols, and reveals as a red thread the concept of their "subjection." The statues are, first, subjected to their artisan's plans and skills (v. 45), contrary to the Babylonian conviction that the gods themselves inspired the artisans, and the limited lifespan of those who construct the statues (v. 46) proves against the divinity of their productions, an idea that seems to presuppose a connection between divinity and eternity. Therefore, the gods can be blamed once again as "false" or deceitful and, in the language of honor and shame, as a disgrace (v. 47b), a burden even to the next generation. The statues are, second, subjected to their Priestly servants' (limited) foresight in times of danger (vv. 48-49; see v. 15 and v. 55). And, third, they will be subjected to a public exposure before all the nations (v. 51) who believed in their divinity (v. 4). In the context of the *Corpus Ieremianum*, one might think of the oracle against Babylon announcing the ruin of this empire and the powerlessness of its gods.

Sub-Passage 6: Unable to Act or Protect (6:53-56)

The sixth sub-passage is linked to the preceding one and also framed in itself by the catchword "king" (vv. 51, 53, and 56). The inauguration and legitimation of a ruler by God is a common idea in the Hebrew Bible. The implied authors of the Letter deny this power to the Babylonian gods (see v. 34), along with the gods' capacity to send rain (v. 53), to procure justice (v. 14), and to protect in times of war (v. 15). They restrict these divine powers, basic for human life, to the God of Israel, the one and only God.

Bar 6:53-56

[53]For they cannot set up a king over a country or give rain to people. [54]They cannot judge their own cause or deliver one who is wronged, for they have no power; [55]they are like crows[41] between heaven and earth. When fire breaks out in a temple of wooden gods overlaid with gold or silver, their priests will flee and escape, but the gods will be burned up like timbers. [56]Besides, they can offer no resistance to king or enemy. Why then must anyone admit or think that they are gods?

The little scene in the center (v. 55) might turn around the idea of the gods' inability to move if "they" now represents the priests: just as the crows flutter around, the fluttering priests flee when there's a fire and leave their gods in the temples as prey to the flames. Of course, the deceptiveness of the coat of precious materials is at stake again: gold and silver do not prevent the fire from consuming the wood of which the statues are made.

Sub-Passage 7: Final Evaluation (6:57-65)

The wording of v. 65 is nearly identical to v. 29b, the last line of part 1 (see also vv. 23 and 16), and has elements of the refrains in vv. 47, 49a, and 52. The formulas in v. 64 resemble the concluding lines in vv. 40, 44b, and 56. The two verses seem to form a sonorous final word not only to the preceding sub-passage but also to the complete second part of the speech.

With regard to the contents of vv. 57-65, this last sub-passage in part 2 might follow the red thread of measuring and evaluating the gods of the Babylonians in comparison to power, expediency, and impressiveness. Three units seem to be discernible. First, while in the preceding section the statues are rhetorically laid bare, exposing their wooden interior (compare v. 57 with v. 55), in this section, "thieves and robbers" physically strip away the precious coat and accessories and expose the "nakedness" of the wooden statues, revealing their helplessness.

---

41. Text-critical matter: v. 55 ὥσπερ γὰρ κορῶναι, *like crows*. Some of those who suppose a Semitic *Vorlage* of the Letter point to the somewhat strange appearance of "crows" here. They suggest that the Hebrew עבים ("clouds") may have been misread as ערבים ("ravens"). Indeed, "clouds" with their unstable consistency fit more easily into the context.

[57]Gods made of wood and overlaid with silver and gold are unable to save themselves from thieves or robbers. [58]Anyone who can will strip them of their gold and silver and of the robes they wear, and go off with this booty, and they will not be able to help themselves. [59]So it is better to be a king who shows his courage, or a household utensil that serves its owner's need, than to be these false gods; better even the door of a house that protects its contents, than these false gods; better also a wooden pillar in a palace, than these false gods.

[60]For sun and moon and stars are bright, and when sent to do a service, they are obedient. [61]So also the lightning, when it flashes, is widely seen; and the wind likewise blows in every land. [62]When God commands the clouds to go over the whole world, they carry out his command. [63]And the fire sent from above to consume mountains and woods does what it is ordered. But these idols are not to be compared with them in appearance or power. [64]Therefore one must not think that they are gods, nor call them gods, for they are not able either to decide a case or to do good to anyone. [65]Since you know then that they are not gods, do not fear them.

Second, the series of comparisons in v. 59 seem to have in common the notion of usefulness or expediency, and the statues of the gods are set in negative contrast to these examples: a door in a house can protect; a pillar in a palace helps to support a building; a king's duty is to show his "manliness," the virtue of courage; a vessel's "duty" is to function for the purpose it was made, either in a household or in a temple. Since the king's virtue is denoted by a noun implying the qualities or acts like a "real man," it is possible to understand the following comparison in a sexual way, the "vessel" being a woman to be "used" (a common scholarly understanding of 1 Thess 4:4).

Third, vv. 60-63 widens the argument and brings into sight cosmic phenomena. The text leaves no doubt that it considers sun, moon, and stars (v. 60) as dependent on divine will, not as divine in themselves or as a cosmic image of a deity. The implied early Jewish authors may well have in mind the creation account of their tradition with its fourth day and God's creation of the heavenly bodies to illuminate the world and to provide it with the structure of time (Gen 1:14-19). Lightning, wind, clouds, and fire are, in all ancient Western Asian cultures, considered to be under the power of the Weather God. The God of Israel has traces of such a Weather God when imagined as riding upon the clouds (Pss 68:5; 104:3-4 [including fire]); coming in a storm (Ps 83:14-15 [including a

---

TRANSLATION MATTERS

6:59 *who shows his courage*: ἐπιδεικνύμενον τὴν ἑαυτοῦ ἀνδρείαν, more literally: "who shows his manliness."

6:59 *a household utensil that serves its owner's need*: σκεῦος ἐν οἰκίᾳ χρήσιμον, ἐφ᾽ ᾧ κεχρήσεται ὁ κεκτημένος, more literally: "a vessel in the house (or: in the temple) that serves the need of the one who uses it."

6:63 *these idols*: see remark on v. 44.

---

consuming fire]); or hurling lightning flashes (Hab 3:11). The Letter of Jeremiah alludes to these traditions in a subtle way to affirm that all these powers are under the control of God, whereas "these things," as the gods with their statues are called in v. 63, are not even comparable to these created or dominated powers. After this attack on the mightiest gods of Babylon the affirmation is most emphatic: do not fear them!

Mockery, Coda (66-69, 70-72)

Sapiential conclusion (6:73)

Like a coda in a piece of music, vv. 66-72 touch on motifs already developed and add some new ideas, all underlining the message that worship of the Babylonian gods is simply stupid and, moreover, again in the vocabulary of honor and shame, disgraceful. The final line[42] draws its conclusion in terminology that comes as a surprise, as it points to wisdom traditions, while the speech as a whole develops mainly along the lines of Priestly/Levitical thinking. It is true that wisdom sentences do close non-sapiential biblical writings, as in the book of Hosea, for example (Hos 14:10). It might have become a stylistic means to round off a text with a wisdom aphorism as a final challenge to the listener or reader.

The verse, though, not only rounds off the Letter but also brings in a new twist of thought, as it is the only verse speaking explicitly of "idols" (εἴδωλα) instead of "deities" (θεοί). Moreover, the individualizing perspective on "someone" (ἄνθρωπος, reflecting the Hebrew אִישׁ, in its

---

42. Most commentators more or less ignore this last verse or merely do not deal with its specific character or function. Carey A. Moore deplores its "abruptness, illogic, and imprecision" in "Epistle of Jeremiah," in *Daniel, Esther, and Jeremiah: The Additions*, AB 44 (Garden City, NY: Doubleday, 1977), 358.

Bar 6:66-69, 70-72

[66] They can neither curse nor bless kings; [67]they cannot show signs in the heavens for the nations, or shine like the sun or give light like the moon. [68]The wild animals are better than they are, for they can flee to shelter and help themselves. [69]So we have no evidence whatever that they are gods; therefore do not fear them.

[70]Like a scarecrow in a cucumber bed,[43] which guards nothing, so are their gods of wood, overlaid with gold and silver. [71]In the same way, their gods of wood, overlaid with gold and silver, are like a thornbush in a garden on which every bird perches; or like a corpse thrown out in the darkness. [72]From the purple and linen[44] that rot upon them you will know that they are not gods; and they will finally be consumed themselves, and be a reproach in the land.

TRANSLATION MATTERS

6:72 *they will . . . be consumed*: αὐτά τε . . . βρωθήσονται, Greek, neuter: "those things will be . . . consumed."

6:72 *be a reproach*: ἔσται ὄνειδος, closer to the "grammar" of honor and shame: "be a matter of disgrace." See also v. 73.

Bar 6:73

[73]Better, therefore, is someone upright who has no idols; such a person will be far above reproach.

broader meaning) having no idols directs the audience's or the reader's attention away from the public cult to personal or familial forms of religion. Now "everybody" is asked to verify whether he or she has idols

43. Text-critical matter: v. 70 Ὥσπερ γὰρ ἐν σικυηράτῳ προβασκάνιον, "like a scarecrow in a cucumber bed." This seems to be a direct quotation of Jer 10:5a MT, missing in LXX, further evidence that the Letter is written with reference to a text of the book of Jeremiah different from the LXX version.

44. Text-critical matter: v. 72, "linen." NRSV presupposes an error or a variant in the Greek translation; the Hebrew word שׁשׁ meaning "byssus" (NRSV takes up this meaning when rendering "linen") and "marble"; the Greek has μαρμάρου, "marble," thinking of marble cult statues.

in his or her house. Besides the official cult of a temple or a king, the religion of the households or even the personal piety (see already v. 6!) comes into focus and the Letter leaves no doubt that "Jeremiah" aims at a radical expelling of every object in use as a cult object representing a deity, be it even the God of Israel. The first and second commandments of the Decalogue come together: to have no idols prevents people from venerating other deities, as the Lord's cult is without images. Men and women alike are challenged.[45]

Looking back

The Letter of Jeremiah can be seen as a powerful rhetorical demystification of cults that rely on splendor reinforcing power and on power in need of being represented by splendor. As such, it has its theological relevance even today, and its satirical mood appropriately fits that message. As a document from Hellenistic times, it might try to solve a problem, to answer a question specific to diasporic existence: how much assimilation in cultic affairs is prudent or necessary? The Letter of Jeremiah is clear: cultic assimilation is stupid as there are no gods besides the one and only God. Such a conviction might convey a strong self-confidence, a freedom to act without fear.

The Letter's most problematic aspect is the implicit construction of a group identity by ridiculing cultic or cult-related practices that in part simply do not correspond to the group's own customs or habits. In particular, women of the "others" and their different behavior serve as "boundary markers" to reinforce the implied audience's own superiority. In today's world, where cultures and religions want to meet with respect, such is not a helpful attitude, although enchantment with pseudo-deities has not become obsolete. The Letter's criteria for such demystification has to be unpacked and revisited on modern terms.

---

45. Wolfgang M. W. Roth suggests that the last verse of the Letter is the most important hint to identify the implied audience: "Jews who privately used images." His categories of religious history are not, however, completely up to date anymore: certainly the idols of personal piety are not a problem "after" the temptation by official cult idols but "alongside." Wolfgang M. W. Roth, "For Life, He Appeals to Death (Wis 13:18): A Study of Old Testament Idol Parodies," *CBQ* 37 (1975): 21–47, at 40–42 (followed by Beentjes, "Satirical Polemics," 129–30, and Saldarini, "The Letter of Jeremiah," 1010).

A Personal Final Conclusion

For me, as a biblical scholar working in an academic context in Germany, the book of Baruch and the Letter of Jeremiah are precious historical documents of an epoch in which "proto-Jewish" and "proto-Christian" structures of conceiving God and the world, of managing communities, and of orientation within a context developing into a "global world" emerged. As a feminist reader, I have to react critically to the precarious position of women in these two books: either women are completely missing and therefore subject to contradictory assignments of their place within the community (Bar), or they are used as shocking examples to demean the religion of the "others" (Ep Jer).

As a Catholic theologian, I consider it crucial for the church not only to face "the guilt of all believers" before God but to be aware that there might be specific failures of "fathers and rulers" (Bar 1:15–3:8)—and that fossilized structures themselves can lead to a pathology of power. As a biblical theologian, I appreciate the centrality of "the Book of God's commandments" as orientation for the community (Bar 4:1). This book, however, needs interpretation for new contexts and new challenges—that is true for Judaism, Christianity, and also Islam. Such new interpretations cannot be done by "experts" only but instead have to be conceived as common work on a "round table" that includes as many voices as possible.

As a person who had the privilege to live one year in Jerusalem as a student, I have been deeply moved by the "spirit" of the city but also shocked by the political and religious power games exercised around

133

her. Could there be space to open up the final line of the book of Baruch, God leading Israel in "mercy [compassion] and righteousness" (Bar 5:9), so that all peoples and religions living today in Jerusalem are included in this divine "mercy [compassion] and righteousness"?

In its strict rejection of "idols," objects of worship without any capacity to refer to the divine reality behind them, the Letter of Jeremiah appears as a predecessor of a basic Jewish, Christian–Reformed, and Muslim conviction while Catholics and Orthodox Christians—ironically those of all the groups that accepted the Letter as a canonical book!—followed a different path based on incarnation theology. In feminist theology, there is a similar discussion between "iconoclasts" who insist on a permanent destruction or deconstruction of all kinds of images of the Divine and those who welcome the diversity and multiplicity of images. Interestingly, the Letter of Jeremiah has no "counter-image" of the God of Israel over against the "gods" it rejects! Its listeners, however, can refer to their tradition, or they have the book of Baruch in mind, with its "images" of the most high and almighty God coming closest to Israel in "mercy and righteousness" (Bar 5:9). When "divine omnipotence" will be freed of arbitrariness or the notion that there is no room for real human liberty; when "mercy" will be freed of condescension and be transformed into compassion; when compassion and justice in God are not opposing principles anymore—then important steps to more appropriate "images of the divine" will have been taken.

Works Cited

1. General

Brenner, Athalya, and Fokkelien van Dijk-Hemmes. *On Gendering Texts: Female and Male Voices in the Hebrew Bible*. BibInt 1. Leiden: Brill, 1993.

Collins, John J., and Daniel C. Harlow, eds. *The Eerdmans Dictionary of Early Judaism*. Grand Rapids, MI: Eerdmans, 2010.

Doering, Lutz. "Jeremia in Babylonien und Ägypten. Mündliche und schriftliche Toraparänese für Exil und Diaspora nach 4QApocryphon of Jeremiah C." In *Frühjudentum und Neues Testament im Horizont Biblischer Theologie*, edited by Wolfgang Kraus and Karl-Wilhelm Niebuhr, 50–79. WUNT 162. Tübingen: Mohr Siebeck, 2003.

———. "Jeremiah and the 'Diaspora Letters' in Ancient Judaism: Epistolary Communication with the Golah as Medium for Dealing with the Present." In *Reading the Present in the Qumran Library: The Perception of the Contemporary by Means of Scriptural Interpretation*, edited by Kristin De Troyer and Armin Lange, 43–72. Atlanta, GA: SBL Press, 2005.

Dube, Musa W. *Postcolonial Feminist Interpretation of the Bible*. St. Louis, MO: Chalice Press, 2000.

Gruen, Erich S. *Diaspora: Jews amidst Greeks and Romans*. Cambridge, MA: Harvard University Press, 2002.

Haker, Hille, Luiz Carlos Susin, and Éloi Messi Metogo, eds. *Concilium: Postcolonial Theologies*. Vol. 49 (London: SCM Press, 2013).

Meyers, Carol. "Was Ancient Israel a Patriarchal Society?" *JBL* 133 (2014): 8–27.

Nehring, Andreas, and Simon Tielesch, eds. *Postkoloniale Theologie. Bibelhermeneutische und kulturwissenschaftliche Beiträge*. Stuttgart: Kohlhammer, 2013.

Schottroff, Luise, and Marie-Theres Wacker, eds. *Feminist Biblical Interpretation: A Compendium of Critical Commentary on the Books of the Bible and Related Literature.* Grand Rapids, MI, and Cambridge: Eerdmans, 2012.

Schüssler Fiorenza, Elisabeth. *The Power of the Word: Scripture and the Rhetoric of Empire.* Minneapolis: Fortress Press, 2007.

———. *Wisdom Ways: Introducing Feminist Biblical Interpretation.* Maryknoll, NY: Orbis Books, 2001.

Sowle Cahill, Lisa, Diego Irarrázaval, and Elaine M. Wainwright, eds. *Concilium: Gender in Theology, Spirituality and Practice.* Vol. 48 (London: SCM Press, 2012), with contributions by Regina Ammicht-Quinn, Rebeka Jadranka Anić, Bendito Ferraro, Luiz Corréa Lima, Heather Eaton, Elsa Támez, Marie-Theres Wacker, Muriel Orevillo-Montenegro, Patricia A. Fox, Susan M. St. Ville, and Anne Arabome.

Stiebert, Johanna. *The Construction of Shame in the Hebrew Bible: The Prophetic Contribution.* JSOTSup 346. Sheffield: Sheffield Academic Press, 2002.

Wacker, Marie-Theres. *Von Göttinnen, Göttern und dem einzigen Gott. Studien zum biblischen Monotheismus aus feministisch-theologischer Sicht.* Theologische Frauenforschung in Europa 14. Münster: Lit, 2004.

2. Publications by Authors of "Contributing Voices"

Ilan, Tal, ed. *A Feminist Commentary on the Babylonian Talmud.* Tübingen: Mohr Siebeck, 2007.

———. *Integrating Women into Second Temple History.* Tübingen: Mohr Siebeck, 1998.

———. *Jewish Women in Greco-Roman Palestine: An Inquiry into Image and Status.* Tübingen: Mohr Siebeck, 1995.

John Baptist, Antony. "Testimonios as Representation of Dalit Women Reality and Their Use in Researches." In *Theology for a New Community: Dalit Consciousness with a Symbolic Universe and Meaning Systems,* edited by T. K. John and James Massey, 173–87. New Delhi: Centre for Dalit/Subaltern Studies, 2013.

———. *Together as Sisters: Hagar and Dalit Women.* Delhi: Indian Society for Promoting Christian Knowledge, 2012.

Lee, Kyung-Sook. "1 & 2 Kings." In *Global Bible Commentary,* edited by Daniel Patte and Teresa Okure, 105–18. Nashville, TN: Abingdon Press, 2005.

———. "Books of Kings: Images of Women without Women's Reality." In *Feminist Biblical Interpretation: A Compendium of Critical Commentary on the Books of the Bible and Related Literature,* edited by Luise Schottroff and Marie-Theres Wacker, 159–77. Grand Rapids, MI, and Cambridge: Eerdmans, 2012.

Lee, Kyung-Sook, and Kyung-Mi Park, eds. *Korean Feminists in Conversation with the Bible, Church and Society.* Sheffield: Sheffield Phoenix Press, 2011.

Mertes, Klaus. *Verlorenes Vertrauen. Katholisch sein in der Kirche.* Freiburg: Herder, 2013.

————. *Widerspruch aus Loyalität*. Würzburg: Echter, 2009.

3. Baruch

Adams, Sean. *Baruch and the Epistle of Jeremiah: A Commentary Based on the Texts in Codex Vaticanus*. Septuagint Commentary Series. Leiden: Brill, 2014.

Alonso Schökel, Luis. "Baruc." In *Daniel – Baruc – Carta de Jeremias – Lamentaciones*, 123–65. Los Libros Sagrados 18. Madrid: Ediciones Cristiandad, 1976.

Assan-Dhôte, Isabelle, and Jacqueline Moatti-Fine. "Baruch." Chap. 1 (pp. 43–126) in *Baruch, Lamentations, Lettre de Jérémie*. La Bible d'Alexandrie 25.2. Paris: Cerf, 2005.

Ballhorn, Egbert. "Baruch—pseudepigraphe Kommunikation." In *Gesellschaft und Religion in der spätbiblischen und deuterokanonischen Literatur*, edited by Renate Egger-Wenzel, Thomas Elßner, and Vincent Reiterer, 229–52. DCLS 20. Berlin and Boston: De Gruyter, 2014.

Baumann, Gerlinde. "Das göttliche Geschlecht. JHWHs Körper und die Genderfrage." In *Körperkonzepte im Ersten Testament. Aspekte einer Feministischen Anthropologie*, edited by Hedwig-Jahnow-Forschungsprojekt, 220–49. Stuttgart: Kohlhammer, 2003.

————. "Die 'Männlichkeit' JHWHs. Ein Neuansatz im Deutungsrahmen altorientalischer Gottesvorstellungen." In *Dem Tod nicht glauben. Sozialgeschichte der Bibel. Festschrift für Luise Schottroff zum 70. Geburtstag*, edited by Frank Crüsemann, Marlene Crüsemann, and Claudia Janssen, 197–213. Gütersloh: Gütersloher Verlagshaus, 2004.

————. "Personified Wisdom: Contexts, Meanings, Theology." In *The Writings and Later Wisdom Books*, edited by Christl Maier and Nuria Calduch-Benages, 57–75. The Bible and Women 1.3. Atlanta, GA: SBL Press, 2014.

Boda, Mark J., Daniel K. Falk, and Rodney A. Werline. *Seeking the Favor of God*. Vol. 2, *The Development of Penitential Prayer in Second Temple Judaism*. EJL 22. Atlanta, GA: SBL Press, 2007.

Burke, David G. *The Poetry of Baruch: A Reconstruction and Analysis of the Original Hebrew Text of Baruch 3:9–5:9*. SBL Septuagint and Cognate Studies 10. Chico, CA: Scholars Press, 1982.

Butting, Klara. *Prophetinnen gefragt. Die Bedeutung der Prophetinnen im Kanon aus Tora und Prophetie*. Wittingen: Erev Rav, 2001.

Calduch-Benages, Nuria. "Jerusalem as Widow (Baruch 4:5–5:9)." In *Biblical Figures in Deuterocanonical and Cognate Literature*, edited by Hermann Lichtenberger and Ulrike Mittmann-Richert, 147–64. Deuterocanonical and Cognate Literature Yearbook 2008. Berlin and New York: Walter de Gruyter, 2009.

Chouraqui, André, and others. "Baroukh/Baruch." In *L'univers de la Bible*, Vol. 7. Paris: Brepols, 1984.

Claassens, Juliana M. *The God Who Provides: Biblical Images of Divine Nourishment*. Nashville, TN: Abingdon Press, 2004.

————. *Mourner, Mother, Midwife: Reimagining God's Delivering Presence in the Old Testament*. Louisville, KY: Westminster John Knox Press, 2012.

Eder, Walter, et al. "Colonization." *Brill's New Pauly*. Antiquity volumes edited by Hubert Cancik and Helmuth Schneider. Brill Online, 2006. http://referenceworks.brillonline.com/entries/brill-s-new-pauly/colonization-e618410.

Feuerstein, Rüdiger. *Das Buch Baruch. Studien zur Textgestalt und Auslegungsgeschichte*. Europäische Hochschul-Schriften XXIII/614. Frankfurt: Peter Lang, 1997.

Fischer, Irmtraud. *Gotteskünderinnen. Zu einer geschlechterfairen Deutung des Phänomens der Prophetie und der Prophetinnen in der Hebräischen Bibel*. Stuttgart: Kohlhammer, 2002.

Floyd, Michael. "Penitential Prayer in the Second Temple Period from the Perspective of Baruch." In *Seeking the Favor of God*. Vol. 2, *The Development of Penitential Prayer in Second Temple Judaism*, edited by Mark J. Boda, Daniel K. Falk, and Rodney A. Werline, 51–81. EJL 22. Atlanta, GA: SBL Press, 2007.

Gäbel, Georg, and Wolfgang Kraus. "Das Buch Baruch." In *Psalmen bis Daniel. Septuaginta deutsch, Erläuterungen und Kommentare 2*, edited by Martin Karrer and Wolfgang Kraus, 2815–26. Stuttgart: Deutsche Bibelgesellschaft, 2011.

Goldstein, Jonathan A. "The Apocryphal Book of I Baruch." *PAAJR* 46–47 (1979–1980): 179–99.

Graham, Alexander J. *Colony and Mother City in Ancient Greece*. 2nd ed. Chicago: Ares Publishers, 1983.

Harrelson, Walther. "Wisdom Hidden and Revealed According to Baruch (Baruch 3.9–4.4)." In *Priests, Prophets and Scribes: Essays on the Formation and Heritage of Second Temple Judaism in Honor of J. Blenkinsopp*, edited by Eugene Ulrich et al., 158–71. JSOTSup 194. Sheffield: University Press, 1992.

Häusl, Maria. "Künderin und Königin. Jerusalem in Bar 4:5–5:9." In *Tochter Zion auf dem Weg zum himmlischen Jerusalem. Rezeptionslinie der "Stadtfrau Jerusalem" von den späten alttestamentlichen Texten bis zu den Werken der Kirchenväter*, edited by Maria Häusl, 103–24. Leipzig: Leipziger Universitätsverlag, 2011.

Keel, Othmar. *Jerusalem und der eine Gott. Eine Religionsgeschichte*. Göttingen: Vandenhoek & Ruprecht, 2001; 2nd ed., 2014.

Knabenbauer, Joseph. "Commentarius in Baruch." In *Commentarius in Danielem prophetam, Lamentationes et Baruch*, 433–520. Cursus Scripturae Sacrae III/2. Paris: Lethielleux, 1889.

Kneucker, Johann Jacob. *Das Buch Baruch. Geschichte und Kritik, Übersetzung und Erklärung auf Grund des wiederhergestellten hebräischen Urtextes*. Leipzig: Brockhaus, 1879.

Kraus, Wolfgang, and Georg Gäbel. "Das Buch Baruch." In *Septuaginta deutsch. Das griechische Alte Testament in deutscher Übersetzung*, edited by Martin Karrer and Wolfgang Kraus, 1343–48. Stuttgart: Deutsche Bibelgesellschaft, 2009.

Maier, Christl M. *Daughter Zion, Mother Zion: Gender, Space, and the Sacred in Ancient Israel*. Minneapolis: Fortress Press, 2008.

Meyer, Ivo. "Das Buch Baruch und der Brief des Jeremia." In *Einleitung in das Alte Testament*, edited by Erich Zenger and Christian Frevel, 585–91. 8th ed. Stuttgart: Kohlhammer, 2012.

Michael, Tony S. L. "Barouch." In *A New English Translation of the Septuagint*, edited by Albert Pietersma and Benjamin G. Wright, 2nd ed., 925–31. New York: Oxford University Press, 2009.

Moore, Carey A. "1 Baruch." In *Daniel, Esther und Jeremiah: The Additions*. 255–316. AB 44. Garden City, NY: Doubleday, 1977.

Mukenge, André Kabasele. *L'unité littéraire du Livre de Baruch*. EBib, N.S. 38. Louvain: Gabalda, 1998.

Reusch, Heinrich. *Erklärung des Buchs Baruch*. Freiburg i. Br.: Herder, 1853.

Rothstein, Johann W. "Das Buch Baruch." In *Die Apokryphen und Pseudepigraphen des Alten Testaments*, vol. 1, edited by Emil Kautzsch, 213–25. Tübingen: Mohr, 1900; repr., 1921.

Saldarini, Anthony J. "The Book of Baruch: Introduction, Commentary, and Reflections." In *Introduction to Prophetic Literature, the Book of Isaiah, the Book of Jeremiah, the Book of Baruch, the Letter of Jeremiah, the Book of Lamentations, the Book of Ezekiel*, edited by Leander E. Keck, 929–82. NIB 6. Nashville, TN: Abingdon Press, 2012.

Schneider, Heinrich. *Das Buch Daniel. Das Buch der Klagelieder. Das Buch Baruch. Die Hl. Schrift für das Leben erklärt*, 131–62. Herders Bibelkommentar IX/2. Freiburg: Herder, 1954.

Schökel, Luis Alonso. "Jerusalén inocente intercede: Baruc 4:9-19." In *Salvación en la Palabra in Tribute to A. Diez Macho*, edited by Domingo Muñoz León, 39–51. Madrid, 1986.

Schreiner, Josef. "Baruch." In *Klagelieder/Baruch*. NEchtB Altes Testament 14, edited by Heinrich Groß and Josef Schreiner, 43–84. Würzburg: Echter, 1986.

Schroer, Silvia. "Wisdom: An Example of Jewish Intercultural Theology." In *Feminist Biblical Interpretation: A Compendium of Critical Commentary on the Books of the Bible and Related Literature*, edited by Luise Schottroff and Marie-Theres Wacker, 555–65. Grand Rapids, MI, and Cambridge: Eerdmans, 2012.

Schroer, Silvia, and Thomas Staubli. "Der göttliche Körper in der Miniaturkunst der südlichen Levante. Einblick in theologisch vernachlässigte Daten." In *„Gott bin ich, kein Mann". Beiträge zur Hermeneutik der biblischen Gottesrede*, edited by Ilona Riedel-Spangenberger and Erich Zenger, 124–55. Paderborn: Schöningh, 2006.

Steck, Odil Hannes. *Das apokryphe Baruchbuch*. FRLANT 160. Göttingen: Vandenhoeck & Ruprecht, 1993.

―――. "Das Buch Baruch." In *ATD Apokryphen*, vol. 5, edited by Otto Kaiser and Lothar Perlitt, 9–68. Göttingen: Vandenhoeck & Ruprecht, 1998.

————. "Israels Gott statt anderer Götter—Israels Gesetz statt fremder Weisheit. Beobachtungen zur Rezeption von Hi 28 in Bar 3,9-4,4." In *„Wer ist wie du, Herr, unter den Göttern?" Studien zur Theologie und Religionsgeschichte Israels*, edited by Ingo Kottsieper, 457–71. Festschrift Otto Kaiser. Göttingen: Vandenhoeck & Ruprecht, 1994.

Tov, Emanuel. *The Septuagint Translation of Jeremiah and Baruch: A Discussion of an Early Revision of the LXX of Jeremiah 29–52 and Baruch 1:1-3:8.* HSM 8. Missoula, MT: Scholars Press, 1976.

Tull, Patricia K. "Baruch." In *Women's Bible Commentary*, edited by Carol A. Newsom and Sharon H. Ringe, 305–8. Exp. ed. Louisville, KY: Westminster John Knox Press, 1998.

Uehlinger, Christoph. "'Powerful Persianisms' in Glyptic Iconography of Persian Period Palestine." In *The Crisis of Israelite Religion: Transformation of Religious Tradition in Exilic and Post Exilic Times*, edited by Bob Becking and Marjo Korpel, 134–82. Leiden: Brill, 1999.

Venter, Pieter M. "Penitential Prayers in the Books of Baruch and Daniel." *OTE* 18 (2005): 406–25.

Vos, Cornelis J. de. "'You Have Forsaken the Fountain of Wisdom': The Function of Law in Baruch 3:9–4:4." *ZABR* 13 (2007): 176–86.

Wacker, Marie-Theres. "Baruch: Mail from Distant Shores." In *Feminist Biblical Interpretation: A Compendium of Critical Commentary on the Books of the Bible and Related Literature*, edited by Luise Schottroff and Marie-Theres Wacker, 431–38. Grand Rapids, MI, and Cambridge: Eerdmans, 2012. Slightly revised and expanded version of a contribution originally published as "Das Buch Baruch. Post aus der Ferne." In *Kompendium feministische Bibelauslegung*, edited by Luise Schottroff and Marie-Theres Wacker, 422–27. 3rd ed. Gütersloh: Gütersloher Verlagshaus, 2007.

————. "Das Buch Baruch." In *Bibel in gerechter Sprache, Taschenausgabe*, edited by Ulrike Bail, Frank Crüsemann, et al., 1281–87. 4th ed. Gütersloh: Gütersloher Verlagshaus, 2011.

Wagner, Andreas. *Gottes Körper. Zur alttestamentlichen Vorstellung der Menschengestaltigkeit Gottes.* Gütersloh: Gütersloher Verlagshaus, 2010.

Wambacq, Benjamin N. "Baruch." In *Jeremias – Klaagliederen – Baruch – Brief van Jeremias*, 365–84. De Boeken van het Oude Testament. Roermond and Maaseik: J. J. Romen & Zonen, 1957.

Whitehouse, Owen C. "The Book of Baruch." In *The Apocrypha and Pseudepigrapha of the Old Testament*, vol. 1, edited by Robert Charles, 569–95. Oxford: Clarendon Press, 1913.

Wischnowsky, Marc. *Tochter Zion. Aufnahme und Überwindung der Stadtklage in den Prophetenschriften des Alten Testaments.* WMANT 89. Neukirchen-Vluyn: Neukirchener Verlag, 2001.

Ziegler, Joseph, ed. "Baruch." *Ieremias, Baruch, Threni, Epistula Ieremiae*, 450–67. 4th ed. Septuaginta: Vetus Testamentum Graecum, auctoritate Academiae

Scientiarum Gottingensis editum 15. Göttingen: Vandenhoeck & Ruprecht, 1957; repr., 2013.

4. Epistle of Jeremiah

Adams, Sean. *Baruch and the Epistle of Jeremiah: A Commentary Based on the Texts in Codex Vaticanus*. Septuagint Commentary Series. Leiden: Brill, 2014.

Alonso Schökel, Luis. "Carta de Jeremias." In *Daniel – Baruc – Carta de Jeremias – Lamentaciones*, 167–78. Los Libros Sagrados 18. Madrid: Ediciones Cristiandad, 1976.

Artom, Elia S. "L'origine, la data e gli scopi dell'Epistola di Geremia." In *Annuario di Studi Ebraici* 1 (1935): 49–74.

Ball, C. J. "Epistle of Jeremy." In *The Apocrypha and Pseudepigrapha of the Old Testament*, vol. 1, edited by Robert Charles, 596–611. Oxford: Clarendon Press, 1913.

Beentjes, Panc C. "Satirical Polemics against Idols and Idolatry in the Letter of Jeremiah (Baruch ch. 6)." In *Aspects of Religious Contact and Conflict in the Ancient World*, edited by Pieter W. van der Horst, 121–33. Utrechtse Theologische Reeks 31. Utrecht: Universiteit Utrecht, 1995.

Berlejung, Angelika. *Die Theologie der Bilder. Herstellung und Einweihung von Kultbildern in Mesopotamien und die alttestamentliche Bilderpolemik*. OBO 162. Fribourg and Göttingen: Universitäts-Verlag, 1998.

———. "Geheimnis und Ereignis. Zur Funktion und Aufgabe der Kultbilder in Mesopotamien." In *Die Macht der Bilder*, edited by Günter Sternberger and Marie-Theres Wacker, 109–44. Jahrbuch für Biblische Theologie 13. Neukirchen-Vluyn: Neukirchener Verlag, 1998.

———. "Washing the Mouth: The Consecration of Divine Images in Mesopotamia." In *The Image and the Book: Iconic Cults, Aniconism, and the Rise of the Book Religion in Israel and the Ancient Near East*, edited by Karel van der Toorn, 45–72. CBET 21. Leuven: Peeters, 1997.

Chouraqui, André, and others. "Lettre d'Irmeyahou/Lettre de Jérémie." In *L'univers de la Bible*, vol. 7, 453–64. Paris: Brepols, 1984.

Erbele-Küster, Dorothea. "Gender and Cult: 'Pure' and 'Impure' as Gender-Relevant Categories." In *Torah: The Bible and the Women*, vol. 1, edited by Irmtraud Fischer and Mercedes Navarro Puerto, 375–406. Atlanta, GA: SBL Press, 2011.

———. *Körper und Geschlecht. Studien zur Anthropologie von Leviticus 12 und 15*. WMANT 121. Neukirchen-Vluyn: Neukirchener Verlag, 2008.

Gäbel, Georg, and Wolfgang Kraus. "Epistole Jeremiu/Epistula Jeremiae/Der Brief des Jeremia." In *Psalmen bis Daniel, Septuaginta deutsch, Erläuterungen und Kommentare 2*, edited by Martin Karrer and Wolfgang Kraus, 2842–48. Stuttgart: Deutsche Bibelgesellschaft, 2011.

Kellermann, Dieter. "Apokryphes Obst. Bemerkungen zur Epistula Jeremiae (Baruch Kap. 6), insbesondere zu Vers 42." *ZDMG* 129 (1979): 23–42.

Kratz, Reinhard G. "Der Brief des Jeremia." In *ATD Apokryphen*, vol. 5, edited by Otto Kaiser and Lothar Perlitt, 69–108. Göttingen: Vandenhoeck & Ruprecht, 1998.

———. "Die Rezeption von Jer. 10 und 29 im Pseudepigraphen Brief des Jeremia." *JSJ* 26 (April 1995): 1–31.

Kraus, Wolfgang, and Georg Gäbel. "Epistole Jeremiu/Der Brief des Jeremias." In *Septuaginta deutsch. Das griechische Alte Testament in deutscher Übersetzung*, edited by Martin Karrer and Wolfgang Kraus, 1358–61. Stuttgart: Deutsche Bibelgesellschaft, 2009.

Moatti-Fine, Jacqueline. "Lettre de Jérémie." In *Baruch, Lamentations, Lettre de Jérémie*, edited by Isabelle Assan-Dhôte and Jacqueline Moatti-Fine, 287–330. La Bible d'Alexandrie 25.2. Paris: Cerf, 2005.

Moore, Carey A. "Epistle of Jeremiah." In *Daniel, Esther und Jeremiah: The Additions*, 317–58. AB 44. Garden City, NY: Doubleday, 1977.

Naumann, Weigand. *Untersuchungen über den apokryphen Jeremiasbrief*. BZAW 25. Gießen: Alfred Töpelmann, 1913.

Reusch, Heinrich. *Erklärung des Buchs Baruch*. Freiburg i. Br.: Herder, 1853.

Roth, Wolfgang M. W. "For Life, He Appeals to Death (Wis 13:18): A Study of Old Testament Idol Parodies." *CBQ* 37 (1975): 21–47.

Rothstein, Johann W. "Der Brief des Jeremia." In *Die Apokryphen und Pseudepigraphen des Alten Testaments*, vol. 1, edited by Emil Kautzsch, 226–29. Tübingen: Mohr, 1900; repr., 1921.

Saldarini, Anthony J. "The Letter of Jeremiah: Introduction, Commentary, and Reflections." In *Introduction to Prophetic Literature, the Book of Isaiah, the Book of Jeremiah, the Book of Baruch, the Letter of Jeremiah, the Book of Lamentations, the Book of Ezekiel*, edited by Leander E. Keck, 983–1010. NIB 6. Nashville, TN: Abingdon Press, 2001.

Scheer, Tanja S. "Tempelprostitution in Korinth?" In *Tempelprostitution im Altertum. Fakten und Fiktionen*, edited by Tanja S. Scheer and Martin Lindner, 221–66. Berlin: Verlag Antike e.K, 2009a.

Scheer, Tanja S., and Martin Lindner, eds. *Tempelprostitution im Altertum. Fakten und Fiktionen*. Berlin: Verlag Antike e.K., 2009.

Stark, Christine. *"Kultprostitution" im Alten Testament? Die Qedeschen der Hebräischen Bibel und das Motiv der Hurerei*. OBO 221. Göttingen: Vandenhoeck & Ruprecht, 2006.

Tull, Patricia K. "Letter of Jeremiah." In *Women's Bible Commentary*, edited by Carol A. Newsom and Sharon H. Ringe, 309–10. Exp. ed. Louisville, KY: Westminster John Knox Press, 1998.

Wacker, Marie-Theres. "Der Brief des Jeremia." In *Bibel in gerechter Sprache, Taschenausgabe*, edited by Ulrike Bail, Frank Crüsemann, et al., 1287–90. 4th ed. Gütersloh: Gütersloher Verlagshaus, 2011.

———. "'Kultprostitution' im Alten Israel? Forschungsmythen, Spuren, Thesen." In *Tempelprostitution im Altertum. Fakten und Fiktionen*, edited by Tanja S. Scheer and Martin Lindner, 55–84. Berlin: Verlag Antike e.K., 2009.

Wambacq, Benjamin N. "De Brief van Jeremias." In *Jeremias – Klaagliederen – Baruch – Brief van Jeremias*, 385–94. De Boeken van het Oude Testament. Roermond and Maaseik: J. J. Romen & Zonen, 1957.

Wright, Benjamin G. "The Epistle of Jeremiah: Translation or Composition?" In *Deuterocanonical Additions of the Old Testament Books*, edited by Géza G. Xeravits et al., 126–41. DCLS 5. Berlin: W. de Gruyter, 2010.

———. "The Letter of Jeremiah," in *A New English Translation of the Septuagint*, edited by Albert Pietersma and Benjamin G. Wright, 2nd ed., 942–45. New York: Oxford University Press, 2009.

Ziegler, Joseph, ed. "Epistula Ieremiae." In *Ieremias, Baruch, Threni, Epistula Ieremiae*. 4th ed. 494–504. Septuaginta: Vetus Testamentum Graecum, auctoritate Academiae Scientiarum Gottingensis editum 15. Göttingen, Vandenhoeck & Ruprecht, 1957; repr., 2013.

5. Dalit/Dalit Women

Imaiyam (Annamalai, V.). *Koveru Kazhudaigal*. Chennai: Crea, 1994.

John Baptist, Antony. "Testimonios as Representation of Dalit Women Reality and Their Use in Researches." In *Theology for a New Community: Dalit Consciousness with a Symbolic Universe and Meaning Systems*, edited by T. K. John (=John K. Thoonunkaparambil) and James Massey, 173–87. New Delhi: Centre for Dalit/Subaltern Studies, 2013.

———. *Together as Sisters: Hagar and Dalit Women*. Delhi: Indian Society for Promoting Christian Knowledge, 2012.

Kamble, Baby. *The Prisons We Broke*. Translated by Maya Pandit. Hyderabad: Orient Longman, 2008.

Mulackal, Shalini. "Dalit Belief Systems and Rituals." In *Theology for a New Community: Dalit Consciousness with a Symbolic Universe and Meaning Systems*, edited by T. K. John and James Massey, 142–72. New Delhi: Centre for Dalit/Subaltern Studies, 2013.

Rege, Sharmila. *Writing Caste, Writing Gender: Narrating Dalit Women's Testimonios*. New Delhi: Zubaan, 2006.

Spivak, Gayatri Shakravorti. "Can the Subaltern Speak?" *Marxism and the Interpretation of Culture*, edited by Cary Nelson and Lawrence Grossberg, 271–313. Chicago: University of Illinois Press, 1988.

Viramma, Josiane Racine, and Jean-Luc Racine. *Viramma: Life of a Dalit*. Translated by Will Hobson. New Delhi: Social Science Press, 2000.

Index of Scripture References and Other Ancient Writings

Syriac Apocalypse of Baruch (2 Baruch)
    xxxviii

Greek Apocalypse of Baruch (3 Baruch)
    xxxviii

Paraleipomena Jeremiou (4 Baruch)
    xxxviii

4QApocryphon Jeremiah
    xxxviii

Philo
De aeternitate mundi
    §112   53
De Cherubim
    §52   53
De opificio mundi
    §21   53

Aristobulus
Eusebius Praeparatio Evangelica
    13.12   60

Herodotus
Histories
    1.181   109
    1.199   124

Index of Subjects

General Editor

Barbara E. Reid, OP, is a Dominican Sister of Grand Rapids, Michigan. She holds a PhD in biblical studies from The Catholic University of America and is vice president and academic dean and professor of New Testament studies at Catholic Theological Union, Chicago. Her most recent publications are *Wisdom's Feast: An Invitation to Feminist Interpretation of the Scriptures* (2016) and *Abiding Word: Sunday Reflections on Year A, B, C* (3 vols.; 2011, 2012, 2013). She served as president of the Catholic Biblical Association in 2014–2015.

Volume Editor

Carol J. Dempsey, OP, PhD, is professor of theology (biblical studies) at the University of Portland, Oregon. Her primary research interest is in prophetic literature as it relates to the ancient and contemporary world. Her recent publications include *The Bible and Literature* (Orbis Books, 2015) and *Amos, Hosea, Micah, Nahum, Habakkuk, and Zephaniah: A Commentary* (Liturgical Press, 2013) and numerous articles related to prophets, gender studies, ethics, and environmental concerns. She is a member of the Dominican Order of Caldwell, New Jersey.

Author

Dr. Marie-Theres Wacker is professor of Old Testament at the Faculty of Catholic Theology, University of Muenster/Germany; she is also director of the Seminar of Old Testament Exegesis and of the unit Feminist Theology and Gender Research at the same faculty. Her research fields include literature of Hellenistic Judaism, history of biblical monotheism, feminist and gender-sensitive hermeneutics of the Hebrew Bible, and questions of Jewish-Christian and Muslim-Christian dialogue. She is a member of the board of directors of the international theological review

Concilium. With Luise Schottroff she edited and co-authored a one-volume commentary on the Christian Bible and related literature, *Feminist Biblical Interpretation: A Compendium* (Grand Rapids, MI: Eerdmans, 2012; German edition: *Kompendium Feministische Theologie*, 3rd ed. [Gütersloh: Gütersloher Verlagshaus, 2007]). In spring 2015 she, along with a group of collaborators, launched the website www.juedischer-friedhof-muenster.de, a photographical, inscriptional, and biographical documentation of the Jewish Cemetery in the city of Muenster with its four hundred tombstones since 1816, to create awareness of that place and to root it in the collective memory of the city as an important site of Jewish presence in Germany before and after the Shoah.